Bon Appétit, Y'all

Bon Appétit, Y'all

Recipes and Stories from Three Generations
of Southern Cooking

Virginia Willis

Photography by Ellen Silverman

TEN SPEED PRESS
Berkeley | Toronto

Ten Speed Press
PO Box 7123
Berkeley, California 94707
www.tenspeed.com

Distributed in Australia by Simon and Schuster Australia, in Canada by
Ten Speed Press Canada, in New Zealand by Southern Publishers Group,
in South Africa by Real Books, and in the United Kingdom and Europe
by Publishers Group UK.

Cover and text design by Betsy Stromberg
Food styling by Virginia Willis
Prop styling by Angie Mosier

Library of Congress Cataloging-in-Publication Data on file with publisher.

Printed in Thailand
First printing, 2008

1 2 3 4 5 6 7 8 9 10 — 12 11 10 09 08

CONTENTS

FOREWORD

I WRITE ABOUT VIRGINIA WILLIS and her new book with pride. Not because I had a hand in the book, but because I was one of Virginia's first teachers. She came to me one day while I was taping one of my cooking shows and asked to apprentice on her days off. I almost said no. But Virginia is determined, passionate about food, and gifted, and she packed every minute with learning—as she has continued to do throughout the fifteen years we've been cooking together.

Since that beginning, Virginia has worked with some of the top names in the food world, from Anne Willan to Martha Stewart. She has had the great gift of allowing herself to be influenced by many brilliant cooks, both French and American. And she has done what every teacher wants of a student—she exceeded my capabilities. (I'm afraid she won't brag on herself, so I must.)

This book reflects Virginia's quintessential Southernness. In the South, the first thing one is asked is, "Who are your people?" She has always claimed her people, her mother and grandmother among them, through her food. You are going to share those people through this book—they will become your own. You will find a cake recipe here, a cheese straw there, that will make you sigh and say, "Oh, if I could only eat that right now," propelling you to the kitchen. In these pages you will receive only the very best, to read, to savor, and to cook.

Nathalie Dupree

INTRODUCTION

RICH IN FOLKLORE AND HISTORY, the cooking of the American South embodies all the glamour, grit, and heartbreak of Southern culture: the sad cruelty of slavery's influence; the joie de vivre of wealthy, well-bred, landed aristocracy; the romance of moonlight and magnolia; the sun-washed wholesomeness of family memories; a note or two of twisted Southern Gothic; fierce attachment to the land; and recently, a prideful sense of place, with chefs boldly championing local, artisanal, and heirloom products and vegetables.

My part in the old and complex story of Southern food began in my grandmother's country kitchen, with its walls made of heart-of-Georgia pine. My maternal grandmother, Emily Louise Wingate Baston, whom I called Meme, was the daughter of a farmer, a true Southern lady, and a wonderful cook. Born in 1907, she grew up near Hephzibah, Georgia. From the time I was in a high chair to when I was a grown woman pulling up a chair to her kitchen table, I loved to hear her stories of milking cows and making butter and cheese, filling a root cellar, killing hogs in the fall, and curing hams in the smokehouse.

Meme graduated from Young Harris College in 1927, a somewhat unusual feat for a woman of her time in the rural South. Her diploma, a real

Meme's recipe book

sheepskin, has hung in the dining room of our family home for as long as I can remember. She met my grandfather at a fish fry on the Savannah River; they were married for almost 65 years, until he passed away. Meme was the president of the Evans Extension Homemakers Club and was famous for pound cake (see page 266); fried chicken; light, buttery yeast rolls; old-fashioned butter beans; turnip and mustard greens with salty, smoky pot liquor; and homemade jams and jellies. Many of these recipes are still scribbled in her handwriting directly on the wooden interior of her kitchen cupboard—a sight that can leave me breathless and even move me to tears.

My mother, Virginia, and her siblings grew up being fed from that same heart-of-pine kitchen that came to mean so much to me. The family raised chickens and cows, though they stopped milking the cows when one surly beast kicked my grandmother (they packed the freezer with beef instead!). Meme served grits every morning for breakfast and Mama said she filled the plates to the rim. The school bus would pull up at the end of the long driveway and my grandmother would make it wait until all the plates were clean. No one, including the Columbia County Board of Education, argued with Meme.

In the 1960s, Mama and Meme both watched Julia Child's first television series and religiously tried the recipes the following week. Years later, I was the grade school child who took leftover *crêpes aux champignons* and *roulade au poulet* to school for lunch. I hated it then, but now see in my mother's explorations the roots of my own passion for food. When I was three years old, my family moved to Louisiana and Mama discovered Cajun recipes, often preparing Red Beans and Rice (page 160), Crawfish Étouffée (page 130), and Shrimp Creole (page 131). So Mama's repertoire covers all the Southern classics that she learned from Meme, but also includes Quail in Red Wine Sauce (page 119), various gumbos (page 132), and French Butter Cookies (page 260).

A love of fresh, home-cooked food and a tradition of unconditional hospitality have always been guiding values in my family—I see them as a testimony to our Southern heritage. I spent much of my childhood in the kitchen with Meme and Mama, absorbing those values and acquiring skills I would later develop into a profession. There are photos of me as young as four in Meme's kitchen, standing on a chair making biscuits, or sitting on the counter with my feet in the cool steel sink, shelling butter beans. From the age of ten I used to sell birthday cakes to the neighborhood moms for their children.

My career began in earnest in Atlanta, where I worked as an unpaid apprentice for Nathalie Dupree, and has since taken me all over the world. I have cooked for President Clinton, chef Roger Vergé, Aretha Franklin, and Jane Fonda—and made *lapin Normandie* with the grande dame, Julia herself. My television work has taken me from the steep cliffs of Amalfi, where I picked plump yellow lemons, to the coast of Connecticut, where I tasted a briny oyster straight from the frigid waters of the Atlantic.

As a Southerner and a graduate of both L'Academie de Cuisine and École de Cuisine La Varenne, my own style of cooking combines my Southern heritage with classical French training. The result is a mélange of new Southern and new American cooking with a heavy dose of classic French technique. As a food writer and cooking teacher, I try to be sensitive to busy lives, hectic schedules, and health concerns. Thus, many of the recipes in this book are adaptations of, and use less fat than, traditional Southern and classic French dishes, while a few are old-timey dishes flavored with hog jowl and bacon, and some are just simple country food that would be equally at home both here and in France. I take French technique into the Southern kitchen—you'll find recipes for Pork Chops with Dried Plums (page 84) as well as Fried Pork Chops with Pan Gravy (page 80), Old-Fashioned Pot Roast (page 89), and Boeuf Bourguignonne (page 91).

My philosophy with most recipes is that simple is best. I try to use the finest ingredients and, by concentrating on sound French technique, do as little to them as possible to let the flavor of the actual food shine through—a style I like to call "refined Southern cuisine." These are recipes to cook in the home kitchen, not restaurant-driven creations. They are recipes for families, for displaced Southerners yearning for a taste of home, for aspiring cooks, and for anyone who simply wants to spend some time in the kitchen working and playing with food.

Some of my favorite memories, stories you will read in this book, happened in the kitchen learning at Mama's or Meme's side. I was learning so much more than food and cooking. Those times were history lessons, math exercises, and instruction in social studies. Food and cooking are always about so much more than just sustenance, of course. For me, they define some of my most precious relationships, root me in my culture, and give me my place in the world. *Bon Appétit, Y'all* is my way of saying welcome to my Southern kitchen. Pull up a chair.

CHAPTER 1
STARTERS AND NIBBLES

HORS D'OEUVRES WHET THE appetite but do not satiate; they are just a "little something" to begin a meal or to nibble on between meals.

In my grandmother's rural South, dainty bites and tea sandwiches would only appear at showers and weddings. This was mostly because there was no need to stimulate the appetite of hardworking farmers and field hands. But also, perhaps, it was that hors d'oeuvres just seemed to marry so naturally with a cocktail, that forbidden elixir of hell to small-town Protestants.

As I'm neither teetotaler nor field hand, I'm glad hors d'oeuvres have become part of the modern Southern table, where they can be as highbrow as a starter of Classic Crab Cakes (page 145) or as down-home as boiled peanuts.

Some Southern hors d'oeuvres, unfortunately, partake of the "trashy" element of Southern cooking that relies on processed foods. I'm here to tell you that a bag of little smokies, a bottle of ketchup, and a jar of grape jelly combined in a slow cooker, served with a box of toothpicks on the side, is not an hors d'oeuvre. I won't be sharing recipes for canned crescent rolls with fake crab or Vienna sausages and cubes of Velveeta speared with a pretzel stick. Nor will I advise you to put out a potato chip–crusted casserole to eat on small plates and call it an hors d'oeuvre.

Because they're not everyday fare, hors d'oeuvres made for a party can require a bit of additional planning and thought. All of the recipes in this chapter have tips on making ahead to help you juggle preparation and serving. And here are a few tips that will help you plan.

Judge how much you'll need. There's a fine balance between generously feeding your guests and wasting food. Remember that the greater the variety, the more likely people are to try at least one of everything. Also, the size of serving utensils and plates is important: the larger the serving utensil, the more your guests will take (and likely not finish).

Consider the time of day. Is it a lady's tea or an afternoon shower or an evening cocktail party? For a daytime event, I suggest five or six food choices, allowing for two pieces of each per guest. At night, their appetites are telling your guests that it is dinnertime, so you need to plan accordingly. As a rule of thumb, I serve a minimum of eight different hors d'oeuvres for an evening event, planning that guests will consume four or five pieces of each. If hors d'oeuvres are served preceding a sit-down dinner, prepare five or six different choices, counting on one or two of each per guest.

Decide the type of service. A stationary buffet is certainly easier for the host, but passing the nibbles allows guests to move about and socialize. A combination of both is an excellent solution. Use six-inch plates for a buffet, even a substantial one. Standing up, it is impossible to balance both a drink and a plate that's any larger.

Create a balanced menu. Choose some simple-to-prepare dishes, such as dips, and some that need only be set out on a platter, such as cheese boards and seasoned olives. Some of my favorite hors d'oeuvres require no recipe: I arrange a country ham on a board and slice it paper thin, heap spiced nuts in a bowl, and serve halved French Breakfast radishes to spread with sexy cultured butter and sprinkle with fleur de sel. A bountiful array of lightly steamed vegetable crudités makes an attractive, tasty, and fairly inexpensive "filler" at an hors d'oeuvres buffet. Steaming or blanching the vegetables, then shocking them (plunging them in ice water to stop the cooking and set color) improves their taste and brightens their appearance.

CRISPY FRIED ASPARAGUS

Makes 12

Meme loved asparagus, which she called "asparagus salad," although there wasn't anything to preparing it other than opening the familiar shiny silver can. Even though I know the flavor of canned asparagus (really, there isn't any) cannot compare to freshly cooked, I enjoy that taste memory.

The ends of fresh asparagus can be tough and woody. I prefer to slice off the last inch or two of the stem instead of snapping it off where the spear breaks naturally. Not only is it more visually appealing when all the spears are exactly the same size, but they will also cook at the same rate.

As these are best fried at the last minute, I suggest you serve them as a first course at a small dinner, not as an hors d'oeuvre at a large party.

12 thick asparagus, ends trimmed

12 very thin slices prosciutto or country ham (about 8 ounces), halved

1/4 cup canola oil, for frying, plus more if needed

1 cup all-purpose flour, for dredging

Coarse salt and freshly ground black pepper

2 large eggs

Prepare an ice-water bath by filling a large bowl with ice and water. Line 2 large plates with paper towels.

To cook the asparagus, bring a large pot of salted water to a boil over high heat. Add the asparagus and boil just until tender, 4 to 6 minutes. Drain well in a colander and transfer to the ice bath to cool. Once cooled, place them on one of the towel-lined plates to drain and pat dry with additional paper towels.

To prepare the asparagus, wrap 1 piece of ham around each spear. Set aside on a plate. Heat the oil in a shallow skillet over medium-high heat until shimmering.

To dredge the spears, place the flour in a shallow bowl and season with salt and pepper. In a second shallow bowl, whisk the eggs. Roll the ham-wrapped asparagus in the flour, dip in the eggs, and transfer to the hot oil.

To cook the spears, fry them, in batches, turning to cook on all sides, until golden brown, 3 to 5 minutes. Transfer to the second towel-lined plate to drain. Season with salt and pepper and serve immediately.

MAKING AHEAD: The asparagus spears can be wrapped with ham and stored in an airtight container at least 24 hours ahead. You can also prepare them completely ahead and hold them at room temperature for up to 1 hour. When ready to serve, re-crisp them in a 450°F oven for about 5 minutes.

THYME TOASTED PECANS

Makes 4 cups

Southerners always seem to have candied and spiced pecans around to nibble on during the holidays. My grandmother always made sweet pecans crusted with egg whites and sugar, using the nuts she and my grandfather had collected in the fall. So this version, with extra-virgin olive oil and herbs, is a real departure for my family. Recipes such as this, with a short ingredients list, are completely determined by the quality of the ingredients. The shorter the list, the better the ingredients must be. Pecans are the star, but the choice of olive oil and salt is crucial to the success of the dish. Use the finest possible. This recipe is splendidly simple, just perfect with apéritifs and for cocktail parties.

4 cups pecan halves

2 teaspoons coarse salt or sea salt

1 teaspoon freshly ground black pepper

1 tablespoon fresh thyme leaves

3 tablespoons extra-virgin olive oil

In a large, dry skillet, toast the pecans over medium heat until golden brown and fragrant, about 5 minutes.

Meanwhile, in a large bowl combine the salt, pepper, thyme leaves, and olive oil.

Add the warm toasted pecans to the thyme-oil mixture. Stir well to combine and evenly coat the pecans. The fragrance is amazing! Taste and adjust for seasoning with salt and pepper.

MAKING AHEAD: Once the seasoned nuts have cooled, store them in an airtight container in the refrigerator for up to 2 weeks. Bring them to room temperature before serving.

MAMA'S SPICED PECANS

Makes 2 cups

In south Georgia, farmland not used for peaches is often planted to pecan groves. Evenings in the fall, we would search for the elusive nuts hidden among the fallen brown leaves, the bare trees black in the evening shadows, the sunset sky a colorful vermillion. We'd return home and store our harvest in large sacks of netting. After shelling and cleaning, Mama and Meme made these nuts for the holidays.

4 cups canola oil

2 cups pecan halves

1 tablespoon unsalted butter

Pinch of cayenne pepper, or to taste

Coarse salt and freshly ground black pepper

Line a plate with paper towels and set near the cooktop. In a large, heavy-bottomed pot, heat the oil over medium heat until the oil reaches 350°F on a deep-fat thermometer. Carefully add the pecans and cook until the color deepens, 2 to 3 minutes. Using a slotted spoon, transfer to a large bowl. While the nuts are still hot, add the butter and cayenne and stir to combine. Season with salt and pepper. Transfer to the prepared plate to drain.

MAKING AHEAD: Once the nuts have cooled, store in an airtight container in the refrigerator for up to 2 weeks. Bring to room temperature before serving.

SPICED PUFF PASTRY CHEESE STRAWS

Makes about
6 dozen

Having grown up on Dede's Cheese Straws (page 15), I never knew this version existed until I went to culinary school.

Like Dede's traditional Southern version, these savory, buttery bites get their kick from cayenne. If cayenne is too hot for you, simply substitute paprika or pimentón (smoked paprika from Spain). Store-bought frozen puff pastry can be gruesome, so choose carefully; I always use Dufour's, available online and at gourmet markets such as Whole Foods.

2/3 cup freshly grated Parmigiano-Reggiano cheese (about 2 ounces)

1/4 teaspoon cayenne pepper

1/4 teaspoon Hungarian paprika

1/2 teaspoon coarse salt

1 large egg

2 tablespoons water

1 sheet frozen puff pastry (from one 14-ounce package), thawed according to package instructions, and unfolded

Preheat the oven to 425°F. Set aside two ungreased rimmed baking sheets.

In a small bowl, combine the cheese, cayenne, paprika, and salt. Set aside. In a second small bowl, whisk together the egg and water. Set aside.

On a lightly floured surface, roll out the thawed pastry sheet 1/8 inch thick, to form a rectangle that is about 10 by 16 inches. Lightly brush the dough with the egg wash.

To shape the straws, halve the pastry crosswise into two 5 by 8-inch rectangles. Sprinkle the cheese mixture over one rectangle and top with the other rectangle, egg-wash side down, pressing firmly to force out any air pockets. Roll out the layered pastry a little further to make the layers adhere (the rectangle should be about 12 by 9 inches). Brush the top of the pastry with additional egg wash and transfer to a baking sheet. Chill until firm, about 10 minutes in the freezer or 30 minutes in the refrigerator.

Remove from the freezer and transfer to a floured work surface. With a large sharp knife, pastry wheel, or pizza cutter, cut the pastry lengthwise into 1/4-inch-wide sticks. Twist the ends of each strip in opposite directions to create a long twirl.

To bake the straws, arrange them about 1 1/2 inches apart on the baking sheets, pressing down the ends to fix the straws to the rimmed edge of the sheet pan. Bake the cheese straws, in batches, in the middle of the oven until golden, 10 to 12 minutes. (While baking in batches, keep the raw dough in the refrigerator.) Transfer the baking sheet to a rack to cool slightly, then transfer the cheese straws to a rack to cool completely.

MAKING AHEAD: Once they have cooled completely, store the cheese straws in an airtight container for up to 2 days. Re-crisp them in a 425°F oven just until heated through, about 5 minutes.

DEVILED EGGS

Makes 2 dozen

I made these once for a political fundraiser at my friend Melita Easter's house, attended by the governor of Georgia, who stood there and practically ate the whole plate. The secret is butter, a tip I picked up in culinary school that takes this Southern staple from delicious to sublime and renders people unable to use the sense God gave a cat to stop eating.

If you don't have a specially designed plate for serving deviled eggs, with cuplike indentations to keep the eggs from rolling, simply trim off a sliver from the bottom of the cooked white before you fill the eggs with the yolk mixture. Garnish the platter with leaves of butter lettuce or herbs and nestle the filled eggs in the greenery.

Very fresh eggs are difficult to peel. Buy and refrigerate eggs about seven days in advance of cooking. This allows the eggs to take in air, which helps separate the membranes from the shells.

12 large eggs

1/3 cup mayonnaise (page 282)

2 tablespoons unsalted butter, at room temperature

1 tablespoon Dijon mustard

Pinch of cayenne pepper

Coarse salt and freshly ground white pepper

2 tablespoons finely chopped fresh tarragon, chives, or chervil, plus leaves for garnish

To hard-cook the eggs, place the eggs in a saucepan and add water to cover them by 1 inch. Bring to a boil over high heat (you will see bubbles around the sides of the pot). Remove from the heat, cover, and let stand for 12 minutes. Drain the eggs and rinse them under cold running water. Set aside to cool completely.

To peel the eggs, once the eggs have cooked and cooled, remove the shells by tapping each egg gently on the counter or sink all over to crackle it. Roll an egg between your hands to loosen the shell. Peel, starting at the large end, while holding the egg under running cold water; this facilitates peeling and also removes any stray shell fragments.

To prepare the filling, halve the peeled eggs lengthwise. Carefully remove the yolks. Set the whites aside. Pass the yolks through a fine-mesh strainer into a bowl or place them in the work bowl of a food processor fitted with the metal blade. Blend the yolks, mayonnaise, butter, mustard, and cayenne, and mix until smooth; season with salt and pepper. Add the finely chopped tarragon.

Place the mixture in a piping bag fitted with a large star tip, or use a medium sealable plastic bag with one of the corner tips snipped off.

To assemble the eggs, when ready to serve, pipe the yolk mixture into the whites. Garnish with additional herbs and serve immediately.

MAKING AHEAD: Unpeeled hard-cooked eggs can be refrigerated for up to 1 week. Or prepare the eggs, but don't assemble, up to 8 hours in advance of serving; refrigerate the whites covered with a damp towel in an airtight plastic container. Store the egg-yolk mixture in the piping bag with the tip also covered in a damp paper towel. Knead the yolk mixture slightly to soften before filling the yolks. The eggs may also be assembled and stored covered in the refrigerator for up to 2 hours. Any longer and the yolk mixture starts to form a crust.

CRAB DIP

Makes about
3 cups

The Eastern seaboard—especially the Chesapeake Bay—is riddled with shallow muddy inlets of brackish water, the perfect home for blue crabs. Grades of crabmeat depend on which part of the crab the meat is from and the size of the pieces. Jumbo lump is the most expensive and is composed of the largest pieces of white body meat. Lump crab is next and is harvested from the back fin. Flake is the smallest pieces of white body meat. Claw meat is the darker meat from the claw and is the least expensive. Look for fresh or pasteurized crab in your seafood department and avoid the canned, shelf-stable product.

Serve this dip with water crackers or toasted slices of baguette.

1 tablespoon unsalted butter, at room temperature, for the dish

4 ounces cream cheese, at room temperature

4 ounces fresh goat cheese, at room temperature

3 tablespoons Mayonnaise (page 282)

1 teaspoon Dijon mustard

1/4 teaspoon cayenne pepper

Coarse salt and freshly ground black pepper

2 tablespoons dry white wine

2 tablespoons chopped mixed fresh herbs (such as flat-leaf parsley, chives, chervil, or tarragon)

1 pound jumbo lump or lump crabmeat, picked over for cartilage

1/2 cup fresh or panko (Japanese) breadcrumbs

Position an oven rack 4 inches below the broiler element. Preheat the broiler. Butter a medium gratin dish.

To make the dip, combine the cream cheese, goat cheese, mayonnaise, mustard, and cayenne pepper in a double boiler over medium heat. Season with salt and pepper. Add the wine and herbs and stir until smooth. Using a large spatula, fold in the crabmeat, taking care not to break the lumps. Taste and adjust the seasoning with salt and pepper. Transfer to the prepared baking dish and top with the breadcrumbs. Broil until golden brown, about 5 minutes, depending on the strength of your broiler. Serve warm.

MAKING AHEAD: Instead of a double boiler, combine the ingredients in the gratin dish. Cover with plastic wrap and refrigerate until ready to cook. When ready to cook, remove from the refrigerator and let warm to room temperature. Top with breadcrumbs and bake at 350°F until heated through, bubbling, and golden brown, about 25 minutes.

VARIATION: You can skip the gratin dish, breadcrumbs, and broiling altogether. Simply transfer the hot mixture from the double boiler into a chafing dish, fondue pot, or the setup described in Caterer's Trick, below, and serve with water crackers or toasted slices of baguette.

Caterer's Trick

Chafing dishes are excellent for a crowd, but are often too large for smaller parties. Here's an alternative that works well for foods like soups, dips, and sauces. On a heatproof surface, make a pot stand out of bricks or glass bricks, arranged in an open square or triangle. Place a sterno cup in the center and rest a heavy-duty pot on the bricks. I like the casual look of aged bricks and an enameled pot for a simple buffet.

MAMA'S SAUSAGE-PECAN BALLS

Makes 3 dozen

Mama found the original of this recipe on the back of a box of Bisquick, a premixed baking product containing flour, shortening, salt, and leavening. According to General Mills, the recipe continues to be one of their most popular. Mama added pecans to the sausage balls, which she served during the holidays and at cocktail parties. I made a few additional changes and developed this "from scratch" version.

This recipe works best if you grate the cheese yourself rather than buying it already grated, which is coated to keep the pieces from sticking together. You can add additional cayenne if you like, or use extra hot sausage.

1 cup pecan halves

10 ounces sharp Cheddar cheese

2 cups all-purpose flour

2 teaspoons baking powder

1 1/2 teaspoons fine sea salt

1/4 teaspoon cayenne pepper

3 tablespoons solid vegetable shortening, preferably Crisco, at room temperature

8 ounces raw mild pork sausage

Preheat the oven to 350°F. Line a baking sheet with a silicone baking sheet or parchment paper.

Place the pecans in the work bowl of a food processor fitted with the metal blade. Pulse until chopped, but not too finely. Remove to a bowl and set aside. Replace the blade with the grating disc and grate the cheese. Remove to a second bowl and set aside.

Switch back to the metal blade. To make the sausage mixture, in the same bowl of the food processor (no need to clean it), combine the flour, baking powder, salt, and cayenne pepper. Pulse to combine. Add the shortening and pulse until the mixture resembles coarse meal. Add the grated cheese and the sausage and pulse until well combined. Transfer the mixture to a bowl. Add the reserved pecans and, using your hands, press the dough together until well combined. (The dough will be very crumbly.)

To form the balls, using a small ice cream scoop and your hands, shape the mixture into 1-inch balls and place about 1 inch apart on the prepared baking sheet. Bake until browned, 20 to 25 minutes. Remove to a rack to cool. Serve immediately.

MAKING AHEAD: The balls can be refrigerated in an airtight container for up to 3 days. To serve, let the balls come to room temperature. Or to serve warm, reheat in a 350°F oven until heated through, 5 to 7 minutes.

DEDE'S CHEESE STRAWS

Makes about
6 dozen

When I was growing up, our nibbles were most often the cheese straws made by my grandfather, whom I called Dede. Dede was a tall, strapping man who knew the secret of a long, happy marriage to his iron-willed wife. As he put it, his blue eyes twinkling, he always got in the last word: "Yes, beloved."

Dede would layer his cheese straws in a tin lined with sheets of butter-stained waxed paper smelling of sharp cheese and peppery cayenne. Everyone loves these cheese straws—I once caught a party guest stuffing his pockets with them.

A cookie press is needed to make these savory crackers. I prefer the version that resembles a caulking gun, although a turn-crank one will do. Some hard-core cheese straw makers invest in the electric version!

1½ cups all-purpose flour

½ teaspoon fine sea salt

Pinch of cayenne pepper, or to taste

½ pound sharp Cheddar cheese, at room temperature, freshly grated

½ cup (1 stick) unsalted butter, at room temperature

Position the oven racks in the top and bottom thirds of the oven. Preheat the oven to 375°F. Butter 2 baking sheets.

To make the dough, in a small bowl, combine the flour, salt, and cayenne. Set aside. In a heavy-duty mixer fitted with the paddle, cream the cheese and butter on medium speed until smooth and well combined. Gradually add the flour mixture. Mix on low speed until smooth. (The dough can also be made in the bowl of a large food processor: grate the cheese with the grating blade, then transfer the cheese to a bowl and insert the metal blade. Pulse the dry ingredients to combine, then add the butter and cheese. Process until smooth.) Cover the bowl with plastic wrap and set aside to rest for about 15 minutes.

To shape the dough, work it in your hands; it should be soft and pliable (like Play-Doh). Shape the dough into a cylinder and pack it into a cookie press fitted with the serrated ribbon disk.

Holding the cookie press at an angle to one of the prepared baking sheets, press the trigger twice, dragging the press away to make a long straw the length of the baking sheet. Repeat until you've covered the sheet, spacing the ribbons of dough 1 inch apart. Using a butter knife or offset spatula, cut each ribbon into 1- to 2-inch pieces. Repeat with the remaining dough and the other baking sheet. (If your cookie press extrudes the dough in fits and spurts, simply pick up the dough and reuse.)

Bake the cheese straws, rotating the baking sheets once, until lightly browned on the edges, about 20 minutes. Remove the baking sheets to a rack to cool slightly. Using an offset or slotted spatula, remove the individual cheese straws to cool completely.

MAKING AHEAD: Store the cheese straws at room temperature in an airtight container between sheets of waxed paper. They will keep for 2 to 3 weeks.

La Varenne Gougères

Makes 20
medium puffs

This is a savory version of the classic French pastry dough pâte à choux used to make profiteroles and éclairs. Gougères are a classic Burgundian treat commonly served with apéritifs at parties, bistros, and wine bars. You can increase the recipe (see Variation, following), but do not double it, as it does not multiply well.

A note of encouragement: don't panic when you are adding the eggs and the dough starts to look awful. Just keep stirring and it will come together.

3/4 cup water

1/3 cup unsalted butter

3/4 teaspoon coarse salt

3/4 cup all-purpose flour

5 large eggs, at room temperature

3/4 cup grated Gruyère cheese
(about 2 1/2 ounces)

Preheat the oven to 375°F. Line a baking sheet with a silicone baking sheet or parchment paper.

To make the dough, in a medium saucepan, bring the water, butter, and 1/2 teaspoon of the salt to a boil over high heat. Immediately remove the pan from the heat, add the flour all at once, and beat vigorously with a wooden spoon until the mixture is smooth and pulls away from the sides of the pan to form a ball, 30 to 60 seconds. (This mixture is called the panade.) Beat the mixture over low heat for an additional 30 to 60 seconds to dry the mixture.

To make the egg wash, whisk 1 of the eggs in a small bowl with the remaining 1/4 teaspoon salt until well mixed; set aside. With a wooden spoon, beat the remaining 4 eggs into the dough, one at a time, beating thoroughly after each addition. (It will come together, I promise.) Beat until the dough is shiny and slides from the spoon. Add the grated cheese.

If using parchment paper to line the baking sheet, "glue" down the paper at this point with a few dabs of the dough.

To form the gougères, use either a tablespoon for a rustic look, or for a more finished appearance, a pastry bag fitted with a 1/2-inch round tip. Spoon or pipe 12 mounds of dough about 2 inches in diameter onto the baking sheet, spacing them at least 2 inches apart. Brush the puffs with the reserved egg wash.

Bake until puffed and golden, 25 to 30 minutes. To test for doneness, remove one puff from the baking sheet and let it cool for 45 to 60 seconds. If it remains crisp and doesn't deflate, it is done. If not, return it to the oven and continue baking 5 to 10 minutes more. Remove to a rack to cool. Let the puffs cool slightly on the sheet, then transfer to a cooling rack. Serve warm or at room temperature.

MAKING AHEAD: These are brilliantly resilient and freeze beautifully. Once cooled, store them in an airtight container in the freezer for up to 4 weeks. Warm and re-crisp in a 350°F oven, 5 to 7 minutes.

VARIATION: To make 30 to 35 medium puffs, adjust the ingredient amounts as follows: 1 1/4 cups flour, 1 cup water, 3/4 teaspoon salt, 6 1/2 tablespoons butter, 5 eggs, and 1 cup cheese.

PIMENTO CHEESE IN CHERRY TOMATOES

Makes about
32 nibbles, or
4 cups filling

The "pâté of the South," pimento cheese is the epitome of a summer picnic delight. Everyone has a slightly different recipe, but the primary ingredients remain the same. Don't be tempted to buy grated cheese, because the end result won't be creamy enough. Try this stuffed in tomatoes, slathered on a celery stick, or (one of my favorites) straight from the bowl on a spoon.

1 1/2 pounds grated extra-sharp Cheddar cheese (about 4 cups)

1/2 onion, preferably Vidalia, grated

1/4 cup mayonnaise (page 282)

1 (4-ounce) jar pimentos, drained and finely chopped

Dash of hot sauce

Coarse salt and freshly ground black pepper

32 bite-size cherry tomatoes

32 small fresh flat-leaf parsley leaves

To make the pimento cheese, combine the cheese, onion, and mayonnaise in a bowl. Stir until well combined. Add the pimentos and hot sauce. Season with salt and pepper and set aside.

Meanwhile, using a serrated knife, slice off the top third of each cherry tomato. Using your index finger or a very small spoon, remove and discard the seeds and inside flesh of the tomatoes.

To fill the tomatoes, place the pimento cheese mixture in a piping bag fitted with a large round tip or use a medium sealable plastic bag with one of the corner tips snipped off. Fill each tomato with the mixture, allowing a little to rise above the tops. Garnish each tomato with a parsley leaf. Serve immediately.

MAKING AHEAD: The prepared cheese filling can be refrigerated in an airtight container for up to 2 weeks. The cherry tomatoes can be prepared up to 24 hours before serving: prep the tomatoes and store them, cut side down, on a baking sheet lined with damp paper towels. Wrap in plastic wrap and refrigerate until ready to fill.

VARIATION: For real comfort food, try warm pimento-cheese toasts. Place slices of sourdough bread on a baking sheet and brown on one side under the broiler. Turn over and thickly spread with pimento cheese. Return to the broiler and toast until the cheese is melted and bubbly, 5 to 7 minutes. Curl up on the sofa and enjoy.

VIDALIA ONION CONFIT WITH GARLIC TOASTS

Makes about
2 cups confit

One of Mama's favorite recipes is to simply peel and quarter Vidalias, top them with a pat of butter, and microwave the pieces until they are tender. This recipe is not much more difficult.

Confit is most often meat, such as duck, that has been cooked and preserved in its own fat, but the term also describes a jamlike condiment of cooked seasoned fruit or vegetables. This confit is wonderful as suggested, served on toasts as a nibble, but it also shines served as a condiment with pork or chicken. It is absolutely incredible with blue cheese.

1 baguette, sliced diagonally 1/4 inch thick

2 tablespoons olive oil

1 clove garlic, halved, for the toasts

1 tablespoon unsalted butter

6 onions, preferably Vidalia, chopped (about 1 1/2 pounds)

1/2 teaspoon firmly packed dark brown sugar

Coarse salt and freshly ground black pepper

1/4 cup dry red wine

1 tablespoon chopped fresh thyme, plus small sprigs for garnish

Position an oven rack 4 inches below the broiler element and preheat the broiler. To make the toasts, arrange the baguette slices on a baking sheet and brush on one side with some of the olive oil. Broil until brown, 2 to 3 minutes. Turn the toasts and broil the other side. Remove the toasts from the oven and while warm, rub one side of each toast with the cut surfaces of the garlic clove. Transfer to a rack to cool.

To make the confit, heat the butter and remaining olive oil in a large skillet over medium heat. Add the onions and sugar, and season with salt and pepper. Cook, stirring occasionally, until the onions are soft, 15 to 20 minutes.

Increase the heat to medium-high. Add the wine and cook, stirring occasionally, until the wine is reduced and the onions are a deep golden brown, 15 to 20 minutes more. Add the thyme; taste and adjust for seasoning with salt and pepper.

To serve, place the reserved toasts on a large serving platter and top each piece with a spoonful of confit. Garnish each with a sprig of thyme.

MAKING AHEAD: The toasts can be made up to 2 days ahead and stored at room temperature in an airtight container. The confit can also be made ahead and will actually improve as the flavors marry. Refrigerate the confit in an airtight container for up to 4 days.

Storing Onions

Onions need circulating air to stay fresh. Vidalia onions are particularly tricky due to their high sugar content. One of the best ways to store Vidalia onions is in the cut-off legs of pantyhose: drop an onion down the leg, tie a knot, and repeat. Hang the onion-filled hose from a hook in a cool, dry place. They will keep for months. Alternatively, wrap them separately in paper towels and refrigerate.

Exotic Mushroom-and-Herb Tart

Serves 4 to 6

There is no doubt that if you used only exotic mushrooms this tart would be delicious. However, white mushrooms, easier to find and less expensive, are fairly bland and will take on the flavors of other types. I suggest using a variety, including white button, for a balance of flavor and cost.

1 tablespoon unsalted butter

1 tablespoon canola oil

1 pound mixed mushrooms (such as cremini, chanterelle, morel, shiitake, and white button), sliced

1 large shallot, finely chopped

2 tablespoons chopped mixed fresh herbs (such as parsley, thyme, and tarragon)

Pinch of freshly ground nutmeg

Coarse salt and freshly ground black pepper

1 large egg, lightly beaten

1 tablespoon water

1 sheet frozen puff pastry (from one 14-ounce package), thawed according to package instructions, and unfolded

1/2 cup fresh goat cheese or cream cheese (about 3 ounces), at room temperature

To prepare the mushrooms, heat the butter and oil in a large, heavy-bottomed skillet over medium heat until shimmering. Add the mushrooms and saute until soft and all the liquid in the pan has evaporated, about 5 minutes. Add the shallot and cook until translucent, about 3 minutes more. Add the herbs and nutmeg. Taste and adjust for seasoning with salt and pepper. Set aside to cool.

Line a baking sheet with a silicone baking sheet or parchment paper. In a small bowl, whisk together the egg and the water to make a wash; set aside.

To prepare the pastry, on a lightly floured surface, roll out the puff pastry to a 12 by 15-inch rectangle. From it, cut one 12 by 5-inch rectangle, two 11 by 1/2-inch strips, and two 5 by 1/2-inch strips. Place the rectangle on the prepared baking sheet and prick all over with a fork. Brush all the pastry strips with the egg wash.

To form the pastry shell, place the short pastry strips, egg-wash side down, along the edges of the short sides of the pastry; place the long strips, egg-wash side down, along the edges of the long sides of the pastry. (Don't worry about making all of this very exact: the goal is to create a rim to contain the mushrooms. For a more rustic look, leave the 12 by 15-inch rectangle intact, and simply create a rim by folding over all 4 edges, and seal with egg wash.) Chill until firm, about 10 minutes in the freezer or 30 minutes in the refrigerator.

Preheat the oven to 400°F. Bake the tart shell until golden, about 15 minutes. Remove from the oven and spread the cheese evenly over bottom of the hot shell. Top with the reserved sauteed mushrooms. Return to the oven and continue to bake until heated through, about 10 minutes. Remove from the oven and let cool slightly. Cut into strips and serve.

MAKING AHEAD: The mushrooms can be prepared completely in advance and reheated. The tart shell can also be prepared to the point of chilling the raw dough. So, all you would need to do before serving is prebake the shell, fill, and finish baking.

BELGIAN ENDIVE WITH GOLD COAST SHRIMP SALAD

Makes about 30 hors d'oeuvres

We sometimes vacation at Jekyll and St. Simons Islands, part of a region that Georgians call the "Golden Isles" or "Gold Coast." For many years, it was the vacation retreat of very wealthy families from the Northeast. But it was another sort of gold that inspired the name: according to a local historian, it was named centuries ago by the first settlers, who were dazzled by the golden glow of the marshes at dusk. These marshes, the clear estuaries, and the surrounding waters are also home to sweet wild Atlantic shrimp.

With the endive leaves arranged in concentric circles on a platter, this is an especially attractive addition to the buffet table.

12 cups water

1 carrot, coarsely chopped

1 stalk celery, coarsely chopped

1 lemon, halved

1/2 onion, preferably Vidalia, peeled

2 bay leaves, preferably fresh

1 tablespoon coarse salt, plus more to taste

1 pound unshelled large shrimp (21/25 count)

4 to 6 heads Belgian endive

3 tablespoons chopped fresh tarragon

2 tablespoons mayonnaise (page 282)

Freshly ground black pepper

30 fresh tarragon leaves, for garnish

To poach the shrimp, combine the water, carrot, celery, lemon, onion, bay leaves, and 1 tablespoon of the salt in a large pot. Bring to a boil over high heat, then decrease the heat to low. Simmer gently for about 10 minutes to make a flavorful court-bouillon.

Have ready a frozen freezer pack sealed in a heavy-duty plastic bag or a large heavy-duty sealable plastic bag filled with ice cubes. Make an ice bath to cool the shrimp: transfer several cups (or more, depending on the quantity of shrimp) of the broth to a large heat-proof bowl. Place the ice pack in the bowl of broth; move the pack around until the broth is well chilled (drain and add more ice to the bag as needed). Return the heat to high and bring the remaining mixture to a rolling boil. Add the shrimp and boil until the shells are pink and the meat is white, 1 to 2 minutes. Do not overcook.

Drain the shrimp in a colander or remove with a slotted spoon, then immediately transfer to the chilled liquid to stop the cooking process. Set aside.

To prepare the endive, cut off and discard the root ends. Pull the heads apart one leaf at a time. Arrange the leaves in concentric circles like a flower on a large platter.

To prepare the salad, peel, devein, and coarsely chop the shrimp. Place in a bowl with the chopped tarragon and mayonnaise; stir to combine. Taste and adjust for seasoning with salt and pepper.

To assemble, place 1 generous teaspoon of shrimp salad near the trimmed bottom edge of each endive leaf. Garnish each with a tarragon leaf. Serve immediately.

MAKING AHEAD: The shrimp salad can be prepared completely ahead and stored in an airtight container in the refrigerator for up to 2 days. The leaves can be prepared and wrapped in damp paper towels in a sealable plastic bag overnight. Finally, up to 2 hours ahead, the filled endive leaves can be arranged on the platter, covered with a damp paper towel, and refrigerated. Serve chilled.

Poached Georgia Shrimp

Serves 4 to 6

Poaching means to gently simmer food in liquid—water, stock, court-bouillon, or even oil. Here, it's court-bouillon, an aromatic stock that transfers its flavors to the food cooked in it, traditionally fish and shellfish. Use the best possible extra-virgin olive oil to make this dish really shine.

12 cups water

1 carrot, coarsely chopped

1 stalk celery, coarsely chopped

1 lemon, halved

1/2 onion, preferably Vidalia, peeled

2 bay leaves, preferably fresh

1 tablespoon coarse salt, plus more to taste

11/2 pounds unshelled large shrimp (21/25 count)

1/2 cup extra-virgin olive oil

Juice of 2 lemons

Freshly ground black pepper

1/4 cup chopped fresh flat-leaf parsley

1 baguette, sliced 1/4 inch thick, for accompaniment

To poach the shrimp, in a large pot, combine the water, carrot, celery, lemon, onion, bay leaves, and 1 tablespoon of the salt. Bring to a boil over high heat, then decrease the heat to low. Simmer gently for about 10 minutes to make a flavorful court-bouillon. Return the heat to high and bring the mixture to a rolling boil. Add the shrimp and boil until the shells are pink and the meat is white, 1 to 2 minutes. Do not overcook.

Drain the shrimp in a colander. As soon as the shrimp are just cool enough to touch, peel and devein them.

To dress the shrimp, while they are still warm, place them in a large bowl with the olive oil and lemon juice. Toss to coat, then season with salt and pepper. Marinate the shrimp at room temperature for at least 30 minutes and up to 1 hour before serving. Add the chopped parsley and adjust for seasoning with salt and pepper.

Serve the shrimp on baguette slices, drizzled with some of the juices.

MAKING AHEAD: The shrimp can be prepared completely ahead and refrigerated in an airtight container in the refrigerator for up to 2 days. (The most important part is bathing them in the lemon mixture while they are still warm.) Bring to room temperature before serving.

Shrimp

Jumbo, large, and medium are all arbitrary designations for shrimp. Chefs buy shrimp according to an industry designation— the count per pound. For example, a count of 41/50 means that there are between 41 and 50 shrimp per pound, while U12 indicates that there are "under 12" shrimp per pound. In general, large shrimp are 21/25 count, extra-large are 16/20 count, and jumbo shrimp are 11/15 count.

COCA-COLA–GLAZED WINGS

Many Southern families, mine included, have recipes that use Coca-Cola, most often shortened to "Co-Cola." Mama still occasionally makes her Coca-Cola cake and Meme would sometimes use Coke when she baked her Easter ham.

These nouveau Southern wings are by no means traditional, but they are lip-smacking good and garnered me a Golden Whisk Award from *The Atlanta Journal-Constitution* as one of the best recipes of 2005. The sweetness of the Coke, combined with the heat of the peppers, is incredible. Wing pieces are available at most supermarkets, but look for whole wings. Not only are these wings less expensive, but the tips may also be used to prepare chicken stock (page 227).

1 cup Coca-Cola Classic

Juice of 2 limes

1½ cups firmly packed light brown sugar

3 jalapeño chiles, finely chopped, plus 2 jalapeño chiles, sliced, for garnish

3 pounds chicken wings (12 to 14 whole wings)

Coarse salt and freshly ground black pepper

Position an oven rack 4 inches below the broiler element. Preheat the broiler. Line a baking sheet with aluminum foil and place an ovenproof rack on the lined baking sheet.

To make the glaze, in a small saucepan, bring the soda, lime juice, brown sugar, and the chopped jalapeño chiles to a boil over high heat. Decrease the heat to medium-low and simmer until syrupy, about 30 minutes; keep warm over low heat.

To prepare the chicken wings, cut off the wing tips (reserve the tips to make stock), and halve the wings at the joint. Place the wing pieces in a large bowl and season with salt and pepper. Pour about half the glaze over the wings and toss to coat. Keep the remaining sauce warm over low heat.

To broil the wings, place the glazed wings on the rack set on the baking sheet. Broil for 10 minutes per side, brushing twice on each side with the reserved glaze.

Transfer to a warm platter, garnish with the sliced jalapeño chiles, and serve immediately.

MAKING AHEAD: The glaze can be made ahead, cooled, and refrigerated in an airtight container for up to 3 days. Bring to room temperature before cooking the wings. The wings can be completely prepared ahead and reheated in a 350°F oven until warmed through, about 10 minutes.

HEIRLOOM TOMATO-AND-OLIVE TARTINES

Serves 4 to 6

In French, tartine means a slice of bread with jam, butter, or other spread. It's a typical after-school snack for children. But there is nothing childlike about this grown-up version: baguette toasts covered with a savory, deliciously salty tapenade, enhanced with capers. Adding capers to olives and anchovies may seem redundantly salty, but they add another layer of flavor.

As Meme grew older, her doctor told her to avoid seeds. She loved all sorts of fresh vegetables and typically "worked around" this restriction. I was happy to help her out by removing tomato seeds. Here is my way: halve the tomato crosswise through its midsection with a serrated knife. Use your index finger to scoop out the seeds from each half, then give the tomato a gentle squeeze to draw out any seeds that remain.

3 large cloves garlic

2 cups pitted kalamata or other brine-cured black olives

4 anchovy fillets, drained

1 tablespoon drained capers

1 teaspoon chopped fresh thyme, plus thyme sprigs for garnish

1 teaspoon chopped fresh rosemary

1/4 cup plus 2 tablespoons extra-virgin olive oil

Coarse salt and freshly ground black pepper

1 baguette, sliced diagonally 1/4 inch thick

2 to 4 ripe heirloom tomatoes, cored, seeded, and chopped

To prepare the tapenade, in the bowl of a food processor fitted with the metal blade, combine 2 of the garlic cloves, the olives, anchovies, capers, thyme, and rosemary. Process until almost smooth. With the machine running, gradually add 1/4 cup of the olive oil. Process the mixture until smooth. Taste and adjust for seasoning with freshly ground black pepper. Transfer to a small bowl and set aside.

Position an oven rack 4 inches below the broiler element and preheat the broiler. To make the toasts, arrange the baguette slices on a baking sheet and brush one side with the 2 tablespoons olive oil. Broil until brown, 2 to 3 minutes. Turn and broil the other side. Halve the remaining clove of garlic. Remove the toast from the oven and while warm, rub one side of each toast with the cut surface of the garlic. Transfer to a rack to cool.

Place the chopped tomatoes in a bowl and season with salt and pepper.

To assemble, spread the toasts with a spoonful or so of tapenade. Press a spoonful of the seasoned chopped tomatoes into the tapenade to cover. Drizzle with a little of the remaining olive oil, and garnish with a small sprig of thyme.

MAKING AHEAD: The tapenade can be prepared ahead and refrigerated in an airtight container for up to 5 days. The toasts can be made up to 2 days ahead and stored at room temperature in an airtight container.

SAUTEED GREENS BRUSCHETTA WITH FRESH MOZZARELLA

Serves 4 to 6

Working the line in a restaurant is usually challenging, often miserable, but always an absolute adrenalin-filled rush. When dinner service is going at full throttle, the only option is to do as instructed by the expediter and hang on. This is a version of an appetizer served from my station many years ago while I was interning for chef Nora Pouillon at her Restaurant Nora, in Washington, D.C. She was an amazing role model for me: not only was she an industry leader and a woman, but also a pioneer in the organic movement. Her restaurant was the first in America to be certified organic.

Fresh mozzarella is radically different from the hard "pizza" cheese commonly found in supermarket refrigerator cases. The fresh version, in the form of balls packed in lightly salted brine or whey, is increasingly available in many local markets.

1 baguette, sliced diagonally 1/4 inch thick

2 tablespoons extra-virgin olive oil

2 cloves garlic, halved, for the toasts, plus 2 more cloves garlic, very finely chopped

1/2 pound dandelion greens, fresh spinach, or arugula, stemmed

Coarse salt and freshly ground black pepper

1/2 cup shredded fresh mozzarella cheese

Position an oven rack 4 inches below the broiler element and pre-heat the broiler. To make the toasts, arrange the baguette slices on a baking sheet and brush on one side with some of the olive oil. Broil until brown, 2 to 3 minutes. Turn the toasts and broil the other side. Remove the toasts from the oven and while warm, rub one side of each toast with the cut surfaces of the halved garlic cloves. Transfer to a rack to cool.

To prepare the greens, in a large, heavy-bottomed saute pan, heat the remaining olive oil over medium heat. Add the chopped garlic and cook until fragrant, 45 to 60 seconds. Increase the heat to medium-high, add the greens, season with salt and pepper, and saute, stirring, until wilted and tender, about 3 minutes. Remove from the heat and pour off any excess liquid. Add the mozzarella and stir to combine. Taste and adjust for seasoning with salt and pepper.

To assemble, place about 1 tablespoon of the greens mixture on the oiled side of each toast. Serve immediately.

MAKING AHEAD: The toasts can be made up to 2 days ahead and stored at room temperature in an airtight container.

CHAPTER 2

SALADS AND SLAWS

THE SOUTH IS OFTEN referred to as the "Bible Belt," but when it comes to cooking, it is undoubtedly the "Mayonnaise Belt." All too often mayonnaise is the first ingredient of an old-fashioned Southern salad or slaw. Then, there is our unfortunate fascination with gelatin and "congealed salads," a legacy of the 1930s, the era of newfangled icebox cooking.

Still, in the smothering heat of summer, a cold salad makes a welcome addition to a buffet. One positive benefit of our unbearably long, hot summer is a blissfully long growing season of fine, fresh vegetables. Summer is the time for shelling peas, picking tomatoes, and trimming green beans, the ingredients of contemporary Southern salads. How better to feature the flavors of these fresh vegetables than with minimal cooking or no cooking at all?

The salads in this chapter reflect a marked Southern or French sensibility, or a marriage of both. My Fingerling Potato Salad (page 48) utilizes the classic French technique of pouring vinegar over hot potatoes to heighten their flavor. The dressing, though, is a typically Southern blend of mayonnaise and sour cream.

That is not to say the recipes are all traditional or served in the expected way. Vodka-spiked watermelon, a mainstay at college fraternity parties, is now all dressed up. Black-eyed peas are not the usual side dish flavored with hog jowl, but tossed in a shallot vinaigrette. In the South, ambrosia is a dessert, but as my version omits the usual canned pineapple in sugary syrup, candy-like marshmallows, or sweetened coconut, I serve it as a fresh-fruit salad (truth is, I will eat it anytime!).

Southern salads once suffered from a scarcity of lettuce greens, as the summer heat is generally too intense for lettuce cultivation. To compensate, the staples of Southern salads were vegetables such as tomatoes, cucumbers, bell peppers, celery, radishes, and onion. Thanks to improved farming techniques, shipping, and refrigeration, that's all changed. Salad greens are now widely available and common on the Southern table.

Making a green salad seems simple, especially now with prepackaged greens that you don't even have to wash—just dress and toss. But that's just a "salad." How do you make a great salad? Use the freshest possible greens and vegetables and treat them with the utmost care. Wash them, if necessary, by swishing in cold water, whether in the sink or a large bowl. Then dry them thoroughly so the salad won't be waterlogged and the dressing diluted. Pat the greens dry with a large kitchen towel, or use a salad spinner, if necessary (in batches, so the tender leaves are not crammed and crushed or broken).

Don't overdress: salad ingredients should be lightly coated, not swimming in liquid. When I prepare any type of dressing, I season both the dressing and the greens, to layer the flavors. Toss the salad and dressing together, gently, in a large bowl, turning the greens over until they are coated. Never, ever just pour the dressing on top of a bed of naked greens and serve. That is like lying in an unmade bed and trying to get the covers straight—it just won't work. Once dressed, always serve the salad immediately or it will wilt from sitting too long in the dressing.

Slaws, on the other hand, usually benefit from a little resting time to wilt the cabbage and let the flavors marry. But don't let them rest too long or they'll get limp. Cole slaw, an absolute must for picnics, and the perfect accompaniment to fried fish and hushpuppies, should be cool, crisp, and fresh. Like salads, a slaw will suffer from too much or too little dressing: too much and it's cold cabbage soup, too little and it won't fully coat a cabbage's wrinkly surface.

MEME'S AMBROSIA

No holiday in our family would be complete without this refreshing fruit salad. My grand-father Dede would patiently grate the fresh coconut on a box grater, also put to use for the obligatory coconut cake. My sister, Jona, would sit, fidgeting, on the stool in the kitchen waiting for a sip of the coconut juice. Once the coconut was grated, Dede would peel and segment enough oranges to make gallons of this exquisite con-coction. Although Dede did all the work (with a little help from Jona), I've named this dish for Meme, because she loved it and he made it for her. Use this simple recipe as the starting point for creating your own version. Always use fresh coconut, not flaked, canned, bagged, or frozen.

6 navel oranges

1 cup shredded fresh coconut
(see below)

1/4 cup sugar (optional)

To section the oranges, using a sharp knife and a cutting board, slice off the tops and bottoms so the oranges will stand upright. For each orange, set the fruit upright on the board. Working from top to bottom, slice off the peel, pith, and outer membranes from the orange to expose the segments. Carefully cut each segment away from its membranes and put in a bowl along with any juice. Squeeze any remaining juice from the membranes, then discard them.

To assemble, add the coconut to the orange segments and gently toss to combine. Add sugar to taste, depending on the sweetness of the oranges. The ambrosia can be refrigerated for up to 2 days, covered.

Preparing Fresh Coconut

To crack the coconut, pierce three holes on the coconut shell with an ice pick or a clean screwdriver and drain out the juice. Place the pierced, drained coconut directly on the rack in a pre-heated 350°F oven for about 10 minutes to crack the shell. Remove it from the oven and wrap it in a kitchen towel; place it either on the floor or on a sturdy work surface that can tolerate hammering. Give the shell a couple of whacks with a hammer to break it completely open. Remove the pieces of broken coconut from the towel. The coconut meat, covered with brown skin, will pull away easily from the cracked shell. Using a vegetable peeler, remove the brown skin from the meat. Grate the skinless meat in a food processor or with a box grater.

MAMA'S SPINACH SALAD WITH MUSHROOMS

Serves 4 to 6

When we lived in small-town South Georgia, we used to travel to Atlanta to visit Aunt Lee, a stylish lady in the glamorous big city. Before we left Atlanta for home, we would stop by the Dekalb Farmer's Market, which opened in the late 1970s as a small produce stand and has now grown into a 140,000-square-foot market, serving up to 100,000 people every week. There, Mama would buy the ingredients for this hearty salad to make after we got home.

ITALIAN SALAD DRESSING

6 tablespoons extra-virgin olive oil

2 tablespoons red wine vinegar

2 tablespoons chopped fresh flat-leaf parsley

1 tablespoon freshly squeezed lemon juice

2 cloves garlic, very finely chopped

1 teaspoon dried basil, crumbled

1/4 teaspoon red pepper flakes

Pinch of dried oregano, crumbled

Coarse salt and freshly ground black pepper

SALAD

6 slices thick-cut bacon, cut into lardons (see page 179)

1/2 red onion, thinly sliced

1 pound fresh spinach, coarse stems removed

12 large white button mushrooms, sliced

2 or 3 hard-cooked eggs (see page 11), peeled and quartered

Coarse salt and freshly ground black pepper

To prepare the dressing, combine the oil, vinegar, parsley, lemon juice, garlic, basil, red pepper, and oregano in a small jar. Shake to blend. Season to taste with salt and pepper.

To prepare the salad, line a plate with paper towels. Heat a large skillet over medium heat. Add the bacon and cook until crisp and brown, 5 to 7 minutes. Using a slotted spoon, transfer the bacon to the plate. Set aside. Drain off all but about 1 tablespoon of the fat from the skillet. Add the red onion and cook until tender, about 2 minutes. Set aside.

To assemble the salad, place the spinach in a large bowl. Add the reserved bacon and onion, mushrooms, and eggs. Drizzle over a little of the salad dressing. Toss to coat, adding more if needed. Taste and adjust for seasoning with salt and pepper. Serve immediately.

Cleaning Mushrooms

When cleaning mushrooms, keep the variety in mind. Wash white button or cremini in a colander under cold running water. Once cleaned, trim the stem end with a fresh cut, and use shortly thereafter or the mushrooms will continue to soak up water. (Do not trim before washing or they will soak up the water.) Look for cremini and white button mushrooms with no bruises, closed gills, and a rounded cap. More expensive mushrooms like chanterelle and morel, and even shiitake, need to be gently wiped with a moist cloth. Most mushrooms stems are edible, except for shiitake, which are very tough and woody and need to be completely removed.

BLACK-EYED PEA SALAD

Serves 4 to 6

I like to serve this salad with vinaigrette, as here, or lightly moistened with a dollop of homemade mayonnaise (page 282). (I seem to have some sort of primal need to combine tomatoes with mayonnaise.) The truth is, this salad really reminds me of how a plate of food looks toward the end of a summer meal when all the vegetables and flavors swim and mingle together.

This salad can be served as is, in lettuce cups, or as a side dish for grilled or fried chicken. Regardless of how you serve it, all of the vegetables should be chopped approximately the same size so each bite is evenly mixed.

3 ears fresh sweet corn, shucked and silks removed

2 cups freshly shelled black-eyed peas (about 1 3/4 pounds unshelled) or frozen black-eyed peas, thawed

2 tomatoes, cored, seeded, and chopped

1 onion, preferably Vidalia, finely chopped

1/2 stalk celery, very finely chopped

1 clove garlic, very finely chopped

1 small bunch basil, stemmed and leaves very thinly sliced into chiffonade (see page 197)

2 tablespoons apple cider vinegar

1 teaspoon Dijon mustard

1/4 cup canola oil

Coarse salt and freshly ground black pepper

Prepare an ice-water bath by filling a large bowl with ice and water. Line a plate with paper towels.

To cook the corn, bring a large pot of salted water to a rolling boil over high heat. Add the corn and cook until tender, 2 to 3 minutes. Remove with tongs to the ice water to cool, then transfer to the towel-lined plate to drain.

To cook the black-eyed peas, add them to the pot and simmer until tender but not mushy, about 20 minutes. (Taste one and see how tender it is; the cooking time will depend on their freshness.)

Meanwhile, cut the corn kernels from the cobs and place in a large bowl. Add the tomatoes, onion, and garlic. When the peas are tender, drain them in a colander, then shock under cold running water to stop the cooking. Once the peas are completely cool, drain very well, shaking to remove all the moisture, and add to the corn mixture, along with the basil. Set aside.

To make the dressing, whisk together the vinegar and mustard in a bowl. Add the oil in a slow steady stream, whisking constantly, until the dressing is creamy and emulsified. Season the dressing with salt and pepper.

To serve, drizzle over a little of the salad dressing. Toss to coat, adding more if needed. Taste and adjust for seasoning with salt and pepper. Serve immediately.

CLASSIC COLE SLAW

There are three kinds of Southern slaws: barbecue slaw, cole slaw, and yellow slaw. Barbecue slaw is a western North Carolina tradition made with chopped cabbage, pungent vinegar, and red pepper. Cole slaw is what most people in Georgia consider slaw—primarily cabbage and mayonnaise. Yellow, or mustard, slaw is more commonly found in South Carolina and eastern North Carolina (its main ingredients are cabbage and mustard). Try a spoonful of this slaw on Pulled Pork Sandwiches with Mama's Barbecue Sauce (page 81) for a sloppy, glorious treat.

1/4 cup sugar

1/3 cup mayonnaise (page 282)

1/4 cup buttermilk

Juice of 1 lemon

1 tablespoon apple cider vinegar

1 teaspoon grated onion (preferably Vidalia)

1/2 teaspoon dry mustard

1/4 small head green cabbage, cored and finely shredded (about 2 cups)

1/4 small head red cabbage, cored and finely shredded (about 2 cups)

1 carrot, finely shredded

Coarse salt and freshly ground black pepper

In a large bowl, combine the sugar, mayonnaise, buttermilk, lemon juice, vinegar, onion, and mustard. Whisk until smooth. Add the green and red cabbages and carrot, and mix well to combine. Season with salt and pepper. Cover with plastic wrap and refrigerate to marinate for at least 2 hours before serving. Adjust for seasoning with salt and pepper before serving.

GRILLED STEAK SALAD WITH GREEN BEANS AND BLUE CHEESE

Serves 4 to 6

Traditional balsamic vinegar, from the Italian region of Emilia-Romagna, takes a minimum of twelve years to produce, and can be very costly. However, I don't think you need to spend a lot if you're going to toss it with a salad or use it for cooking. One that is traditionally barrel-aged, then mixed with a lesser-quality vinegar works very well and is typically about fifteen dollars. A good blue cheese, such as Roquefort, Maytag, or Stilton, would be wonderful here.

1 pound haricots verts or slender green beans, trimmed

$1/2$ cup extra-virgin olive oil

3 tablespoons balsamic vinegar

3 (8-ounce) boneless rib-eye or sirloin steaks

Coarse salt and freshly ground black pepper

6 cups arugula (about 6 ounces)

4 cups grape tomatoes, halved

$11/4$ cups pitted kalamata or other brine-cured black olives

1 cup crumbled blue cheese (about $31/2$ ounces)

Prepare a charcoal fire using about 6 pounds of charcoal and burn until the coals are completely covered with a thin coating of light gray ash, 20 to 30 minutes. Spread the coals evenly over the grill bottom, position the grill rack above the coals, and heat until medium-hot (when you can hold your hand 5 inches above the grill surface for no longer than 3 or 4 seconds). Or, for a gas grill, turn on all burners to High, close the lid, and heat until very hot, 10 to 15 minutes.

Meanwhile, prepare an ice-water bath by filling a large bowl with ice and water. Line a plate with paper towels.

To cook the beans, bring a large pot of salted water to a boil over high heat. Add the beans to the pot and cook until tender, 5 to 7 minutes. Drain well in a colander, then set the colander with the beans in the ice bath (to set the color and stop the cooking), making sure the beans are submerged. (By setting the colander in the ice bath, you won't have to fish the beans out of the ice water.) Once chilled, remove the beans to the prepared plate to drain.

To make the dressing, combine the oil and vinegar in a bowl. Remove 2 tablespoons of the dressing to a small bowl. Season the steaks with salt and pepper; brush both sides with the reserved 2 tablespoons of dressing.

Grill the steaks to your desired doneness, about 4 minutes per side for medium-rare. Remove to a clean plate and set aside for 2 to 3 minutes to rest and let the juices redistribute. Slice the steaks crosswise into $1/4$-inch strips.

To serve, place the green beans, arugula, tomatoes, and olives in large bowl. Drizzle over the remaining dressing and toss to coat. Season with salt and pepper. Divide the salad among individual serving plates. Top each with some steak strips and crumbled blue cheese.

VEGETABLE SLAW WITH CREAMY ASIAN DRESSING

Serves 4 to 6

Except for the mayonnaise, this Asian-inspired slaw is very un-Southern. The combination of flavors and colors makes a grand addition to any summer picnic. Mirin is a sweet, low-alcohol rice wine, essentially "cooking sake."

Believe it or not, soy sauce actually did make it into Meme's kitchen. She was once featured in an article in the local newspaper, and, I suppose, thinking her simple country recipes were not appropriate for the "big time," she included a recipe for her stir-fry. It was a combination of broccoli, carrots, and snow peas, with soy sauce as a seasoning. The recipe might have been "exotic" back then, but Meme's stir-fry technique was pure South: the vegetables cooked for a very un-stir-fry length of time—20 minutes!

1/4 cup mayonnaise (page 282)

2 tablespoons rice vinegar

1 tablespoon mirin

1 tablespoon soy sauce

Juice of 1 lemon

1 small jalapeño chile, seeded and very finely chopped

1/2 English (hothouse) cucumber, partially peeled (to form vertical stripes of green peel and white flesh)

1/4 small head red cabbage, cored and very finely shredded

1/4 small head napa (Chinese) cabbage, very finely shredded

4 red, icicle, or French Breakfast radishes, trimmed and very thinly sliced

2 carrots, grated

1 red bell pepper, cored, seeded, and cut into thin strips

2 green onions, white and green parts, thinly sliced

2 tablespoons sesame seed, preferably black

Coarse salt and freshly ground black pepper

To make the dressing, combine the mayonnaise, rice vinegar, mirin, soy sauce, lemon juice, and jalapeño in a small bowl. Set aside.

To prepare the salad, halve the cucumber lengthwise and scrape off the seeds with a teaspoon. Slice the cucumber into 1/8-inch-thick half-moons. Place the slices in a large bowl. Add the red and napa cabbages, radishes, carrots, red pepper, green onions, and sesame seed. Pour over just enough dressing to lightly coat. Season with salt and pepper and toss well to combine. Serve immediately.

Sesame Seed

Sesame seed was brought to America by African slaves, whose word for it, *benne*, became part of the vernacular in the American South, specifically in the Low Country around Charleston, South Carolina. Black, brown, and even red sesame seed is available, but the most common color is a pale ivory-yellow. I like to use black when I want to make a bold visual statement. Sesame seed has a nutty, sweet flavor and is used in both sweet and savory cooking. (Mama, oddly enough, dislikes it so much that she picks the seeds off of her hamburger bun.)

ARUGULA WITH ROASTED PEARS AND GOAT CHEESE

Serves 4 to 6

Not that long ago, for most of America, "cheese" meant pre-sliced singles wrapped in plastic, or insipidly flavored orange wheels produced in America's heartland. Any cheeses considered "gourmet" were imported from Europe. Fortunately, artisanal cheesemaking is now thriving all over the country, including the South. I love the fresh goat cheese from the Wehner family's Green Hill Dairy and Sweet Grass Dairy in Thomasville, Georgia. Their cows and goats roam freely in the woods and graze in lush, green pastures. This idyllic existence, the family maintains, makes them so content that they produce the most delicious milk, which, in turn, makes the best cheese. Sweet, roasted Bosc pears, tender baby arugula, and mild creamy goat cheese make this simple, elegant salad sing.

2 tablespoons unsalted butter, melted

2 or 3 firm Bosc pears, halved lengthwise and cored

Sea salt and freshly ground black pepper

4 to 6 cups baby arugula (about 4 ounces)

1 tablespoon sherry or balsamic vinegar

2 tablespoons extra-virgin olive oil

4 to 6 ounces fresh goat cheese, at room temperature

1/4 cup honey (preferably tupelo, orange blossom, or sweet clover)

Preheat the oven to 400°F. Brush a baking sheet with some of the melted butter.

To roast the pears, arrange the pear halves, cut sides down, on the buttered sheet. Brush the tops with the remaining melted butter. Season with salt and pepper. Roast until just tender to the point of a knife, 20 to 25 minutes.

To dress the greens, place the arugula in a large bowl. Drizzle with the vinegar and olive oil. Season with salt and pepper and toss to combine and coat.

To serve, divide the greens among 4 to 6 individual serving plates. Top each with a warm roasted pear half, cut side up. Place a spoonful of goat cheese on each pear. Drizzle with honey. Season with salt and freshly ground black pepper. Serve immediately.

Bosc Pears

Bosc pears are the archetypical pear, with an elongated neck and round, bell-shaped bottom. Their firm, sweet flesh is suitable for fresh eating, salads, and cooking. They are harvested in the fall. Look for firm fruit with a golden bronze color.

ROASTED BEET SALAD WITH WALNUTS AND WALNUT OIL

Serves 4 to 6

These beets are roasted, and very delicious! But if you have a mandoline, a professional tool that will slice vegetables evenly and very thinly, skip the roasting process and slice the beets raw (this works only with beets at the peak of seasonal freshness—sweet, dry, and tender). When really fresh beets are sliced so thin as to be almost shaved, there is no need to cook them. Toasted walnut oil adds a classic French flavor to the salad, but you could also use almond or pecan oil, available online and at gourmet or specialty markets. Store nut oils in the refrigerator; they turn rancid fairly quickly.

4 medium fresh beets

¼ cup walnuts, for garnish

1 shallot, very finely chopped

1 tablespoon Dijon mustard

2 tablespoons sherry or walnut vinegar

3 tablespoons extra-virgin olive oil

2 tablespoons walnut oil

Coarse salt and freshly ground black pepper

6 to 8 ounces mâche or tender young greens

4 to 6 ounces fresh goat cheese

Preheat the oven to 375°F. Wrap the beets individually in aluminum foil and bake them directly on the oven rack until completely tender, 1 to 1¹/₂ hours. Remove from the oven. When cool enough to handle, slip off the skins and slice the beets ¹/₄ inch thick. Set aside.

While the beets are roasting, toast the walnuts on a baking sheet in the same oven until brown, about 10 minutes. Let the nuts cool slightly, coarsely chop them, and transfer to a small bowl; set aside.

To prepare the dressing, whisk together the shallot, mustard, and vinegar in a small bowl. Add the olive and walnut oils in a slow stream, whisking constantly, until creamy and emulsified; season with salt and pepper.

Just before serving, toss the beets in a little of the dressing to coat. Taste and adjust for seasoning with salt and pepper. In a separate bowl, toss the mâche with just enough dressing to coat. Taste and adjust for seasoning with salt and pepper.

To serve, divide the greens and beets among the serving plates. Top with a spoonful of goat cheese and a sprinkling of toasted walnuts. Serve immediately.

CARROT AND BEET SALAD WITH LEMON VINAIGRETTE

Serves 4 to 6

We bought my grandmother a food processor, but she continued to use her hand-cranked shredder for grating. Made of cast aluminum, it was a sturdy beast that attached to the counter with a vise. She would peel the carrots and Dede would patiently shred them into a large bowl for carrot slaw.

This recipe is a bit more complex in flavor and technique than Meme's, and I use a food processor to shred the vegetables. Just make sure you shred the carrots first! To prevent the beets from staining the carrots when mixed in the salad, the key is to dress the beets before combining with the carrots. This seals in their red pigments (betalains), which don't dissolve in oil.

2 small shallots, finely chopped

1 clove garlic, finely chopped

1 tablespoon Dijon mustard

Juice of 2 lemons

1/2 cup walnut oil

Coarse salt and freshly ground black pepper

1/4 cup finely chopped walnuts

5 large carrots, finely shredded

6 small to medium fresh beets, peeled and finely shredded

To make the dressing, whisk together the shallot, garlic, mustard, and lemon juice in a bowl. Add the walnut oil in a slow stream and blend until smooth. Season with salt and pepper; mix in the chopped walnuts. Set aside.

In separate bowls, toss the carrots with half the dressing and the beets with the remainder. Taste each and adjust for seasoning with salt and pepper.

Once the vegetables are separately dressed, they may be combined and served, or refrigerated and held separately for up to several hours before combining (you may either bring to room temperature or serve chilled). Serve immediately after the carrots and beets are mixed.

CELERIAC SLAW

Serves 4 to 6

Céleri rémoulade—shredded celeriac (celery root) in a mayonnaise-based dressing—is the French version of slaw. Peel a celeriac bulb with a chef's knife, trimming away the gnarled brown skin to expose the pale flesh. Once peeled, it should be rubbed with lemon or soaked in acidulated water to prevent browning.

1 medium bulb celeriac (about 1½ pounds), peeled and grated

½ cup mayonnaise (page 282)

1 tablespoon Dijon mustard

1 tablespoon capers, rinsed and chopped

1 tablespoon chopped fresh tarragon

1 tablespoon chopped fresh flat-leaf parsley

Grated zest and juice of 1 lemon

Coarse salt and freshly ground black pepper

In a bowl, combine the celeriac, mayonnaise, mustard, capers, tarragon, parsley, and lemon zest and juice. Toss to combine. Taste and adjust for seasoning with salt and pepper. Cover with plastic wrap and chill for up to 8 hours until ready to serve.

HEART-HEALTHY COLE SLAW

Serves 4 to 6

My friend Shelly shared this recipe, her aunt Mimi's, at a cookout one summer. It's lighter and healthier than most, and since it is essentially vinegar and oil, it is safe to have on a buffet for hours.

½ head green cabbage, cored and finely chopped (about 4 cups)

½ green bell pepper, cored, seeded, and finely chopped

1 onion, preferably Vidalia, very finely chopped

2 tablespoons sugar

Coarse salt and freshly ground black pepper

¼ cup canola oil

¼ cup distilled white vinegar

½ teaspoon dry mustard

½ teaspoon celery seed

Place the cabbage, bell pepper, and onion in a large bowl. Sprinkle over the sugar and season with salt and pepper. Set aside.

In a small saucepan, combine the oil, vinegar, dry mustard, and celery seed. Season with salt and pepper. Bring to a boil over high heat, then reduce the heat and let simmer for 1 minute. Pour the hot dressing over the cabbage and toss to combine. Cover with plastic wrap and marinate in the refrigerator for 2 hours. To serve, remove from the refrigerator and taste and adjust for seasoning with salt and pepper.

FRISÉE SALAD WITH POACHED EGGS AND BACON

Practically every bistro in France has a version of this salad—*salade frisée aux lardons*—on the menu. Made with frisée, a frilly green in the chicory family, and traditionally topped with a poached egg, it is very rich—not the sort of salad to eat every day, but wonderful occasionally as a substantial lunch or a light supper.

4 to 6 thick slices hearty country bread

2 tablespoons extra-virgin olive oil

Coarse salt and freshly ground black pepper

1 clove garlic, halved, for the toasts, plus 1 clove garlic, very finely chopped

3 tablespoons distilled white vinegar

4 to 6 large eggs

6 slices thick-cut bacon, cut into lardons (see page 179)

1 large shallot, chopped

2 tablespoons best-quality red wine vinegar

2 heads frisée (about 8 ounces), washed, dried, and torn

Preheat the broiler. To make the toasts, arrange the bread slices on a baking sheet and brush one side with the olive oil and season with salt and pepper. Broil about 4 inches from the heat until golden brown, 2 to 3 minutes. Turn the slices over and toast. Remove from the oven and while warm, rub one side of each toast with the cut surface of the halved garlic clove. Transfer to a rack and set aside.

Fill a large bowl with water and set aside (use hot water if serving the salad immediately, cold if making the eggs ahead). To poach the eggs, fill a large saucepan with 3 inches of water, add the white vinegar, and bring to a boil over medium-high heat. Break one of the eggs into a ramekin or teacup. Using the handle (not the bowl) of a wooden spoon, swirl the water to create a whirlpool effect, which will help the eggs hold their shape. Decrease the heat to medium-low so the water is at a gentle boil and slide the egg into the center. Reduce the heat and poach the egg until the white is solid and the yolk is firm but still soft to the touch, 3 to 4 minutes. Using a slotted spoon, remove the egg and transfer to the bowl of water; set aside. Return the water to a gentle boil, and repeat the process with the other eggs. The eggs can be poached up to 12 hours ahead and refrigerated in a sealed container. To serve them, reheat briefly in hot water.

Line a plate with paper towels. To cook the bacon, heat a large skillet over medium heat. Add the bacon and cook until crisp and brown, 5 to 7 minutes. Using a slotted spoon, transfer the bacon to the prepared plate; set aside.

To make the dressing, drain off all but about 2 tablespoons of the bacon fat from the skillet. Add the shallot and cook until translucent, about 1 minute. Add the chopped garlic and cook until fragrant, 45 to 60 seconds. Add the red wine vinegar and stir to combine (the vinegar will emit strong fumes, so keep your face back from the pan).

Add the greens to the skillet and toss to coat and wilt slightly. Taste and adjust for seasoning with salt and pepper.

To serve, divide the salad among individual serving plates. Using a slotted spoon, transfer the eggs from the bowl of water to paper towels; gently pat them dry. Place an egg on top of each bed of dressed greens. Garnish with the reserved bacon and season with pepper. Serve with the garlic toasts.

HEIRLOOM TOMATO SALAD WITH GOAT CHEESE

Serves 4 to 6

No salad screams "summer" louder than this one. The combination of tomatoes with freshly chopped herbs is a testament to my philosophy of simple recipes executed with the best possible ingredients. Heirloom tomatoes are grown from non-hybrid, open-pollinated seeds, and are the varieties that have been passed down through the generations by farmers and gardeners around the world. They are far superior to the red-colored tennis balls available in most grocery stores. If you cannot find heirloom tomatoes, use a ripe tomato from your garden, a good produce market, or a farmer's market. Be sure to look for a regional goat cheese and support your local farmer. Other cheeses to consider for this recipe include briny cubes of feta or mild, creamy fresh mozzarella.

1$\frac{1}{2}$ tablespoons red wine vinegar

$\frac{1}{2}$ teaspoon Dijon mustard

2 tablespoons extra-virgin olive oil

2 tablespoons canola oil

Coarse salt and freshly ground black pepper

2 pounds mixed heirloom tomatoes, cored and cut into $\frac{1}{2}$-inch wedges

$\frac{1}{4}$ cup chopped mixed fresh herbs such as basil, parsley, and chives

4 to 6 ounces fresh goat cheese, crumbled

$\frac{1}{4}$ cup microgreens, such as basil, arugula, or beet (optional)

To make the dressing, whisk the vinegar and mustard together in a large bowl. Add the oils in a slow steady stream, whisking constantly, until the dressing is creamy and emulsified. Season with salt and pepper. Add the tomato wedges and gently toss to coat.

Add the herbs and goat cheese and toss to coat. Taste and adjust for seasoning with salt and pepper. Divide among chilled serving plates. Top with the greens. Serve immediately.

Microgreens

Microgreens are the plant's first true leaves and are exceptionally tender. The young seedlings are harvested when less than fourteen days old, often with the stems attached. The tiny leaves are exact miniatures of how they would look if left to mature. They are often very intense in flavor. Common varieties include arugula, basil, beet, collard, mustard, daikon, chard, and celery. Microgreens are available at upscale and natural grocery stores such as Whole Foods and many farmer's markets.

HERB GARDEN SALAD

Serves 4 to 6

Alain Passard is the chef-owner of the Parisian restaurant L'Arpège, awarded three Michelin stars, the highest possible rating from the most prestigious organization. He caused quite a stir when he "went vegetarian," as he had come from the classic French tradition of cooking with meat stocks. This salad is inspired by a dish he created when he entered his veggie phase.

This is well suited for cooks who grow their own herbs or are able to purchase good quality fresh herbs from their farmer's market—otherwise, it can be somewhat costly at a traditional grocery store. Rinse the herbs under cold running water, then spin them dry in a salad spinner. Carefully remove the leaves from the stems (don't cheat: use only the leaves, discard the stems). Use more herbs than lettuce. Nasturtiums (both leaves and flowers), cilantro, basil, and chervil are other herb suggestions.

4 to 6 thick slices hearty country bread

2 tablespoons extra-virgin olive oil

Coarse salt and freshly ground black pepper

1 clove garlic, halved

1 teaspoon sherry wine vinegar

1 teaspoon red wine vinegar

2 cups mixed young tender greens

1 cup fresh flat-leaf parsley leaves

1 cup fresh chives, snipped in 1/2-inch lengths

1/2 cup fresh dill leaves

1/2 cup fresh tarragon leaves

1/2 cup fresh mint leaves

1/4 cup microgreens, such as basil, arugula, or beet (optional)

Preheat the broiler. To make the toasts, arrange the bread slices on a baking sheet and brush one side with one tablespoon of the olive oil and season with salt and pepper. Broil about 4 inches from the heat until golden brown, 2 to 3 minutes. Turn the slices over and toast. Remove from the oven while warm, and rub one side of each toast with the cut surface of the garlic. Transfer to a rack and set aside.

To prepare the salad, combine the sherry and red wine vinegars and the remaining 1 tablespoon olive oil in a large bowl. Add the greens, parsley, chives, dill, tarragon, mint, and microgreens. Season with salt and pepper and toss to evenly coat the greens with the dressing. Place the garlic toasts on serving plates. Divide the salad on top of the toasts.

Fresh and Dried Herbs

Herbs are the leaves and sometimes the flowers of a plant. Spices are seeds, bark, and dried berries. Some recipes and cookbooks will specify 1 teaspoon of a freshly chopped herb or 1/2 teaspoon of a dried herb. This substitution ratio assumes that the herbs are freshly dried and very potent with essential oils. The truth is, many dried herbs and spices are not stored correctly or not replaced often enough, so the herbs are actually less potent than their fresh counterparts. I almost always use fresh herbs.

Mama's Potato Salad

Serves 6 to 8

Russet (also called Idaho) potatoes are not usually recommended for potato salad. They can become waterlogged when boiled and fall apart easily. Their high-starch, low-moisture content makes them inclined to absorb too much dressing. But that is the beauty of this dish. This is the archetypical summer potato salad that has been served on paper plates across the country for generations. When Mama prepares this salad, she lets the potatoes cool just enough, but not completely. The cubes break down slightly and the salad is a blend of larger pieces of potato with a little bit of creamy mash. This is one of my sister's favorite dishes, a comforting classic that echoes with childhood memories whenever Mama makes it, so she always makes a big batch. The recipe halves beautifully.

7 russet potatoes (about 3 pounds)

Coarse salt

$1^1/2$ cups mayonnaise (page 282)

5 large hard-cooked eggs (see page 11), peeled and grated

1 small onion, preferably Vidalia, finely chopped

4 stalks celery, finely chopped

$1/4$ cup sweet pickle or dill pickle relish

Freshly ground black pepper

To cook the potatoes, peel them and cut into $1/2$-inch cubes. Immediately place them in a large pot with water to cover; season with salt. Bring to a boil over high heat, and then decrease the heat to low. Simmer until tender, about 30 minutes. Drain the potatoes in a colander and transfer them to a large shallow bowl to cool.

Meanwhile, to make the dressing, combine the mayonnaise, grated eggs, onion, celery, and pickle relish in a bowl. Once the potatoes have cooled completely, pour the dressing over the potatoes and stir to combine. Taste and adjust for seasoning with salt and pepper. Serve at room temperature or chilled.

FINGERLING POTATO SALAD

Serves 4 to 6

While I lived and worked at La Varenne, we often dined outside on a terrace overlooking miles of Burgundian countryside. One memorable day, I cut off the tip of my left thumb while preparing potato salad for one of our outdoor feasts. I quickly wrapped my hand in a towel and raised it above my head. I grabbed the severed bit from the cutting board in my right hand, walked into Anne Willan's office, and told her I had cut myself. She asked to see it. I refused. She insisted. Finally, opening my right palm, I said, "Well, here it is." The grand dame Anne blanched and replied, "Oh dear, I think we need a Cognac." After a trip to the hospital I did enjoy the feast, but declined a serving of the potato salad.

3½ pounds fingerling or red bliss potatoes, halved

½ cup white wine vinegar

¾ cup mayonnaise (page 282)

¾ cup sour cream

1 tablespoon Dijon mustard

Coarse salt and freshly ground black pepper

1 onion, preferably Vidalia, chopped

1 stalk celery, finely chopped

½ cup chopped fresh flat-leaf parsley

To cook the potatoes, place them in a large pot of cold, salted water. Bring to a boil over high heat, then decrease the heat to medium-low. Simmer until the potatoes are tender, 10 to 15 minutes. Drain well in a colander. While still warm, transfer the potatoes to a baking sheet and drizzle with the vinegar. Set aside to cool to room temperature.

To make the dressing, combine the mayonnaise, sour cream, and mustard in a large bowl. Season with salt and pepper.

To assemble the salad, add the cooled potatoes, onion, celery, and parsley to the dressing and stir to combine and coat. Taste and adjust for seasoning with salt and pepper. Serve at room temperature or chilled.

Tarragon Tomato Salad

Here is my version of a recipe taught by Anne Willan. Her version uses small cherry tomatoes, which are scored, blanched, and peeled. The combination is incredible, as the peeled tomatoes soak up the flavorful vinaigrette and explode in your mouth. However, the number of people I would peel cherry tomatoes for is fairly limited.

The wine may seem a little surprising, but tomatoes contain alcohol-soluble flavors that can only be delivered to your taste receptors in the presence of alcohol. As the salad marinates, the tomatoes begin to exude their juices, so don't make this more than 2 or 3 hours before serving. Serve this pretty combination in a butterhead lettuce cup with plenty of bread to soak up the juices.

1/2 cup walnuts

1 1/2 pounds grape tomatoes, halved

2 tablespoons chopped fresh tarragon

1 tablespoon chopped fresh chives

2 tablespoons dry white wine

2 tablespoons balsamic vinegar

1 tablespoon Dijon mustard

6 tablespoons extra-virgin olive oil

2 tablespoons walnut oil

Coarse salt and freshly ground black pepper

1/4 cup microgreens, such as basil, arugula, or beet (optional)

Preheat the oven to 350°F. Toast the walnuts on a baking sheet until brown, about 10 minutes. Let cool slightly, then coarsely chop. Set aside.

To marinate the tomatoes, place the tomatoes, tarragon, and chives in a large bowl. Drizzle over the wine and stir to combine. Set aside.

To prepare the dressing, whisk the vinegar and mustard together in a small bowl. Add the oils in a slow steady steam, whisking constantly, until the dressing is creamy and emulsified. Season with salt and pepper.

To assemble the salad, pour enough of the dressing over the tomatoes to lightly coat. Add the walnuts and stir to combine. Taste and adjust for seasoning with salt and pepper.

To serve, divide the salad among chilled serving plates. Garnish with microgreens. Serve immediately.

Tarragon

Tarragon is an essential seasoning in classic French cuisine and is wonderful with a range of foods, including eggs, chicken, and fish. Many sauces include it, like Sauce Béarnaise, served with steak, and Sauce Rémoulade, served with cold meats and seafood. When married with chopped fresh parsley, chives, and chervil, it forms the traditional seasoning blend *fines herbes*.

TIPSY WATERMELON SALAD

Serves 6 to 8

Summer is unthinkable without watermelon. As children, my sister and I would stand for what seemed like hours on the back steps and eat and eat and eat chilled wedges of homegrown watermelon. The seed-spitting contests were fierce. As we were often barefoot and playing in the dirt, the watermelon juice served as an adhesive for a fine dusting of red Georgia clay. We would get so sticky and messy, we were barred from the house until we'd washed off with the hose. And, if we didn't do a good job, Meme was more than happy to help.

This watermelon salad is decidedly grown-up enough to eat indoors (barring any seed-spitting challenges). Spiking watermelon with vodka is an old trick, but the crème de cassis—a Burgundian liqueur made from black currants—elevates this to the extraordinary.

1 (6-pound) watermelon, halved lengthwise

1 cup lemon juice

2/3 cup sugar

1/2 cup vodka

1/3 cup crème de cassis

Pinch of fine sea salt

1/4 cup chopped fresh mint

To prepare the watermelon, using a large ice cream scoop, remove the watermelon flesh from the rind and place the balls in a large bowl. Reserve the scooped-out rind of one of the watermelon halves to use as serving bowl.

To make the dressing, whisk the lemon juice and sugar in a bowl until the sugar dissolves. Whisk in the vodka and crème de cassis. Season the mixture with a pinch of salt. Pour the mixture over the watermelon and gently stir to combine and coat the balls. Cover with plastic wrap and chill for at least 1 hour and up to 2 hours.

When ready to serve, gently toss the watermelon balls once again to redistribute the liquid. Transfer them to the reserved scooped-out watermelon "bowl." Sprinkle with chopped fresh mint and serve.

Warm Pecan-crusted Goat Cheese Toasts with Mixed Baby Greens

Serves 4 to 6

I cannot serve this salad without thinking of my friend Stephanie Stuckey-Benfield. Her family is the Stuckey's of the roadside stores and Pecan Log Rolls. Her grandfather opened his first pecan stand in 1937. This simple stand evolved into a veritable empire of Stuckey's Pecan Shoppes, the highway heaven of souvenirs, cold drinks, and pecan candy.

The pecan log roll, for the uninitiated, is a secret combination of sweet, fluffy goo in a coating of crushed pecans, created by Stephanie's grandmother. In this recipe, once the goat cheese is rolled in pecans it looks undeniably like the candied confection, although the taste is savory.

1 cup very finely chopped pecans

Coarse salt and freshly ground black pepper

1 (6-ounce) log fresh goat cheese

4 to 6 thick slices country bread

1/4 cup extra-virgin olive oil, plus more for drizzling

1 shallot, very finely chopped

1 teaspoon Dijon mustard

2 tablespoons red wine vinegar

4 to 6 cups mesclun greens (about 4 ounces)

Preheat the broiler. Place the chopped pecans in a shallow dish and season with salt and pepper. Roll the goat cheese log in the pecans to coat evenly. Refrigerate until firm, if necessary, then cut into 4 to 6 uniform rounds.

To heat the goat cheese toasts, place the bread slices on a baking sheet and drizzle with some of the olive oil. Place a round of goat cheese atop a piece of bread. Broil until the cheese is melted and browned, 3 to 5 minutes.

Meanwhile, to make the dressing, whisk the shallot, mustard, and vinegar together in a small bowl. Add the remaining 1/4 cup oil in a slow steady stream, whisking constantly, until the dressing is creamy and emulsified. Season with salt and pepper.

To serve, toss the salad greens with just enough dressing to coat. Taste and adjust for seasoning with salt and pepper. Divide among serving plates and top each salad with a warm goat cheese toast.

ZESTY GREEN BEAN SALAD

Serves 4 to 6

Fresh and colorful, this salad is a far cry from the concoction made with canned green beans and pinto beans. Wax beans are a yellow version of the snap bean. They remain pale yellow once cooked and are a nice color contrast to the green beans and red tomatoes.

3/4 pound wax beans, trimmed

3/4 pound haricots verts or slender green beans, trimmed

1/2 pint grape, teardrop, or pear tomatoes, halved

2 tablespoons chopped fresh mint

Juice of 2 lemons

2 shallots, finely chopped

1/2 cup extra-virgin olive oil

Coarse salt and freshly ground black pepper

Prepare an ice-water bath by filling a large bowl with ice and water. Line a plate with paper towels.

Bring a large pot of salted water to a boil over high heat. Add the wax beans and cook until just tender, about 3 minutes. Add the haricots verts and cook until both beans are tender, an additional 3 to 5 minutes.

Drain well in a colander, then set the colander with beans in the ice-water bath (to set the color and stop the cooking), making sure the beans are submerged. Once chilled, transfer the beans to the prepared plate.

To assemble the salad, combine the beans, tomatoes, and mint in a large bowl. Set aside.

To prepare the dressing, whisk the lemon juice, shallots, and olive oil together in a small bowl. Season with salt and pepper.

Just before serving, drizzle a little of the dressing over the bean mixture. (Do not combine ahead, as the beans will discolor from the acid in the vinaigrette.) Toss to coat, adding more dressing if needed. Taste and adjust for seasoning with salt and pepper. Serve immediately.

Blanching

Blanching is a cooking term for parboiling, lightly cooking ingredients in boiling water just until tender—usually vegetables. The ingredients are then refreshed under ice-cold water, which is known as shocking, and drained. Shocking stops the cooking and helps set the color. Blanching and shocking help vegetables keep their texture and color and also remove bitterness.

Broccoli and Grape-Tomato Salad

Serves 4 to 6

Most Junior League cookbooks have at least Broccoli Salads I and II, and often III and IV. It's the diplomatic way of not having to decide whose version is best. The amusing part is they are all, in essence, the same salad and contain, besides broccoli (and mayonnaise, of course), red onion, bacon, and often raisins. Really racy ones with a modern twist might also contain crushed ramen noodles.

This salad is colorful and satisfying in a very simple way. To really make the flavors and colors pop, it is imperative to blanch and shock the broccoli. Otherwise, it is like grazing in the produce bin.

4 slices thick-cut bacon, cut into lardons (see page 179; optional)

1 head broccoli (about 1 pound)

1/2 pint grape tomatoes, halved

1/2 red onion, very thinly sliced

Coarse salt and freshly ground black pepper

2 tablespoons sherry vinegar

1 clove garlic, very finely chopped

1/4 cup extra-virgin olive oil

Line two plates with paper towels. Prepare an ice-water bath by filling a large bowl with ice and water.

In a skillet, cook the bacon over medium heat, stirring frequently, until crisp and brown, 5 to 7 minutes. Using a slotted spoon, transfer the bacon to one of the prepared plates to drain. Set aside.

To prepare the broccoli, separate the head into bite-size florets, reserving the stems for another use. Bring a large pot of salted water to a boil over high heat. Cook the florets until just tender, 2 to 3 minutes. Remove with a slotted spoon and transfer to the ice-water bath to set the color and stop the cooking. Once chilled, transfer to the second prepared plate and pat dry with paper towels.

Combine the broccoli, tomatoes, and onion in a large bowl. Season with salt and pepper and set aside.

To prepare the dressing, whisk the vinegar and garlic together in a small bowl. Add the oil in a slow steady stream, whisking constantly, until the dressing is creamy and emulsified. Season with salt and pepper.

Just before serving, drizzle the dressing over the vegetables and toss to combine and coat. Add the bacon, and taste and adjust for seasoning with salt and pepper.

HONEY FIGS WITH GOAT CHEESE AND PECANS

Serves 4 to 6

Honey is a fine example of the French concept of *terroir*—quite literally, a little bit of the earth of the surrounding area is imparted to every jar of honey. Dede loved honey and enjoyed it on his toast or biscuits. When I grew older and started to travel, I would always bring home a jar of the local honey as a gift for him. Although he has long since passed away, I have continued the tradition and always bring home a jar of local honey as a memento when I travel. The shelf in my cupboard resembles an amber rainbow.

I once had a bit of pecan-crusted goat cheese left over from another recipe and served it the next day, nestled in a quartered fresh fig and drizzled with honey—that's how this recipe was born.

1 cup chopped pecans

Coarse salt and freshly ground black pepper

1 (6-ounce) log fresh goat cheese

12 to 18 fresh figs (such as Brown Turkey, Calimyrna, or Black Mission)

3/4 cup honey (preferably tupelo, orange blossom, or sweet clover)

To prepare the goat cheese, place the chopped pecans in a shallow dish and season with salt and pepper. Roll the goat cheese log in the pecans to coat evenly. Refrigerate until firm, if necessary, then cut into 4 to 6 uniform rounds.

To prepare the figs, using a small paring knife and starting at the stem end, quarter the figs, but don't quite cut all the way though the bottom. Open them slightly to form a flower.

To serve, divide the figs evenly among 4 or 6 shallow bowls. Top each fig with a round of pecan-crusted goat cheese. Drizzle the honey over the figs and cheese. Season with salt and pepper and serve.

Measuring Honey

When measuring out sticky ingredients such as honey, first spray a little nonstick spray into the measuring utensil, then fill with the ingredient. The sticky substance will slide right out.

CHAPTER 3
EGGS AND DAIRY

For years, an egg stand at the Union Square Farmer's Market in Manhattan posted a handwritten cardboard sign with the following chastisement: "New Yorkers—Milk does not come from Chickens." It seems that everyone stopped there for both fresh eggs and milk, and this particular stand only sold the eggs. It's good for a chuckle, but even the city slickers dressed in black were not too far off. Eggs and dairy go together.

The South has always been a predominantly agrarian society, and farmyard animals including cows and chickens have supplied part of our diet since Colonial times. However, before improvements in shipping and refrigeration, cheese and milk products were not common to all and were considered a luxury unless you lived on a farm. Indeed, to the farm women who did the work, the action of procuring the milk and making the cheese and butter never felt too luxurious.

When Mama was very young, she and her two sisters hand-churned butter, fed the chickens, and collected the eggs. Their home was not a working farm; they simply lived in the country and that was part of life. Churning butter is physical exercise, and an exercise in patience. It is important to keep the same tempo, neither too fast nor too slow. Meme stayed on her young charges to make sure they did the job right, pounding the dasher up and down until she felt the butter had formed. Then they collected and kneaded the butter to remove any pockets of buttermilk trapped inside.

Finally, the butter was washed and placed into small wooden boxes for pressing, boxes my grandmother had used when she was young. The churn made of thick, pale-gray pottery now sits in my office, and the dovetailed butter boxes are on a shelf in my kitchen, reminders of what my mother would most certainly argue were not "simpler times."

French cooking is virtually synonymous with butter. The region of Normandy is famous for its rich cream, milk, and butter. Many classic French sauces are based on or finished with butter, and fish and chicken are often sauteed in butter. I once witnessed a French chef deep-fry butter. He cut the butter into logs the size of a pencil, then coated the logs in flour, egg wash, and breadcrumbs. The crusted batons were transferred to the freezer. Once the logs were frozen solid, he deep-fried them in oil to a rich golden brown and alternated them on the serving plate with blanched asparagus. They looked like bad bar food, mozzarella cheese sticks. Oh, but no, when the tines of the fork cracked the crunchy crust, the butter, which had liquefied, flooded the plate to coat the asparagus. It was obscenely delicious.

Not long ago, a Southern breakfast was a massive meal of eggs, grits, fried country ham or bacon, and buttery biscuits. Rib-sticking breakfasts were a robust way to start a long day of hard work on the farm. This has changed; not only do we skip big breakfast productions for lack of time, but we are also, as a whole, much more sedentary and need to eat less fat. Eggs are high-quality protein, and they've regained a place in a balanced diet after years of controversy over their cholesterol content. Look for farm-fresh or free-range organic eggs for the best and tastiest results.

SIMPLIFYING SOUFFLÉS

Soufflés are among the most elegant egg-based dishes in cuisine—and they tend to intimidate even skilled cooks, even though they are really not that hard to make. If your soufflé skills are shaky or nonexistent, read this section before you make any of the soufflé recipes in this book.

There are two basic kinds of baked soufflés: savory, which are served as a first course or a light meal, and sweet, which are served as desserts. (Cold soufflés are sweet and are not really soufflés at all, but an illusion. They are frozen concoctions, often held together with gelatin, that mimic the tall "top hat" of a properly prepared baked soufflé.) The name itself originates from the French *souffler*, which means "to blow up." It is controlling the "blowing up" that can be tricky. Simple baked soufflés are best served as a main-course lunch, a light supper, or an elegant starter, and of course, as the pièce de résistance for dessert.

Savory soufflés are composed of stiffly beaten egg whites and a flavored base made from a very thick, well-seasoned béchamel sauce. The sauce must be highly seasoned with flavorings and aromatics to compensate for the blandness of the egg whites. A savory soufflé may also contain finely chopped, well-drained additions such as spinach, tomato, or fish. Large, wet chunks of food will not only sink, but they will also weigh down a soufflé and hamper its rise.

Baked dessert soufflés are made by one of two methods: by preparing a flavored meringue by simply adding fruit puree or melted chocolate to a cooked meringue or by preparing a flavored base of crème pâtissière (pastry cream) that performs similarly to the béchamel sauce. (Pastry cream is a sweet, thick, flour-based egg custard that is then combined with stiffly beaten egg whites.) Dessert soufflés are very simple, since the sugar and chocolate help create a very stable foam.

Choosing the Soufflé Mold: the classic soufflé mold is a porcelain dish with straight sides. One common mistake is baking a soufflé in a dish that is either too large or too small for the mixture. When egg whites are beaten, they increase in volume seven to eight times. Therefore, a soufflé mixture should fill to the absolute rim of the dish since it will increase in volume two to three times as it bakes. In general, a soufflé made with five egg whites needs a $1^1/_2$-quart dish, and a soufflé made with seven to eight egg whites needs a $2^1/_2$-quart dish.

Preparing the Soufflé Mold: the dish must also be well coated with softened (not melted), room temperature butter to ensure the soufflé will climb the sides of the dish and not stick as the mixture rises and expands. Often when the mixture sticks, it will create a lopsided soufflé. To coat the dish, brush the inside of the soufflé mold with butter and place it in the refrigerator. As the butter chills and firms, you can very clearly see any spots you might have missed. Then dust the well-buttered dish evenly with grated Parmigiano-Reggiano cheese, fine dry breadcrumbs, or cornmeal; or, for dessert soufflés, cookie crumbs, finely chopped nuts, or granulated sugar. Turn the mold upside down and tap to remove excess crumbs.

Properly beaten egg whites are the key to a masterful soufflé. While the soufflé is in the oven, the air trapped inside the egg whites expands, causing the soufflé to rise. Beating egg whites is quite simply incorporating air into the egg white foam. Fresh eggs will produce a more stable foam. A downy mass of beaten egg whites is actually thousands of minute air bubbles connected by a film of egg white—a foam. To create a stable foam, it is imperative that the whites be absolutely free of any yolk or fat. Even a mere drop of yolk or fat will hinder the foam formation. The bowl and beaters must be spotlessly clean; use only glass or stainless steel bowls, as plastic bowls can retain a film of oil.

It is easier to separate eggs when they are cold and straight from the refrigerator; the whites and yolks are firmer and less likely to break. When separating eggs, crack one egg at a time into a cup, transferring each white to the mixing bowl only after it is successfully separated. There is nothing worse that ruining the entire batch on the last egg! Many soufflé recipes will call for one or two more whites than yolks to enhance the volume. Even though it is best to separate eggs when they are cold, egg whites will whip to greater volume when they have had a chance to warm slightly. To achieve this, let the egg whites stand at room temperature in the mixing bowl while you assemble the remaining ingredients.

When ready to beat the whites, start slowly. In the clean metal bowl of a heavy-duty mixer fitted with the whisk, beat the egg whites on low speed until foamy. Add a bit of cream of tartar or vinegar. Adding acid helps create a stable foam that will hold up until heat cooks the egg proteins and sets the soufflé.

After adding the acid, increase the speed to high and continue beating just until the whites are stiff, but not dry, and no longer slip when the bowl is tilted. (My mentor Nathalie Dupree used to hold the bowl upside down over my head to test whether I had properly whipped the whites!) If the whites are under-beaten, they won't achieve full volume. If overbeaten, the whites will appear "rocky" and can't hold air well because all of the bubbles are smashed. Rocky, overbeaten whites will not expand properly when heated. Sometimes beating in an additional egg white might bring back a batch of overbeaten whites.

How to Fold: once you have gone to the trouble of putting all that air in the whites, it is important not to deflate the whites when mixing them with the soufflé base. Folding is folding, not stirring. Gentle folding is the key to maintaining volume. I sacrifice about a quarter of the beaten egg whites into the yolk mixture to lighten the yolk mixture before adding the rest of the whites. This helps blend the whites with the base and makes the real folding easier. Then add the remaining whites. Using a large rubber spatula, gradually combine the mixtures with a downward stroke into the bowl, continuing across the bottom, up the side, and over the top of the mixture. Come up through the center every few strokes and rotate the bowl often as

you fold. You are bringing a bit of the soufflé mixture at the bottom of the bowl up and over the egg whites. Fold just until there are no streaks remaining. Then, gently pour the mixture into the prepared dish. Lastly, run your thumb around the inside rim of the dish, making a shallow trough around the edge of the batter. This will help the soufflés rise up straight and tall.

Placement in the Oven: put the soufflé on the lower to middle rack of a preheated nonconvection oven and leave it alone. Most large soufflés are baked at 400°F, or are started at 400°F, then reduced to 375°F. Small, individual soufflés are baked at 400°F. The soufflé needs that burst of high heat to rise. Don't dare open the oven door while the soufflé is baking: a cool draft or a slammed oven door will make the soufflé fall.

Don't fret if it does fall while baking, for whatever reason. For a quick fix for a savory soufflé, turn the mixture into another baking dish, drizzle some heavy cream over it, sprinkle freshly grated Parmigiano-Reggiano on top, and return it to the oven for 10 minutes. It will miraculously rise again for a delicious twice-baked soufflé!

When It's Done: a soufflé is finished cooking when it has risen two to three inches above the rim of the mold and is golden brown on top. The French prefer soufflés with slightly runny centers that are spooned over portions as a sauce. These soufflés are not quite cooked through all the way and are more fragile, but delicious! It's an age-old rule that diners wait for the soufflé, not the soufflé for the diners! Whisk it out of the oven to the table immediately. Serve a large soufflé by gently breaking the top crust into portions with two spoons held back to back. Then, lightly spoon it out, including some of the soft center and crisp crust in each portion.

VIDALIA ONION QUICHE

Makes one
10-inch quiche

Mama often prepared quiche during the time that coincided with that ridiculous phrase and tongue-in-cheek bestseller, *Real Men Don't Eat Quiche*. I thought it was absurd then, and still do. Cheesy, yummy, eggy goodness encased in rich, golden pastry? What's not to like?

French Pie Pastry (recipe follows), blind baked

1½ cups Vidalia Onion Confit (page 18)

3 large eggs

3 large egg yolks

2 cups whole milk

½ cup heavy cream

2 tablespoons chopped fresh flat-leaf parsley

Pinch of cayenne pepper

Coarse salt and freshly ground white pepper

Prepare the pastry shell and the onion confit; let both cool.

Preheat the oven to 350°F. To make the custard, whisk together the eggs, egg yolks, milk, cream, parsley, and cayenne pepper in a large bowl. Season with salt and pepper. Set aside.

Spread the cooled onion confit in the pastry shell. Pour the custard over the onions. Bake until the custard is lightly browned and set, 30 to 35 minutes. Remove to a rack to cool slightly. Serve warm or at room temperature.

FRENCH PIE PASTRY

Makes one (10-inch) tart shell

2 cups all-purpose flour

1 teaspoon fine sea salt

½ cup (1 stick) unsalted butter, cut into bits and chilled

2 large egg yolks

5 to 6 tablespoons cold water

To prepare the dough, combine the flour and salt in the bowl of a food processor fitted with the metal blade. Add the butter. Process until the mixture resembles coarse meal, 8 to 10 seconds. Add the egg yolks and pulse to combine.

With the processor on pulse, add the ice water a tablespoon at a time. Pulse until the mixture holds together as a soft, but not crumbly or sticky, dough. Shape the dough into a disk, wrap in plastic wrap, and refrigerate until firm and evenly moist, about 30 minutes.

To prepare the dough, lightly flour a clean work surface and rolling pin. Place the dough disk in the center of the floured surface. Roll out the dough, starting in the center and rolling up to, but not over, the top edge of the dough. Return to the center, and roll down to, but not over, the bottom edge. Give the dough a quarter turn, and continue rolling, repeating the quarter turns until you have a disk about 1/8 inch thick.

continued

Drape the dough over the rolling pin and transfer to a 10-inch tart pan with a removable bottom, unrolling over the tin. With one hand lift the pastry and with the other gently tuck it into the pan, being careful not to stretch or pull the dough. Let the pastry settle into the bottom of the pan. Take a small piece of dough and shape it into a ball. Press the ball of dough around the bottom edges of the tart pan, snugly shaping the pastry to the pan without tearing it. Remove any excess pastry by rolling the pin across the top of the pan.

Prick the bottom of the pastry all over with the tines of a fork to help prevent shrinkage during baking. Chill until firm, about 30 minutes.

To blind bake, preheat the oven to 425°F. Crumple a piece of parchment paper, then lay it out flat over the bottom of the pastry. Weight the paper with pie weights, dried beans, or uncooked rice. This will keep the unfilled pie crust from puffing up in the oven.

For a partially baked shell that will be filled and baked further, bake for 20 minutes. Remove from the oven and remove the paper and weights. (You can reuse the rice or beans for blind-baking a number of times.) The shell can now be filled and baked further, according to the recipe directions. For a fully baked shell that will hold an uncooked filling, bake the empty shell until a deep golden brown, about 30 minutes total.

ANNE'S TWICE-BAKED SPINACH SOUFFLÉS

Serves 6

The first time I cooked a soufflé for my teacher, culinary authority and soufflé master Anne Willan, I opened the oven door to discover a lopsided, exploding disaster. Determined to learn, I cooked a soufflé once a week for months with the leftover bits of cheese from the cheeseboard. It was brutal, but I finally mastered the soufflé.

That said, cast your fears aside: adapted from one of Anne's recipes, this soufflé is the absolute perfect recipe for beginners because it demonstrates how easy soufflés are to make and to manipulate. Even if everything does go wrong, no one will know, as the soufflés are hidden under a glorious blanket of rich creamy sauce and melted cheese.

SPINACH

1 tablespoon canola oil

1 shallot, finely chopped

1 clove garlic, very finely chopped

1 (10-ounce) package frozen chopped spinach, thawed and very well drained

Pinch of cayenne pepper

Coarse salt and freshly ground black pepper

BÉCHAMEL SAUCE BASE

4 tablespoons (1/2 stick) unsalted butter

1/4 cup all-purpose flour

11/2 cups milk, warmed

Pinch of freshly grated nutmeg

Coarse salt and freshly ground black pepper

1 cup half-and-half

5 large egg yolks

SOUFFLÉ AND TOPPING

7 large egg whites

Coarse salt

2 tablespoons Dijon mustard

1/2 cup grated Gruyère cheese (about 2 ounces)

Freshly ground black pepper

Preheat the oven to 400°F. Generously butter six 8-ounce ramekins or one 6-cup jumbo muffin tin or silicone muffin mold.

To prepare the spinach, in a skillet, heat the oil over medium heat. Add the shallot and cook until soft and translucent, 2 to 3 minutes. Add the garlic and cook until fragrant, 45 to 60 seconds. Add the well-drained spinach and season with cayenne, salt, and pepper. Continue cooking, stirring, until the mixture is well combined and all the moisture has evaporated, 2 to 3 minutes. Set aside.

To prepare the béchamel sauce, in a heavy-bottomed saucepan, melt the butter over medium heat. Whisk in the flour, and cook until foaming but not browned, about 1 minute. Whisk in the warmed milk. Bring to a boil over high heat. Once it is at a boil, continue cooking, stirring constantly, until the sauce thickens, about 2 minutes. Season with nutmeg, salt, and pepper.

You will use two-thirds of this sauce as the base for the soufflés. The remaining one-third will be the coating sauce at the end. Transfer one-third of the sauce to a small saucepan. Add the half-and-half and stir to combine. Set aside.

Stir the spinach into the larger amount of sauce; taste and adjust the seasoning with salt and pepper. Add the egg yolks one at a time, stirring between each addition. Set aside.

To make the soufflés, in the bowl of a heavy-duty mixer fitted with the whisk, beat the egg whites with a pinch of salt on medium speed until foamy. Increase the speed to high and whip until stiff peaks form, 2 to 3 minutes.

To lighten the soufflé, add about one-fourth of the beaten egg whites to the spinach-sauce mixture and whisk until well mixed. Pour this mixture over the remaining whites and fold together until smooth.

Fill the prepared ramekins with the mixture. Place them on a baking sheet and bake until the soufflés are puffed and browned, 12 to 15 minutes. Leave the oven on.

Transfer the soufflés to a rack and cool slightly. Turn out each soufflé into a large gratin dish or casserole. If the soufflés stick, release them by running a butter knife or offset spatula around the rims. Set aside.

To finish the soufflés, bring the reserved cream sauce to a boil over medium-high heat. Add the mustard and $1/4$ cup of the Gruyère cheese. Stir to combine, then taste and adjust for seasoning with salt and pepper. Spoon the sauce over the soufflés to coat, then sprinkle each evenly with the remaining $1/4$ cup Gruyère. (The dish may be made to this point and held at room temperature for up to 1 hour or covered in the refrigerator for up 24 hours. However, it is important to bring the dish to room temperature before browning.)

Bake the sauce-covered soufflés in the gratin dish until browned and bubbling, 7 to 10 minutes. Serve immediately.

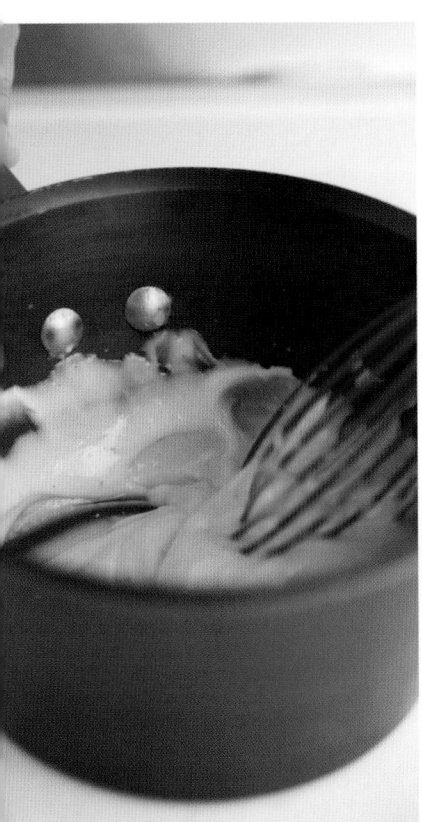

Béchamel Sauce

Whether called béchamel (French), balsamella (Italian), or white sauce, this classic sauce is based on a thickener (a roux) made of butter and flour that is whisked together with milk. Simple seasonings include nutmeg, salt, and pepper, but the flavor is improved if the milk is first infused with aromatics like bay leaf and peppercorns. It is as simple as making tea: place the milk and aromatics in a pot and bring to a simmer over medium heat. Remove from the heat and let rest for about 10 minutes; strain out and discard the aromatics.

Béchamel sauce is the workhorse of cuisine. You can change its consistency by varying the proportions of roux to milk. The more roux, the thicker the sauce, and vice versa. Thin sauces are used as bases for soups and other sauces. Add cheese, for example, and it's Sauce Mornay. A medium béchamel sauce is used for coating and in vegetarian lasagna. Thick béchamel is the base for savory soufflés.

BREAKFAST STRATA WITH COUNTRY SAUSAGE

Serves 8

Strata is the plural of stratum, and whether we're talking about rocks or recipes, it refers to layering. Here, it is a breakfast casserole layered and bound with custard, almost like a savory bread pudding. What's great about a strata is that it should be prepared and refrigerated the night before. The next morning, all you need to do is let it come to room temperature on the counter and bake.

I've used fresh sage, an herb with soft, fuzzy gray-green leaves and a slightly bitter finish, to complement the flavor of the sausage and create another layer of flavor. It goes well with poultry, pork, and veal. Look for fresh bunches with no bruising and a clean, pungent aroma.

1 tablespoon canola oil, plus more for the dish

1/2 pound bulk pork or turkey country sausage

1 onion, preferably Vidalia, chopped

1 red bell pepper, cored, seeded and chopped

1 yellow bell pepper, cored, seeded and chopped

2 cloves garlic, very finely chopped

2 baguettes, cubed

1/2 cup grated Parmigiano-Reggiano cheese (about 1 1/2 ounces)

6 large eggs

2 1/2 cups whole milk

1 tablespoon chopped fresh sage

1 tablespoon chopped fresh flat-leaf parsley

Coarse salt and freshly ground black pepper

Brush a large gratin dish with some of the oil.

To cook the sausage, in a large skillet, heat the remaining 1 tablespoon of oil over medium heat. Add the sausage and cook until it begins to brown, 3 to 5 minutes. Add the onion and red and yellow bell peppers and saute until the onion is golden, about 5 minutes. Add the garlic and cook until fragrant, 45 to 60 seconds.

To assemble the strata, place half of the bread cubes in the prepared gratin dish and top with half of the sausage mixture. Sprinkle 1/4 cup of the grated cheese over the sausage mixture and top with the remaining bread cubes and sausage.

Whisk together the eggs, milk, sage, and parsley in a medium bowl. Season with salt and pepper. Pour the custard over the strata. Cover with plastic wrap and refrigerate for at least 3 hours and up to 12 hours.

Preheat the oven to 350°F. Let the chilled strata stand at room temperature for 20 minutes.

Bake the strata for 30 minutes. Remove from the oven and sprinkle with the remaining 1/4 cup cheese; continue baking until the strata is puffed and golden brown, an additional 20 to 25 minutes. (If the top of the strata starts to get too brown, cover it with aluminum foil.) Remove to a rack to cool slightly. Serve hot or warm.

HAM-AND-SWISS FRITTATA

Serves 4 to 6

An Italian frittata is an open-faced omelet similar to a Spanish tortilla. A French omelet is cooked very quickly over high heat, and additions like herbs, cheese, or vegetables are enclosed in the center of a two- or three-part fold. Frittatas and tortillas are cooked more slowly. The additional ingredients are whisked into the eggs and cooked at the same time. This delicious and easy dish makes a satisfying, simple supper with a side salad. Or take the Spanish approach, and cut the frittata into bite-size cubes and serve it skewered as a simple hors d'oeuvre. Ham and eggs are, of course, a marriage made in heaven. Used cured ham in this recipe, or if using country ham, halve the amount, so it will not be too salty.

1½ tablespoons canola oil

1 onion, preferably Vidalia, chopped

4 to 6 slices cured ham, finely chopped (about 1 cup)

5 large eggs, lightly beaten

¾ cup grated sharp Cheddar or Gruyère cheese (about 2½ ounces)

1 tablespoon snipped fresh chives

Coarse salt and freshly ground black pepper

Place the top rack about 6 inches from the broiler element. Preheat the broiler. In a large, ovenproof skillet, heat the oil over medium heat. Add the onion and ham and cook until the onion is soft and translucent, 3 minutes. In a bowl, whisk together the eggs, half of the cheese, and the chives. Season the mixture with salt and pepper.

Pour the egg mixture into the skillet and cook for 3 minutes, occasionally lifting the cooked egg around the edge with a wooden spoon or silicone spatula to let the raw egg flow underneath. Decrease the heat to low and cook, covered, until the underside is golden, about 5 minutes more. Remove from the heat.

Sprinkle the remaining half of the cheese on the top of the frittata. Broil the frittata in the skillet until the cheese is melted and bubbling, about 1 minute, depending on the strength of your broiler. Let cool slightly. Cut into wedges and serve immediately.

Country Ham

Ham can be fresh, cured, or cured and smoked. Fresh ham is pale pink to beige after cooking. Cured ham is usually deep pink as a result of the curing process. Dry-cured ham like country ham, Italian prosciutto, or Spanish Serrano is deep pink to mahogany red. Most country hams meet the same U.S. Department of Agriculture requirements as prosciutto or Serrano. As long as you slice it thinly enough, you can do everything with a country ham that you can do with prosciutto. Mass producers use nitrates, but the real old-fashioned, handcrafted hams are a beautiful marriage of salt, smoke, and patience. The salt eventually pulls so much moisture from the ham that bacteria cannot multiply. As with certain aged cheeses, mold often forms on the surface of whole, dry-cured hams. The mold is harmless; just scrub it off.

FRENCH TOAST CASSEROLE

Serves 8

When my sister and I were young, our favorite mornings were when Mama would prepare French toast for breakfast. The smell of butter, kissed with cinnamon, combined with the heady scent of sizzling egg was a most welcome greeting as we bounded down the stairs. This version is made the night before, so you won't find yourself camped in front of a hot griddle in the early morning, groggy and in need of caffeine. The next morning, remove it from the fridge to take the chill off. Grab a cup of coffee and pop it in the oven. By the time the table is set, the family is assembled, and you're ready for your second cup, breakfast is ready. Brioche and challah are yeast breads, rich with egg and butter, and make superlative French toast.

4 tablespoons (1/2 stick) unsalted butter, melted

3/4 cup firmly packed light brown sugar

1 loaf brioche or challah, sliced 1 1/2 inches thick (about 1 1/2 pounds)

8 large eggs, lightly beaten

1 cup whole milk

1 tablespoon pure vanilla extract

1/2 teaspoon ground cinnamon

1/4 teaspoon ground ginger

Pinch of salt

1/2 cup chopped pecans

Confectioners' sugar, for accompaniment

Sorghum, cane, or maple syrup, for accompaniment (see page 182)

Combine the melted butter and brown sugar in a baking dish. Arrange the bread slices in the dish. Whisk together the eggs, milk, vanilla, cinnamon, ginger, and salt in a bowl. Pour over the bread, letting it soak in. Top with the pecans. Cover with plastic wrap and refrigerate for at least 3 hours and up to 12 hours.

Preheat the oven to 350°F. Let the chilled casserole stand at room temperature for 20 minutes.

Bake until browned and set, 30 to 45 minutes. Remove to a rack to cool slightly. Sift over confectioners' sugar. Serve hot or warm with sorghum, cane, or maple syrup.

GOAT-CHEESE GRATIN WITH TARRAGON TOAST

Serves 4 to 6

Hot, bubbly cheese, buttery toast, and fresh snipped herbs are a captivating combination for a first course. Serve this in individual dishes for a more elegant presentation. In the summer, it is incredible with chopped fresh tomato. In the winter it takes on a completely different taste and feel topped with your favorite tomato sauce.

Compound butters (see page 281) are flavored with herbs or spices. This recipe features tarragon butter, which is a classic French combination that makes this simple recipe taste spectacular. The flavoring possibilities for compound butters are vast: I once worked with a cowboy chef who made a compound butter for steak with freshly chopped cilantro, fresh lime juice, and finely chopped jalapeño. Mix it up!

1/2 cup (1 stick) unsalted butter, room temperature

Juice of 1/2 lemon

3 tablespoons chopped fresh tarragon

2 cloves garlic, finely chopped

1 shallot, chopped

Coarse salt and freshly ground black pepper

1 baguette, sliced 1/4 inch thick

1 (6-ounce) log fresh goat cheese, crumbled

2 tomatoes, cored, seeded, and chopped, or 1 cup of your favorite tomato, marinara, or pasta sauce

15 kalamata or other brine-cured black olives, pitted

Position an oven rack 4 inches below the broiler element and preheat the broiler. To make the compound butter, stir the butter, lemon juice, tarragon, garlic, and shallot together in a bowl. Season with salt and pepper. Mix until thoroughly combined.

Arrange the bread slices on a baking sheet. Spread the butter mixture on one side of each slice to coat. (Reserve the remaining butter in a sealable container in the refrigerator for up to 2 days. Use it to saute vegetables or make buttery herbed rice or pasta.) Broil until golden brown, 2 to 3 minutes. Turn the toasts and broil the other side. Remove the toasts from the oven and transfer to a rack to cool.

Scatter the goat cheese on the bottoms of individual shallow gratin dishes or one ovenproof gratin dish or casserole. Top with the tomatoes and olives, and season with salt and pepper. Broil until bubbling and hot, 3 to 5 minutes.

Serve with the reserved herb toasts.

CHEESE SOUFFLÉ

Southerners have a bad habit of calling any dish with whipped egg white in it a soufflé—hence all those recipes for cheese grits soufflé and sweet potato soufflé. Believe me, there is way too much butter in both of those concoctions for them to ever rise, especially the latter, which is typically topped with marshmallows.

This classic French soufflé is the real thing, and uses the béchamel method (see page 67). It is very important to use low-moisture cheese when making soufflés. Gruyère and Parmigiano-Reggiano are perfect because they are very flavorful, but dry and not overly fatty. Rich, fatty cheeses like blue or Brie are too heavy and your soufflé won't rise as tall.

5 tablespoons unsalted butter

1/4 cup finely grated Parmigiano-Reggiano cheese (about 1 ounce), plus more for the soufflé dish

3 tablespoons all-purpose flour

1 1/2 cups whole milk, warmed

Pinch of cayenne pepper

Pinch of freshly ground nutmeg

Coarse salt and freshly ground black pepper

4 large egg yolks

3/4 cup grated Gruyère cheese (about 2 1/2 ounces)

3 tablespoons finely chopped fresh herbs (such as chervil, chives, or parsley)

6 large egg whites

Position an oven rack in the middle of the oven. Preheat the oven to 400°F. Using 2 tablespoons of the butter, grease a 1-quart soufflé dish or four 8-ounce soufflé ramekins and sprinkle with Parmigiano-Reggiano cheese to coat. (If using the ramekins, place them on a baking sheet.)

To make the béchamel sauce, in a heavy-bottomed saucepan, melt the remaining 3 tablespoons of butter over medium heat. Whisk in the flour, and cook until foaming but not browned, about 1 minute. Whisk in the milk. Add the cayenne and nutmeg, and season with salt and pepper; bring to a boil over high heat. Once it is at a boil, continue cooking, stirring constantly, until the sauce thickens, about 2 minutes.

Whisk together the yolks and a bit more salt and pepper in a small bowl. Temper the yolks so they won't curdle from the heat of the sauce: first, add a little of the hot sauce to the yolks and whisk to combine. Add the yolk mixture a little at a time to the béchamel sauce and whisk quickly to blend. Fold in the Gruyère, the remaining 1/4 cup Parmigiano-Reggiano, and the herbs. Taste and adjust for seasoning with salt and pepper. Set aside.

To beat the egg whites, in the bowl of a heavy-duty mixer fitted with the whisk, beat the egg whites with a pinch of salt on medium speed until foamy. Increase the speed to high and whip until stiff peaks form, 2 to 3 minutes.

Add about one-fourth of the beaten egg whites to the sauce mixture and stir until well mixed. Pour this lightened mixture over the remaining whites and fold them together as gently as possible.

Fill the prepared dish with the mixture, smoothing the top with a metal spatula. Run your thumb around the inside edge of the rim, making a shallow channel around the batter.

Place the soufflé in the oven, reduce the heat to 375°F, and bake until puffed, golden, and just set in the center, about 25 minutes for one large soufflé or 12 to 15 minutes for individual soufflés. Remove from the oven and serve immediately.

CHAPTER 4

PORK, BEEF, AND LAMB

ALTHOUGH TODAY'S SOUTHERN MENU includes pork, beef, and lamb, this has not always been the case. Beef has only become a regular addition to the Southern table in the last fifty or so years. Farmland was considered too valuable to share with cows and sheep. Pigs, however, were happy in the woods or living in a pen as four-legged garbage disposals, eating leftovers and scraps.

The faithful pig has sustained rich and poor alike through generations of Southern feast and famine. Living "high on the hog" means being pretty well off, and eating what are generally regarded as the superior cuts of pork, such as chops, hams, and shoulders instead of feet, knuckles, and jowls.

Many old-time Southerners will eat, head to tail, every bit of the pig but the squeal. As a child, I was terrified by the preparations for head cheese, which is not a cheese at all, but essentially a sausage made from the meaty bits of the pig's head. The pink head boiling and bobbing in the cast-iron cauldron frightened me. I only learned to love thinly sliced *fromage de tête* later, in France.

Barbecue was, and always has been, the one exception to the relative lack of meat on the Southern table. And in Georgia, barbecue means pork. There is simply nothing in this world or the next that tastes like pig kissed by fire and bathed in smoke. When I was a child, my grandfather would pit-cook a pig every Memorial Day. It was a grand event, the huge beast split and spatchcocked on a large metal grate. He would sit up all night under the pecan trees, sipping coffee and furtively chewing tobacco (hiding that sin from my grandmother). He would make a basting mop out of a branch and a handful of rags, patiently brushing the pig's skin with a potent combination of vinegar and salt, letting heat and smoke slowly transform a hunk of pork into a moist, tender delicacy.

Although my grandparents did not raise pigs, when I was very young, they had a small herd of cattle that lived in the pasture between the house and the pond. These grand, snorting beasts were as effective as a pack of snarling guard dogs in keeping my cousins and me away from the pond, which was off-limits without a grown-up present. (I'm still unsure if the adults thought the danger was that we would drown or that we would, as my grandmother would say, "get on a snake.")

Periodically, Dede would load his shotgun and kill one of the animals, which he would then take to the processing plant. It was free-range, grass-fed beef, now all the rage, but back then, simply considered tough and inferior. Later, I lived and worked for several years in an area of France known for Charolais cattle, a breed whose prized meat reminded me of the meat from my grandfather's cattle. Now older and wiser, I appreciate the tough but very flavorful meat that's raised on grass and have learned how to properly cook it to elicit all its superior goodness.

Many Southerners have Scotch-Irish roots, and it would seem logical that their old family recipes would include ones for lamb, a traditional ingredient from those countries. But lamb is not considered a particularly Southern meat, perhaps because it's too fatty to be fried, the technique of choice for traditional Southern cooking. Another explanation could be that the hot, humid Southern summers are not conducive to raising sheep.

On the other hand, thanks to cooler weather, sheep are raised in France. Lamb is common in French cooking, in traditional stews and daubes, for example, as well as chops enhanced with flavorful marinades, as in Provençal Lamb Chops (page 94). And, with a nod at new Southern cooking, which takes influences and ingredients from outside regional traditions, I'm also including a recipe for Pecan Lamb Chops (page 95).

HERB-CRUSTED FRESH HAM

Serves 6 to 8

Mama and I now share the cooking at the holidays. I usually prepare the main courses, we share the side dishes, and she prepares the desserts. This ham is an Easter favorite.

You may be surprised to see lavender listed as an ingredient in this herb crust. Although very commonly found in desserts, lavender—especially sweet English lavender—is an incredibly versatile herb for savory cooking. Be sure to use only pesticide-free, food-grade leaves and blossoms from an organic farmer's market or online; lavender from florists, spas, or home décor shops are probably not appropriate to eat. The key to cooking with lavender is to start out with a small amount of flowers, and add more as you go. A little amount of the sweet, perfumed herb is wonderful, but adding too much lavender to your recipe is much like eating a bar of soap. A little goes a long way.

1 tablespoon chopped fresh thyme

1 teaspoon chopped fresh rosemary

1 teaspoon chopped fresh tarragon

1/2 teaspoon dried untreated lavender flowers

Half of a fresh bone-in ham (6 to 8 pounds), preferably shank end, with skin (see page 78)

Coarse salt and freshly ground black pepper

2 cups chicken stock (page 227) or low-fat, reduced-sodium chicken broth

To prepare the ham, in a small bowl, combine the thyme, rosemary, tarragon, and lavender. Season the ham with salt and pepper. Rub the herb mixture all over the ham and set aside to marinate and come to room temperature, 30 to 45 minutes.

Preheat the oven to 350°F. Place the herb-crusted ham in a roasting pan. Bake approximately 25 minutes per pound, or until the internal temperature reaches 150°F on an instant-read thermometer inserted near the bone, 2 to 2 1/2 hours. Remove from the oven to a rack. Tent the ham loosely with aluminum foil and let stand until the center of the ham registers 155° to 160°F on the instant-read thermometer, 25 to 30 minutes.

Meanwhile, to make the sauce, pour the pan drippings into a fat separator. Remove and discard the fat. Transfer the drippings into a small saucepan to make the jus. Add the chicken stock and bring to a boil over high heat. Decrease the heat to medium to keep warm until serving. Taste and adjust for seasoning with salt and pepper.

Once the ham has rested, transfer to a cutting board, carve, and serve with the jus on the side.

BOURBON BAKED HAM

Serves 10 to 12

Meme made a paste of mustard, brown sugar, and sometimes Coca-Cola when she baked a ham. She baked it in a heatproof oven bag to avoid having a messy pan to scrub. Adding bourbon, which I use here, would have never crossed her mind. Only when she baked fruitcake was she anywhere near a bottle of bourbon. She and her neighbor, Cousin Eunice, would drive to the liquor store every November to acquire the spirits for the holiday baking—she would have never gone by herself.

1 tablespoon canola oil, plus more for the pan

Half of a semi-boneless, ready-to-eat ham (5 to 6 pounds), preferably shank end (see below)

1 cup honey (preferably tupelo, orange blossom, or sweet clover)

1/2 cup sorghum, cane syrup, or molasses

1/2 cup bourbon

1/4 cup freshly squeezed orange juice

2 tablespoons Dijon mustard

Preheat the oven to 350°F. Brush a large roasting pan with some of the oil.

To prepare the ham, remove the skin and fat. Using a sharp knife make 1/4-inch-deep cuts in the meat in a diamond pattern. Place the ham in the prepared roasting pan. Meanwhile, to make the glaze, heat the honey, sorghum, bourbon, orange juice, and mustard in a saucepan over medium heat until melted and combined.

Pour over the prepared ham the warm bourbon glaze. Transfer to the oven and cook, basting every 30 minutes or so with the glaze on the bottom of the pan, for 2 to 2 1/2 hours, or until an instant-read thermometer inserted into the thickest portion registers 140°F. If the ham starts to overbrown, loosely tent with aluminum foil to prevent it from burning.

Remove from the oven to a rack. Tent the ham loosely with aluminum foil and let it rest for 20 to 30 minutes to allow the juices to redistribute.

Transfer to a cutting board, carve, and serve.

Ham Basics

A whole ham is essentially the entire back leg of a hog, weighs about 20 pounds, and at 1/2 to 3/4 pound per serving, will feed a small army. Unless you need to feed a small army, buy a half ham instead. Half hams come as butt end and shank end. The butt end comes from the upper thigh and has a rounded end, whereas the shank end comes from the lower portion of the leg and has a pointed or tapered end. Look for bone-in hams over boneless hams for more flavor (and a bone for the soup pot). Hams are sometimes labeled "fully cooked," "ready-to-eat," or "heat-and-serve." These may be eaten as is, but are more often heated to an internal temperature of 140°F for fuller flavor.

Coca-Cola–Glazed Baby Back Ribs

Makes about 20 pieces

Coca-Cola is to Atlanta as Guinness is to Dublin. Friends and family liked my Coca-Cola–Glazed Wings (page 24) so much that I decided to try a similar combination on pork. Pork has a natural affinity for sweet, rich caramel flavors. These "nouveau" Southern ribs are by no means traditional, but they are lip-smacking good.

Scotch bonnet peppers are intensely hot, but their fire is tempered by the sweetness of the sugar and Coke. To tone down the heat, substitute jalapeños instead.

1 cup Coca-Cola Classic

1/4 cup apple cider vinegar

1 1/2 cups firmly packed light brown sugar

2 Scotch bonnet chiles, chopped

2 racks baby back ribs (3 pounds total)

Coarse salt and freshly ground black pepper

To make the glaze, in a small saucepan, bring the Coca-Cola, vinegar, brown sugar, and chiles to a boil over high heat; reduce the heat to medium-low and simmer until syrupy, about 10 minutes. Decrease the heat to low and keep the sauce warm while the ribs cook.

Preheat the oven to 325°F. Liberally season both sides of the ribs with salt and pepper. Place the ribs on a broiler pan and bake for 30 minutes, glazing the ribs occasionally with the Coca-Cola mixture. Turn the ribs over and continue to cook for an additional 30 minutes, glazing occasionally, or until the ribs are tender and the meat is starting to pull away from the bone.

When the ribs are cooked through, set the oven to broil. Liberally spoon half of the remaining glaze over the ribs and broil until glazed a deep mahogany brown, 5 to 7 minutes. Turn over; repeat with the remaining glaze, an additional 5 to 7 minutes.

Serve immediately with lots of napkins.

FRIED PORK CHOPS WITH PAN GRAVY

Serves 4 to 6

One of the keys to frying meat is having the oil at the right temperature (about 375°F) so it "sings" when you add the meat. At a lower temperature, meat will cook slowly and stew rather than fry, absorbing the oil and becoming greasy and heavy.

Meat, fish, and vegetables begin to brown at around 230°F. The transformation that develops the characteristic brown color of foods cooked on the grill, in the oven, or in oil is called the "Maillard reaction."

4 to 6 (8- to 10-ounce) bone-in, center-cut pork chops, cut 3/4 inch thick

Coarse salt and freshly ground black pepper

1 cup all-purpose flour

1/4 teaspoon cayenne pepper, or to taste

1/2 cup canola oil

2 cups chicken stock (page 227) or low-fat, reduced-sodium chicken broth, or 1 cup milk plus 1 cup chicken stock or broth

Season the pork chops generously with salt and pepper. Set aside. Place the flour in a shallow plate and mix with cayenne, salt, and pepper. Set aside.

In a large skillet, preferably cast iron, heat the oil over medium-high heat until the temperature reaches 375°F on a deep-fat thermometer.

Meanwhile, to cook the pork chops, add the chops, one piece at a time, to the seasoned flour and turn to coat both sides. Shake to remove excess flour.

Add the pork chops to the hot oil without crowding. Fry until golden brown on one side and the juices are starting to pool on the surface of the meat, about 4 minutes. Using tongs, turn the chops. Cover the skillet, decrease the heat to low, and cook until the center of each chop registers 140°F on an instant-read thermometer, an additional 3 to 4 minutes. Using tongs, remove the chops to a warm platter and tent loosely with aluminum foil to keep warm.

Pour off most of the grease, leaving 2 tablespoons in the pan along with any browned bits. Add 2 tablespoons of the remaining seasoned flour. Using a wooden spoon, cook the roux over moderate heat, stirring constantly, until nutty brown, about 3 minutes. Whisk in the chicken stock and bring to a boil over high heat. Decrease the heat to medium-low, and simmer, whisking occasionally, until thickened, 3 to 5 minutes. Taste and adjust for seasoning with salt and pepper.

VARIATION: To give the chops a little crunch, I sometimes add a few tablespoons of fine cornmeal to the seasoned flour. You can also season the mixture with paprika in addition to the cayenne.

PULLED PORK SANDWICHES WITH MAMA'S BARBECUE SAUCE

Serves 4 to 6

There is an old wooden-handled cleaver hanging from a hook in Mama's kitchen, the cleaver Meme and Dede used to chop the barbecued pork. Pig roasts were better than the fair or carnival when I was a child. Uncle Raymond would chase the children with the pig's tail and Meme would always let me sneak a piece of the crisp, golden brown skin.

This quick and easy pulled pork tenderloin is a far cry from pit-cooked shoulder, but it is a very good imitation. It is a perfect recipe for a busy week when there is less time to cook. The key to the brief cooking time is to first sear the meat to a dark brown, not tan or beige, but a nice crusty brown.

1 (1-pound) pork tenderloin

Coarse salt and freshly ground black pepper

1 tablespoon canola oil

2 1/4 cups Mama's Barbecue Sauce (page 285) or your favorite sauce

4 to 6 hamburger buns, or 8 to 12 slices white bread

Preheat the oven to 350°F. Line a baking sheet with heavy-duty aluminum foil.

To prepare the pork, trim off the fat and silver skin: insert the tip of a sharp boning knife just under the silver skin about 1/2 inch from the edge of the meat where the silver skin begins. Keep the knife closer to the membrane than the meat, and pulling up slightly with the knife, slide the knife along the length of the meat to remove a strip of the membrane. Repeat until no silver skin remains. Season the pork with salt and pepper.

To sear the pork, in a large skillet, heat the oil over medium-high heat until shimmering. Sear the tenderloin until well browned on all sides, 5 to 7 minutes.

Remove from the heat and place lengthwise on the prepared baking sheet. Top with about 1 cup of the barbecue sauce and roll to fully coat. Fold the foil over the top of the meat and pinch the ends of the foil to seal well. Bake until very tender, 30 to 45 minutes.

Remove from the oven and transfer the pork to a large bowl. Discard the cooking juices remaining in the foil. Using 2 forks, shred the pork tenderloin into strips. Add barbecue sauce to taste, about 1 cup. Taste and adjust for seasoning with salt and pepper. Serve on the split buns with the remaining 1/4 cup of sauce on the side.

MUSTARD-CRUSTED PORK LOIN WITH HERB PAN SAUCE

Serves 4 to 6

After a couple of decades advertising pork as "the other white meat," during which pork chops become as lean as chicken, a new type of fattier, richer-tasting pork is finally infiltrating the butcher's case and restaurant menus. This "new" pork is from older breeds not suited for large-scale intensive farming, so it's mostly raised by small farmers who use natural farming methods and fewer antibiotics, and allow the pigs to roam freely. This heritage-heirloom-rare breed-pedigreed pork tends to be darker and redder than conventional supermarket pork. Look for it at your local farmer's market or CSA (Community Supported Agriculture program), online, or at gourmet markets.

Regardless of whether you use heirloom or traditionally farmed pork, it is important not to overcook the loin, a fairly lean cut of meat. Be sure to use an instant-read thermometer to gauge the internal temperature.

3 large cloves garlic, finely chopped

1 bay leaf, preferably fresh

1/4 cup Dijon mustard

1 tablespoon chopped fresh thyme

1 (3-pound) boneless center-cut pork loin

1/2 cup yellow mustard seed

1/2 cup brown mustard seed

Coarse salt and freshly ground black pepper

2 tablespoons canola oil (optional)

2 shallots, finely chopped

1/2 cup dry white wine

1 1/2 cups chicken stock (page 227) or low-fat, reduced-sodium chicken broth

4 tablespoons unsalted butter, cut into pieces (optional)

To season the pork loin, combine the garlic, bay leaf, mustard, and thyme in a large bowl or sealable plastic bag. Add the meat and turn to coat evenly. Let rest at room temperature for 30 minutes, or refrigerate up to overnight, turning the pork occasionally.

Preheat the oven to 350°F. Place the mustard seeds on a baking sheet. Remove the meat from the bowl, season it with salt and pepper, and roll it in the mustard seed to coat evenly. Place the roast in a shallow roasting pan.

Roast until an instant-read thermometer inserted into the center of the meat registers 140° to 145°F, 1 hour to 1 hour and 15 minutes. The pork will be slightly pink in the center (this is desirable).

Remove from the oven and transfer the pork to a warm platter; cover loosely with aluminum foil and let rest for 10 to 15 minutes to let the juices redistribute (the internal temperature of the roast will rise to 150°F from carryover cooking).

Remove all but a couple of tablespoons of fat from the roasting pan and place the pan on the cooktop over medium heat. (If there is no fat, add 2 tablespoons of canola oil.) Add the shallots and saute, stirring frequently, until softened, about 2 minutes. Add the white wine and cook until reduced by half, 3 to 5 minutes. Add the chicken stock and increase the heat to high, scraping the skillet with a wooden spoon to loosen the browned bits.

Cook until the sauce is slightly reduced, an additional 5 minutes. Thinly slice the pork and transfer to a warmed serving platter. Pour any accumulated pork juices from the cutting board into the roasting pan and stir to combine; decrease the heat to medium. Taste and adjust for seasoning with salt and pepper. To finish the sauce with butter, remove the skillet from the heat. Whisk in the butter one piece at a time. Taste and adjust for seasoning with salt and pepper.

Spoon the sauce over the pork slices; serve immediately.

MEME'S FRIED FATBACK

Serves 4 to 6

A simple meal of fried fatback, braised cabbage, and a wedge of cornmeal was one of Meme's stand-by suppers and is seriously old-fashioned country food. Fatback is the layer of fat that extends the length of a hog's back. It is available fresh, meaning unsalted, uncured, and unsmoked. Fatback with the rind is used for making cracklings, which are fried pork skins with a bit of tooth to them, commonly eaten as a snack (yes, still), or baked into cornbread.

1/2 pound fatback, sliced 1/4 inch thick

Line a plate with paper towels. Place the fatback in a cold heavy-duty skillet, preferably cast iron. Heat over medium-low heat. Cook, turning occasionally, until crisp, 10 to 12 minutes. Using tongs, remove the fatback to the prepared plate to drain. Serve immediately.

PORK CHOPS WITH DRIED PLUMS

Serves 4 to 6

Doesn't the phrase "dried plums" sound much more appealing than "prunes"? The slightly sweet flavor of the pork combines nicely with tender, fruity dried plums and is based on a classic French combination. This recipe calls for pork chops on the bone. When you cook meat on the bone, the bone essentially becomes a heat conductor. The meat cooks more evenly and tender with less loss of juices. Serve these chops with quick-cooking polenta for a delicious meal in minutes.

4 to 6 (8- to 10-ounce) bone-in, center-cut pork chops, cut 3/4 inch thick

Coarse salt and freshly ground black pepper

1 tablespoon canola oil

2 large cloves garlic, finely chopped

12 dried plums, pitted and halved (1/2 cup, packed, or 4 ounces)

1/2 cup beef stock (page 227) or reduced-fat, low-sodium beef broth

1 teaspoon chopped fresh thyme

To cook the pork chops, season with salt and pepper. In a large skillet, heat the oil over high heat until shimmering. Place the chops in the skillet and decrease the heat to medium. Cook on both sides until browned and the center of each chop registers 140°F on an instant-read thermometer, about 6 to 8 minutes. Transfer the chops to a warm platter; cover with aluminum foil and keep warm.

To make the sauce, in the same skillet, sauté the garlic over medium heat until fragrant, 45 to 60 seconds. Add the plums and stir to combine. Add the broth and thyme and stir to combine, scraping up any browned bits from the bottom of the pan. Increase the heat to high and cook until the sauce is reduced by half, about 2 minutes. Taste and adjust for seasoning with salt and pepper.

To serve, pour the sauce over the chops and serve immediately.

Meme's Fried Fatback (this page) with Meme's Braised Cabbage (page 176) and Meme's Cornmeal Griddle Cakes (page 216)

MAMA'S COUNTRY-FRIED VENISON STEAK

Serves 4 to 6

For years, I assumed that since my grandfather was a country boy who had grown up on the river, he had hunted his entire life. But he only started hunting deer as an adult. Actually, he killed his first deer while fishing. A deer started swimming toward the boat. Dede had a fishing pole, but no gun. The story goes that he reached out with his mammoth hands, grabbed the deer's rack of antlers, and held the large buck's head under water until he quit fighting. Dede then towed the deer back to shore, old man and the sea, Southern style.

The quality of venison depends on the age of the animal, its diet, and the time of the year the animal was hunted. The meat is very lean, yet the flavor is more assertive than beef. If you are unable to find venison, substitute boneless rib-eye steaks rather than top round, the more common cut for country-fried steak, and too tough. I've jazzed Mama's recipe up a little bit with mustard and panko.

1 1/2 pounds venison, cut into 1/4-inch-thick, serving-size portions, or 4 (6-ounce) rib-eye steaks, pounded 1/4 inch thick

Coarse salt and freshly ground black pepper

3 tablespoons Dijon mustard

1 cup fresh or panko (Japanese) breadcrumbs

1/2 cup all-purpose flour

2 large egg whites

3 tablespoons canola oil, plus more if needed

To prepare the venison, season both sides of the meat with salt and pepper, then brush both sides with mustard to coat. Combine the breadcrumbs and flour in a shallow plate. Season with salt and pepper. Place the egg whites in a separate shallow bowl or pie plate and whisk lightly. Dip the meat first into the egg whites, allowing the excess to drip off. Then dip into the breadcrumb mixture, patting on both sides to coat.

Line a plate with paper towels. To cook the venison, in a large, heavy-duty skillet, preferably cast iron, heat the oil over medium-high heat. Add the meat to the skillet without crowding, in batches, if necessary, and cook on both sides until dark brown, 2 to 3 minutes per side; transfer to the prepared plate once cooked. Serve immediately.

BRAISED SHORT RIBS

Short ribs are the meaty ends of the beef rib from the chuck, rib, and brisket. They are rich and succulent, but fairly fatty, so before braising, it is very important to first brown them well to render the excess fat. Short ribs are available cut two ways: English—cut between the bones so each piece consists of one rib, or flanken—cut across the bones, so each piece consists of several bones. Either cut is appropriate for this dish.

4 to 6 pounds beef short ribs

Coarse salt and freshly ground black pepper

2 tablespoons canola oil

2 onions, preferably Vidalia, chopped

2 carrots, chopped

2 stalks celery, chopped

1 tablespoon tomato paste

3 tablespoons all-purpose flour

1/2 cup red wine vinegar

1 (750-ml) bottle red wine, preferably Pinot Noir

6 cloves garlic, crushed

Bouquet garni (4 sprigs of thyme, 4 of sprigs flat-leaf parsley, 2 bay leaves, preferably fresh, tied together in cheesecloth)

2 to 2 1/2 cups beef stock (page 227) or low-fat, reduced-sodium beef broth

Preheat the oven to 375°F. To brown the short ribs, season them generously with salt and pepper. In a large, heavy-duty Dutch oven, heat the oil over medium-high heat until shimmering. Brown the ribs on all sides, in two or three batches so as not to crowd them, 5 to 7 minutes. Remove to a plate and set aside.

To make the sauce, remove all but 1 tablespoon of the oil from the Dutch oven. Add the onions, carrots, and celery. Cook, stirring occasionally, until the onions are golden brown, 5 to 7 minutes. Decrease the heat to medium. Add the tomato paste and flour and stir to combine. Cook, stirring constantly, for 2 to 3 minutes.

Add the vinegar and wine to deglaze the pan, using a wooden spoon to loosen the browned bits from the bottom of the pan. Cook, uncovered, until the wine is reduced, 5 to 7 minutes.

Return the short ribs to the pan and add the garlic, bouquet garni, and enough stock to cover. Bring to a boil over high heat. Cover, and transfer to the oven. Cook until the meat is tender, 2 1/2 to 3 hours.

To make the sauce, using a slotted spoon, transfer the cooked short ribs to a warm platter and cover loosely with aluminum foil to keep warm. Spoon off any excess oil left on the surface of the pan and discard along with the bouquet garni. In the Dutch oven, using an immersion blender, puree the sauce and vegetables until smooth. Or, once the beef is removed, ladle the sauce and vegetables into a blender and puree a little at a time until smooth. Cook over medium-high heat until the sauce coats the back of a spoon; thin with more stock, if needed, to achieve this consistency. Taste and adjust for seasoning with salt and pepper.

To serve, return the short ribs to the sauce and turn to coat. Heat briefly over medium heat if necessary to rewarm, then serve.

BRISKET WITH VIDALIA ONION PUREE

Serves 6

Brisket is tough, and it is best suited for braising and slow cooking, which tenderizes the meat from within by dissolving the cut's plentiful collagen and fat. Brisket is very often smoked in the South; in fact, barbecue means brisket in Texas, as barbecue means pork in the Southeast. Buy fresh brisket (not corned or brined), ideally the flat or first cut, which is leaner than point or second cut, and has a layer of fat running across it to help keep it moist.

Hungarian paprika, ground from dried sweet peppers, gives the sauce another layer of flavor and a slightly reddish color. There are six types of Hungarian paprika, ranging from delicate to hot; any of them would be fine in this dish. My mother and Aunt Lee took a whirlwind trip to Eastern Europe several years ago. True to their natures, they did have enough time, however, to shop. Knowing how much I like to purchase local ingredients when I travel, Mama brought me paprika as a gift. It's basically a lifetime supply. I store it in the freezer in an airtight container to help it last as long as possible and not become stale and flavorless.

2 tablespoons canola oil

1 (3 1/2- to 4-pound) beef brisket, preferably first cut (see headnote)

Coarse salt and freshly ground black pepper

3 onions, preferably Vidalia, thickly sliced

4 cloves garlic, finely chopped

1 tablespoon Hungarian paprika

2 bay leaves, preferably fresh

12 ounces dark beer or ale

2 cups beef stock (page 227) or low-fat, reduced-sodium beef broth, plus more if needed

Preheat the oven to 375°F. To cook the brisket, in a large, heavy-bottomed Dutch oven, heat the oil over high heat. Pat the brisket dry with paper towels and season with salt and pepper. Sear the brisket until a rich, dark brown on both sides, 8 to 10 minutes total. Remove to a plate.

Decrease the heat to medium, add the onions and cook, stirring constantly, until they begin to color and soften, 5 to 7 minutes. Add the garlic and cook until fragrant, 45 to 60 seconds. Add the paprika, bay leaves, and seared brisket. Add the beer and stock and bring to a boil over medium-high heat. Cover and bake until tender, 2 1/2 to 3 1/2 hours, adding more stock, if needed, so the meat does not dry out.

Remove the brisket from the oven and transfer to a cutting board. Remove and discard the bay leaves. In the Dutch oven, using an immersion blender, puree the onions until smooth. Or, once the beef is removed, ladle the sauce and vegetables into a blender and puree a little at a time until smooth. Taste and adjust for seasoning with salt and pepper.

To serve, slice the brisket against the grain and serve with the onion puree.

OLD-FASHIONED POT ROAST

Serves 4 to 6

Julia Child was quoted as saying, "Once you have mastered a technique, you hardly need look at a recipe again." The technique for cooking tough cuts of meat is braising: the meat is seared until dark brown for flavor, then removed from the pot. Aromatics such as herbs and vegetables are cooked in the same pot in a small amount of the remaining fat. The pan is subsequently deglazed with liquid to help remove any brown bits of flavor from the bottom of the pan, then the meat is returned and liquid is added to come up to the meat's "shoulders." Pot roast is a classic braised dish.

3 tablespoons canola oil

1 (4-pound) boneless chuck roast or rump roast

3 medium onions, preferably Vidalia, thickly sliced

1 cup dry red wine

2 tablespoons Hungarian paprika

2 teaspoons chopped fresh thyme

1 bay leaf, preferably fresh

4 cloves garlic, crushed

3 cups beef stock (page 227) or low-fat, reduced-sodium beef broth, plus more if needed

2 pounds new potatoes, scrubbed

6 carrots, cut into 1 1/2-inch-thick pieces

Coarse salt and freshly ground black pepper

Preheat the oven to 300°F. To cook the roast, in a large, heavy-bottomed Dutch oven, heat the oil over high heat. Sear the meat until it's a rich, dark brown on both sides, 8 to 10 minutes total. Remove to a plate.

Decrease the heat to medium, add the onions and cook, stirring frequently, until a deep, golden brown, 8 to 10 minutes. Add the wine and cook, stirring to loosen any brown bits. Add the paprika, thyme, bay leaf, and garlic. Stir to combine and cook until fragrant, 45 to 60 seconds. Return the seared roast to the pan. Add the stock and bring to a boil over medium-high heat. Cover and bake for 1 hour.

Remove from the oven and turn the roast in the liquid to moisten. Add the potatoes and carrots, cover, and bake an additional 1 to 1 1/2 hours, or until both the meat and vegetables are tender.

Transfer the roast to a warm platter. Using a slotted spoon, place the vegetables around the roast. Cover the platter loosely with aluminum foil to keep warm. Remove the bay leaf from the sauce and discard. If the sauce is too thin, bring it to a boil over high heat to reduce and thicken. If the sauce is too thick, add a little wine or stock to achieve the correct consistency. Taste the sauce and adjust for seasoning with salt and pepper.

To serve, slice the roast against the grain, and spoon the sauce over the roast and vegetables.

BOEUF BOURGUIGNONNE

Serves 4 to 6

In classic French cooking, each dish has a name that indicates its precise ingredients and correct garnish. Bourguignonne is a term for dishes cooked in red wine, as some of the most famous French wines are from Bourgogne (Burgundy). These dishes are garnished with pearl onions, button mushrooms, and lardons of bacon. Never choose stew meat already in precut cubes. It's more expensive and you have no idea if you're getting, for example, leftover bits from the shoulder or rib-eye, two wildly different cuts that won't cook at the same rate.

3 pounds lean rump roast, chuck pot roast, sirloin tip, top round, or bottom round, cut into 2-inch cubes

1 (750-ml) bottle red wine, preferably Pinot Noir

1 carrot, cut into 1-inch pieces

1 stalk celery, cut into 1-inch pieces

1 onion, preferably Vidalia, coarsely chopped

4 slices thick-cut bacon, cut into lardons (see page 179)

3 tablespoons canola oil, plus more if needed

Coarse salt and freshly ground black pepper

1 tablespoon all-purpose flour

2 1/2 cups beef stock (page 227) or low-fat, reduced-sodium beef broth

Bouquet garni (5 sprigs of thyme, 4 sprigs of flat-leaf parsley, 2 bay leaves, preferably fresh, 10 black peppercorns, tied together in cheesecloth)

1 tablespoon tomato paste

2 cloves garlic, finely chopped

1 tablespoon unsalted butter

24 pearl onions, trimmed and peeled

8 ounces white button mushrooms, halved or quartered if large

To marinate the beef, place the cubes in a large nonreactive bowl. Add the wine, carrot, celery, and onion. Cover and refrigerate for at least 2 hours or overnight.

Line both a baking sheet and a large plate with paper towels.

Remove the beef from the marinade and transfer to the prepared baking sheet. Pat the meat dry with paper towels. Strain the marinade, reserving separately both the vegetables and the liquid.

Preheat the oven to 350°F. To cook the beef, heat a large, heavy-duty Dutch oven over medium-high heat. Add the bacon and cook until the fat is rendered and the bacon is crisp, about 5 minutes. Remove the bacon with a slotted spoon to the prepared plate to drain. Pour off all but 1 tablespoon of the bacon fat from the pan. Decrease the heat to medium, add 2 tablespoons of the canola oil and heat until shimmering.

Season the beef with salt and pepper. Sear the beef in two or three batches without crowding until nicely browned on all sides, about 5 minutes; transfer to the prepared baking sheet when done. Add the reserved vegetables from the marinade and cook until they start to color, 5 to 7 minutes. Sprinkle on the flour and toss again to lightly coat. Cook, stirring constantly, until the flour turns brown, 2 to 3 minutes. Return the beef to the Dutch oven. Add the reserved marinade liquid and enough stock to barely cover the meat.

Add the bouquet garni, tomato paste, and garlic to the pan. Bring to a boil on high heat on the cooktop. Cover and transfer to the oven. Cook until the meat is tender, 2 1/2 to 3 hours.

Meanwhile, to make the garnish, in a large skillet, heat the remaining 1 tablespoon of oil and the butter over medium heat. Add the peeled onions, mushrooms, the remaining sprig of thyme, and the remaining bay leaf. Season with salt and pepper. Saute until the vegetables are lightly browned and tender, 5 to 7 minutes. Set aside and keep warm.

Remove the bouquet garni from the Dutch oven and discard. Transfer the beef with a slotted spoon to a bowl. In the Dutch oven,

continued

using an immersion blender, puree the sauce and vegetables until smooth. Or, once the beef is removed, ladle the sauce and vegetables into a blender and puree until smooth a little at a time. Cook the pureed sauce over medium-high heat until the sauce coats the back of a spoon; if needed, thin with more stock to achieve this consistency. Taste and adjust for seasoning with salt and pepper. Return the beef to the sauce and turn to coat.

Remove the sprig of thyme and the bay leaf from the mushrooms and onions in the skillet. Add the sauteed mushrooms, onions, and reserved bacon to the beef and sauce. Stir to combine. Bring to a simmer over medium heat and cook until warm and the flavors marry and blend, 5 to 7 minutes. Taste and adjust for seasoning with salt and pepper. Serve immediately.

SKIRT STEAK WITH SHALLOTS

Serves 4 to 6

Skirt steak is a long, flat, flavorful piece of beef cut from the diaphragm muscle in the plate section of a cow—essentially where the waist would be if a cow had a waist. Also known as plate steak, it is used for making fajitas.

1 tablespoon canola oil, plus more if needed

1 1/2 pounds skirt steak

Coarse salt and freshly ground black pepper

2 tablespoons unsalted butter

2 shallots, peeled and thinly sliced

1 tablespoon red wine vinegar

1/4 cup dry red wine

To cook the steak, in a heavy-duty skillet, heat the oil over medium-high heat until shimmering. Season the steaks with salt and pepper. Add the meat to the skillet without crowding, in batches, if necessary, and cook on both sides until well browned and medium-rare, about 3 minutes per side. Transfer to a warm plate and cover loosely with aluminum foil to keep warm while preparing the sauce.

To prepare the sauce, return the pan to the cooktop over medium heat. Add 1 tablespoon of the butter and the shallots. Cook until the shallots are soft and translucent, 3 to 5 minutes. Add the vinegar and stir to combine. Cook until the vinegar evaporates, 30 to 45 seconds. Add the red wine and cook until reduced by half, 1 to 2 minutes. Remove the pan from the heat and add the remaining 1 tablespoon of butter; swirl to coat. Taste and adjust for seasoning with salt and pepper.

To serve, slice the steak into thin strips against the grain. Overlap the slices on a plate and pour over the red wine glaze.

PEPPER-CRUSTED BEEF WITH COGNAC AND GOLDEN RAISINS

Serves 4 to 6

Pepper, made from the small dried berries of a tropical vine native to India, has been the most widely used spice in the world for centuries. Green peppercorns are harvested when not quite ripe, and are most often dried or cured in brine or vinegar. Black peppercorns are picked when ripe, allowed to ferment, and then dried until they shrivel and turn brownish black. White pepper is allowed to ripen more fully on the vine before the black outer husk is removed. The husks are removed in a steady stream of water, so the peppercorns are very white and very clean.

To crust a beef filet with a combination of crushed peppercorns is a traditional French cooking technique known as *au poivre*. Here, the bite of the pepper is tempered by the sharp cognac and fruity golden raisins.

1/2 cup cognac, brandy, or bourbon

1/2 cup golden raisins

1 teaspoon whole white peppercorns, crushed

1 teaspoon whole black peppercorns, crushed

1 teaspoon whole green peppercorns, crushed

1 whole allspice berry, crushed

4 to 6 (6-ounce) boneless rib-eye or tenderloin steaks, (cut about 1¼ inches thick)

Coarse salt

2 tablespoons canola oil

1/3 cup beef stock (page 227) or low-fat, reduced-sodium beef broth

2 tablespoons unsalted butter, cut into bits (optional)

To plump the raisins, heat the cognac in a small saucepan over low heat just to simmering. Remove from the heat. Add the raisins and set aside to plump, about 30 minutes.

To pan-fry the steak, combine the white, black, and green peppercorns and allspice in a shallow bowl. Season the steaks with salt on both sides and press the peppercorns into one side of the steak.

In a large skillet, heat the oil over medium-high heat. Add the steaks, without crowding, pepper side down first, and cook each side for 3 to 5 minutes for medium-rare. Transfer the meat to a warm platter and cover with aluminum foil to keep warm.

To make the pan sauce, pour off the fat from the skillet. Remove the skillet from the heat and add the raisins and cognac. Return the pan to high heat and bring to a boil. (If you have a gas cooktop especially, watch for flame-ups.) Cook until the mixture is reduced by half, about 2 minutes. Add the beef stock, decrease the heat to medium, and cook until slightly reduced, an additional 2 minutes.

To finish the sauce with butter, remove the pan from the heat and whisk in the butter, one piece at a time. Taste and adjust for seasoning with salt. No additional pepper is necessary.

To serve, return the steaks and any accumulated juices to the skillet and baste with the sauce. Serve immediately.

PROVENÇAL LAMB CHOPS

Serves 4 to 6

Lamb rib chops have a dandy handle (the rib bone), and are excellent served as lamb "lollipops" for delicious, but rather extravagant, hors d'oeuvres. As the ribs get closer to the neck and shoulder, the nugget of meat becomes smaller, perfect for hors d'oeuvres. The larger ones are best as a main course served with a knife and a fork. Loin lamb chops are cut from the loin and look more like miniature T-bone steaks, with a bit of the loin and tenderloin on either side, and take a little longer to cook, but may be substituted in this recipe.

3 cloves garlic, finely chopped

3 tablespoons olive oil

1 tablespoon chopped fresh oregano

Grated zest and juice of 1 lemon

12 (4-ounce) lamb rib chops, cut 1 inch thick

Coarse salt and freshly ground black pepper

In a bowl or sealable plastic bag, combine the garlic, oil, oregano, lemon zest, and lemon juice. Season the lamb chops with salt and pepper. Add the chops to the marinade and turn to coat. Marinate for about 30 minutes at room temperature or refrigerate, covered, overnight, turning the meat occasionally.

When ready to cook, heat the broiler or prepare a charcoal fire using about 6 pounds of charcoal and burn until the coals are completely covered with a thin coating of light gray ash, 20 to 30 minutes. Spread the coals evenly over the grill bottom, position the grill rack above the coals, and heat until medium-hot (when you can hold your hand 5 inches above the grill surface for no longer than 3 or 4 seconds). Or, for a gas grill, turn on all burners to High, close the lid, and heat until very hot, 10 to 15 minutes.

Remove the chops from the marinade, scraping away the excess. Broil about 3 inches from the heat or grill over medium-hot coals (medium-high on a gas grill), 3 to 5 minutes per side, turning once or twice. For rare to medium-rare, the internal temperature should register 120° to 135°F on an instant-read thermometer. Serve immediately.

PECAN LAMB CHOPS

Most members of my family have never been fond of lamb. Dede always called it "sheepy-sheepy" and Mama thinks they look too gentle and sweet to eat. I was inducted into the lamb fan club when testing recipes for Nathalie Dupree.

Lamb chops are earthy, rich, and faintly sweet. However, the fat can be overwhelming and strong, especially when chilled or at room temperature. Remove as much fat as possible before cooking, and serve the chops immediately so they don't have a chance to cool.

1 cup pecan halves

1 tablespoon chopped fresh thyme

Coarse salt and freshly ground black pepper

2 large egg whites, lightly beaten

1/2 cup all-purpose flour

8 (6-ounce) lamb loin chops, cut 1 1/2 inches thick

1/4 cup canola oil

Preheat the oven to 500°F. In the bowl of a food processor fitted with the metal blade, process the pecans and thyme until finely chopped. Spread on a large plate and season with salt and pepper. Whisk the egg whites in a medium bowl until light and frothy. Place the flour in a shallow bowl and season generously with salt and pepper.

To prepare the chops, dredge them in the flour mixture to coat, shaking off the excess flour. Then dip them into the beaten egg white, and finally into the herbed ground pecans, coating all sides.

To cook the chops, in a large, nonstick saute pan, heat 2 tablespoons of the oil over medium-high heat. Add the chops to the skillet without crowding and cook, in batches, if necessary, on both sides until browned, 1 to 2 minutes per side. (Be careful not to let the pecans burn.)

Place the browned chops on a baking sheet and bake an additional 2 to 3 minutes for rare, or until the internal temperature registers 120° to 135°F on an instant-read thermometer. Serve immediately.

CHAPTER 5

GOSPEL BIRDS AND GAME BIRDS

FRIED CHICKEN IS GENERALLY recognized as the South's irresistible gift to cuisine, its ultimate comfort food. Fried chicken is in my soul. Both Mama and my grandmother would fix it for Sunday dinner. Dede called it "gospel bird," as once upon a time, chicken was only served on Sunday. I remember cast-iron skillets that looked like satin—slick and midnight black—pulling the wishbone with my mother, and fighting with my sister over the drumsticks.

Georgia, where I live, is the biggest chicken producer in the United States (Americans eat a lot of chicken—almost ninety pounds a year per person). Several years ago, I visited a chicken facility and saw every last facet of chicken production, from egg to flash-frozen cooked chicken nuggets. I asked to see how they were killed; as someone who eats chicken, I felt it was important to remind myself that the platter of wings represents twelve actual chickens and that those cleanly wrapped boneless, skinless breasts came from animals.

The chickens were hung upside down by their feet in metal shackles, stunned, then passed through a machine that slit their necks. Not all were killed, so there was a man positioned at the end of a narrow room to finish the job. A double conveyor moved the hanging chickens along. On a platform about shoulder high, a man wearing a gas mask and a blue rubber hazmat suit, drenched in blood, was illuminated by a single beam of light. The scene was overwhelming, and one of the most powerful things I have ever witnessed. When I tell this story people often ask me if I still eat chicken. I do. But rarely will you ever hear me complain about my job.

At the market in France, it is possible to buy freshly killed chickens with feathers intact and even a little barnyard residue on their feet. Perhaps the most famous chickens in the world are from Bresse, an area in Burgundy just north of Lyon. White feathers, blue feet, and red combs—the colors of the French flag—make the birds appear especially French. They are the only poultry in the world with an AOC (*appellation d'origine contrôlée*), a government regulated certification that guarantees that certain agricultural products are held to a rigorous set of standards. The birds are fed a diet solely of corn and milk and allowed free range with over ten square meters of space per bird in flocks no larger than five hundred, a far cry from factory farms. These birds are pricey. Metal bands are attached to their legs and a tricolor seal is placed on their necks for identification. When the birds are served in even the finest restaurants, these tags are not removed so that the customer is assured authenticity.

In the United States, chickens are classified according to their best uses: broiler-fryers are young chickens up to seven weeks old that weigh three to five pounds. (Smaller two- to three-pound chickens that were preferred for frying were once available, but these have seemingly disappeared, perhaps because it's hard for producers to earn enough on smaller birds.) Roasters are three to five months old and weigh six to eight pounds. Stewing chickens are breeder hens no longer able to produce eggs. These older hens, ten to eighteen months old and weighing five to six pounds, are less tender because of their age. This makes them suitable for long, slow, cooking. A capon is a castrated rooster that weighs anywhere from four to ten pounds and is especially meaty and tender.

Modern farming has rendered some cooking techniques obsolete. Young chickens are bred to cook very quickly, and breasts from chickens are now larger, answering our demand for white meat. Factory-farmed chickens also contain plenty of fat, so it is no longer necessary to use lots of oil or butter to moisten the flesh or to truss our chickens tightly for roasting to keep the juices in the bird during the long cooking time and protect the leaner breast meat from drying out.

I find that people in general, terrified of salmonella, overcook chicken, especially the boneless, skinless breasts that are so low in fat and lack protective skin and bone. Many of the recipes in this chapter can be adjusted to use boneless, skinless chicken breasts. What's important to remember when adapting the recipes is that chicken is cooked when the juices run clear. If the juices run pink, it's not quite done. If there are no juices, it's overcooked. So, for example, when frying the chicken for Meme's Fried Chicken and Gravy (page 106), boneless, skinless chicken breasts will only need eight to ten minutes for those juices to run clear, not thirty. When adapting the stew-like recipes such as Coq au Vin (page 108) to boneless, skinless breasts, the chicken will be cooked long before the sauce has had a chance to thicken. So, cook the breasts in the sauce until the juices run clear, then remove them to a warm plate and cover with aluminum foil while you continue cooking and reducing the sauce. When the sauce is at the right consistency, return the breasts to the sauce to gently heat through.

HOW TO CUT UP A CHICKEN

Precut chicken pieces are often not uniform in size and shape, and they sometimes contain bits of shattered bone. It's also more economical to cut it yourself. This exercise often elicits squeamish faces when I teach it in class. I've seen chicken cut into parts I never knew existed. Granted, it can be a bit challenging at first. Follow this step-by-step method. With practice, you will eventually master the technique. The key is to cut between the joints; in most instances, if you are struggling too much, your knife is not between a joint, but on a bone.

Finally, only touch the chicken with the hand not holding the knife. This will keep your knife hand clean and dry so the knife is less likely to slip and perhaps cut you, instead of the chicken.

Place the whole chicken, breast side up, on a clean cutting board. Remove the giblets and neck bone from the cavity and set aside. Position the chicken with the cavity facing away from you. Using a chef's knife, remove the wing tips at the joints. Use the neck bone and wing tips for stock.

Pull the drumstick and thigh away from the body. Using a chef's knife, cut through the skin only until your knife meets the thigh joint. Bend the leg-thigh portion back until the thigh bone pops out of the socket. Then, with the tip of your knife, cut around and through the joint at that point, to detach the leg-thigh portion from the body. Place the removed leg quarter on the board, skin side down, and look for a thin line of fat between the leg

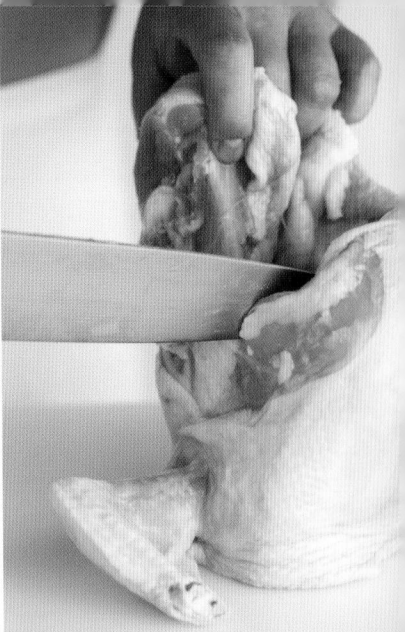

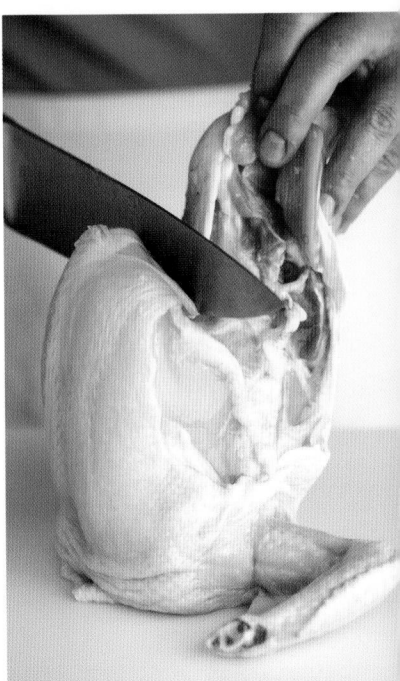

and thigh; this is the joint. With your knife, cut directly thought the joint. Repeat the process on the opposite side. Remove the pieces from the board and set aside.

Next, separate the breast from the back. Tip the chicken so that the neck end is on the board. Cut down through the rib cage, starting from the tail end and cutting to the neck. There is often a second thin line of fat you can use as a guide. Repeat on the other side. The breast and back should still be connected at the neck. Return the chicken to the board, breast side up, with the cavity facing you. Insert the knife into the cavity immediately to the right of the neck. Place the tip of the knife on the cutting board and forcefully bring down the handle of the knife, cutting through the bone to separate. Repeat on the opposite side. The chest and back are now separated. Set the back aside.

Place the chicken breast on the board, skin side down, and sternum facing up. At the tip of the breast, there is a pointed bit of cartilage that is easy to cut through. Cut the cartilage in half so that only the sternum remains uncut. Place the tip of your knife on the board, lined up with the cut in the cartilage. Align the blade on the sternum and forcefully bring down the handle, cutting through the bone. The breast is now separated into two pieces with wings still attached. Halve the breasts to create two pieces each for a total of four breast pieces.

BRINING

Brining—soaking meat, poultry, and shellfish in a saltwater solution—is the key to a juicy, tender result. Salt causes the food proteins to form a complex mesh that traps the brine so the muscle fibers absorb additional liquid during the brining period. Some of this liquid is lost during cooking, but since the meat is juicier to begin with, it cooks up juicier at the end. Think of a cup filled "over the rim."

The size of the salt grains used in a brine is very important. Grains of table salt are very fine, while those of kosher salt are larger. So, 1 teaspoon of kosher salt is equal to about $1/2$ teaspoon of fine salt. The crystals of the two most widely available brands of kosher salt, Morton's and Diamond Brand, differ. Half a cup of table salt is equal to 1 cup of Diamond Brand kosher salt or $3/4$ cup of Morton's kosher salt. My recipes call for Diamond Brand because the conversion is easy at 2:1.

There's no hard-and-fast rule for brining. But keep in mind that the more concentrated the brining solution and the smaller the piece of meat, the shorter the brining period. Common sense dictates that a turkey is going to take more time to brine than a pound of shrimp. A turkey is best brined in a weak solution for a longer period of time than needed for a whole chicken or breasts. It's fairly easy to plan an overnight brine for a holiday turkey, but who has time to do the same for the main course of a weeknight supper? For smaller pieces of meat, my philosophy is to use a strong brine that takes an hour or less.

For turkey: for a 4- to 6-hour brine, dissolve 2 cups Diamond Brand kosher salt and 1 cup sugar per 2 gallons cold water. For a 12- to 14-hour brine, dissolve 1 cup Diamond Brand kosher salt and $1/2$ cup sugar per 2 gallons cold water.

For whole chickens, chicken pieces, and pork: for a 1-hour brine, dissolve 1 cup Diamond Brand kosher salt and $1/2$ cup sugar per 2 quarts water.

OVEN-FRIED CHICKEN BREASTS WITH PECAN CRUST

Serves 4 to 6

Brining, or soaking poultry in salted water before cooking, is the answer to dry, taste-less white meat and rubbery dark meat: brined poultry loses only half as much mois-ture during cooking as unbrined. In this recipe, I use buttermilk instead of water for the brine. Buttermilk is traditional in some fried chicken recipes and has the added benefit of acting as a tenderizer. If doubling this recipe, do not double the amount of salt, as the chicken will be too salty. Serve this with a dollop of Vidalia Honey Mustard Dressing (page 284) as a sweet complement to its savory flavors.

1/4 cup coarse salt

2 tablespoons sugar

1 tablespoon sweet Hungarian paprika

4 cloves garlic, smashed

2 bay leaves, preferably fresh

4 cups buttermilk

4 to 6 (8-ounce) boneless, skinless chicken breasts

1/2 cup fresh or panko (Japanese) breadcrumbs

3/4 cup finely chopped pecans

2 tablespoons canola oil

2 large eggs

2 tablespoons Dijon mustard

1 teaspoon chopped fresh thyme leaves

Freshly ground black pepper

Vidalia Honey Mustard Dressing (page 284), for accompaniment

Preheat the oven to 350°F. Line a rimmed baking sheet with alumi-num foil, then set a large wire rack on the foil.

To make the brine, combine the salt, sugar, paprika, garlic, and bay leaves in a large nonreactive container. Add the buttermilk and stir until the salt is completely dissolved. Immerse the chicken breasts in the brine and marinate at room temperature for 30 min-utes. (Do not brine any longer or refrigerate, or the chicken will be too salty.)

Meanwhile, combine the panko and pecans in a shallow dish. Add the oil and toss well to coat. In a second shallow dish, combine the eggs, mustard, and thyme. Season both mixtures with pepper.

Working with one piece at a time, remove the chicken from the brine and shake off any excess liquid. Dip the chicken into the egg mixture, coating both sides. Place the breasts in the breadcrumb mixture, sprinkle with crumbs to cover, and press so the coating adheres; turn the chicken over and repeat the process. Gently shake off any excess crumbs. Place the coated breasts on the rack set on the baking sheet. Bake until the chicken is golden brown and the juices run clear, 20 to 25 minutes.

Serve each breast with a spoonful of dressing.

COUNTRY CAPTAIN CHICKEN

Serves 4 to 6

This is not a family recipe, but one I was introduced to while testing recipes as an apprentice for Nathalie Dupree. Country Captain is said to have taken its name from a British army officer who brought the recipe back from India.

Curry powder is actually quite common in Southern cooking due to the seaports of Charleston and Savannah. The term describes any of a number of Indian spice blends from mild to fiery that typically contain, among other spices, ground coriander, nutmeg, ginger, cumin, pepper, and chiles. Commercial curry powder comes in two types: standard, which is a golden color and mild, and Madras, which is red and spicy hot.

1 (4- to 5-pound) chicken, cut into 8 pieces (see page 99)

Coarse salt and freshly ground black pepper

1 cup all-purpose flour, plus more if needed

1/2 teaspoon Hungarian paprika

1/2 teaspoon cayenne pepper

3 tablespoons unsalted butter

3 tablespoons canola oil

1 large onion, preferably Vidalia, chopped

1/2 green bell pepper, cored, seeded, and chopped

1/2 red bell pepper, cored, seeded, and chopped

2 cloves garlic, finely chopped

1 tablespoon curry powder, preferably Madras

1 teaspoon ground cumin

1/2 teaspoon ground turmeric

1/4 teaspoon ground cinnamon

1 (28-ounce) can whole tomatoes with juice

1 cup golden raisins

1/2 cup sliced or slivered almonds, lightly toasted (see page 196), for garnish

2 tablespoons chopped fresh parsley, for garnish

$20,000 Rice Pilaf (page 158), for accompaniment

Season the chicken with salt and pepper. Combine the flour, paprika, and cayenne in a shallow bowl, and season with salt and pepper. Turn the chicken pieces in the flour mixture until coated. Shake off the excess flour. Set aside.

Line a plate with paper towels. To prepare the chicken, in a large skillet, heat the butter and oil over medium-high heat until sizzling. Without crowding the skillet, cook the chicken, in batches, if necessary, until a rich, golden brown on both sides, about 3 minutes per side. Remove the chicken pieces to the prepared plate to drain.

Decrease the heat to medium-low, and allow the fat to cool a little. Add the onion, green and red bell peppers, and garlic to the pan and stir until soft, but not browned, 3 to 5 minutes. Add the curry powder, cumin, turmeric, cinnamon, tomatoes with juice, and raisins. Season with salt and pepper.

Return the chicken to the pan, cover, and cook over low heat for 25 to 30 minutes, or until the chicken is tender and the juices run clear when pierced with a knife. Remove the chicken pieces to a shallow bowl or platter with a lip. Tent the chicken with aluminum foil to keep warm.

To finish the sauce, increase the heat to high and reduce the liquid until thickened, stirring frequently, 5 to 7 minutes. Taste and adjust for seasoning with salt and pepper.

To serve, spoon the sauce over the chicken and top with the toasted almonds and chopped parsley. Accompany with rice pilaf.

VARIATION: You can make this recipe with boneless, skinless breasts instead of bone-in pieces. Simmer the breasts as directed on top of the stove along with the other ingredients, but just until the juices run clear, only 8 to 10 additional minutes. Remove the breasts to a warm plate and cover with aluminum foil. Let the sauce continue to simmer until the vegetables are tender and the sauce is thick enough to coat a spoon. Return the breasts to the sauce and finish as directed.

CHICKEN FRICASSEE WITH GARLIC AND RED WINE VINEGAR

Serves 4 to 6

This country French recipe was one of my final exam dishes in culinary school. Delicious and simple, it has become a real family favorite. It's very important to use the best quality red wine vinegar. We made our own at school with the leftover dribbles and drabs of wine.

Many years later, I was cleaning the kitchen at the television studio where Martha Stewart's show was produced, and noticed a cloudy substance in one of the bottles that I was about to recycle. I realized that it was a "mother," a live bacterial culture that turns wine into wine vinegar. I took it home, transferred it to a glass cookie jar, and added red wine. That was over ten years ago. My tasty biology project is still alive and well, producing incredible vinegar.

In France, this dish is often made with guinea hen, which has rich, dark meat, and much more complex flavor than chicken. Meme used to raise guinea hens; they would roost in the trees and make a huge fuss if anyone came into the yard.

1 (4- to 5-pound) chicken, cut into 8 pieces (see page 99)

Coarse salt and freshly ground black pepper

2 tablespoons unsalted butter

1 tablespoon canola oil

4 cloves garlic, crushed

1 cup red wine vinegar

1 (15-ounce) can whole tomatoes, crushed, with liquid

1 cup chicken stock (page 227) or reduced-fat, low-sodium chicken broth

1 bay leaf, preferably fresh

2 sprigs of flat-leaf parsley

2 sprigs of thyme

To cook the chicken, season with salt and pepper. Heat the butter and oil over medium heat in a large, straight-sided skillet or saucepan (not cast iron, as it will interact with the acidic tomatoes and vinegar). Add the chicken, skin side down, without crowding the pan. Cook without crowding until a rich, golden brown on both sides, 3 to 5 minutes per side. Remove the chicken to a plate.

Pour off all but 1 tablespoon of fat. Add the garlic and cook until fragrant, 45 to 60 seconds. Add the vinegar and scrape with a wooden spoon to loosen any brown bits from the bottom of the skillet. Stand back when adding the vinegar, because when it hits the hot pan it will produce strong vinegar fumes. Return the chicken to the skillet. Add the tomatoes with their liquid, chicken stock, bay leaf, parsley, and thyme. Bring to a boil, then decrease the heat to medium-low, cover, and cook until the chicken is tender and the juices run clear, an additional 30 to 45 minutes. Taste and adjust for seasoning with salt and pepper.

To make the sauce, remove the chicken pieces to a warm serving dish. Increase the heat to high, and cook the sauce until reduced and lightly thickened, about 5 minutes. Taste and adjust for seasoning with salt and pepper. Remove and discard the herbs. Spoon the sauce over the chicken and serve.

VARIATION: You can make this recipe with boneless, skinless breasts instead of bone-in pieces. Simmer the breasts as directed on top of the stove along with the other ingredients, but just until the juices run clear, only 8 to 10 additional minutes. Remove the breasts to a warm plate and cover with aluminum foil. Let the sauce continue to simmer until the vegetables are tender and the sauce is thick enough to coat a spoon. Return the breasts to the sauce and finish as directed.

MEME'S FRIED CHICKEN AND GRAVY

Serves 4 to 6

Fried chicken is as deeply rooted in Southern culture as kudzu. It would be my hands-down choice for my last supper. Meme knew how much I loved it and spoiled me. When I lived far away and flew home to visit, it didn't matter what time of the day or night I arrived—2:00 P.M. or 2:00 A.M.—she would be at the stove frying chicken to welcome me home.

1 (4-pound) chicken, cut into pieces (see page 99)

Coarse salt and freshly ground black pepper

2 cups all-purpose flour, plus more if needed

1/4 teaspoon cayenne pepper

1 pound (2 cups) solid vegetable shortening, preferably Crisco, for frying, plus more if needed

2 tablespoons unsalted butter

2 cups chicken stock (page 227) or low-fat, reduced-sodium chicken broth, or 1 cup milk plus 1 cup chicken stock or broth

Season the chicken generously with salt and pepper. Set aside. Place the flour in a shallow plate and season with cayenne, salt, and pepper. Set aside. Line a baking sheet or large plate with brown paper bags or several layers of paper towels.

Heat the shortening in a large skillet, preferably cast iron, over medium-high heat until the temperature measures 375°F on a deep-fat thermometer.

Meanwhile, to fry the chicken, starting with the dark meat (since it takes longer to cook) and working one piece at a time, dredge the chicken in the seasoned flour, turning to coat. Shake to remove excess flour. Reserve any leftover seasoned flour for the gravy.

One piece at a time, slip the chicken into the hot fat without crowding; the fat should not quite cover the chicken. Adjust the heat as necessary to maintain the temperature at 375°F. At this stage, a splatter guard (a wire cover laid over the pan) may prove useful to contain the hot grease. The guard lets the steam escape, while allowing the chicken to brown nicely.

Fry the pieces, turning them once or twice, until the coating is a rich, golden brown on all sides, 10 to 14 minutes. Decrease the heat to medium-low and cover the skillet. Continue cooking until the chicken is cooked all the way through and the juices run clear when pricked with a knife, an additional 10 to 15 minutes. (An instant-read thermometer inserted into a thigh should register 170°F.) Remove the pieces and drain on the prepared baking sheet. (Do not hold the chicken in a warm oven; it will get soggy.)

To make the gravy, remove the skillet from the heat. Pour off most of the grease, leaving 2 to 3 tablespoons and any browned bits. Decrease the heat to very low. Add the butter and cook until foaming. Add 4 tablespoons of the reserved seasoned flour and stir to combine. Cook, whisking constantly, until golden brown, 2 to 3 minutes. Whisk in the stock. Increase the heat to medium and bring to a boil. Cook, stirring often, until the gravy is smooth and thick enough to coat the back of a spoon. Add more stock or water to achieve the correct consistency. Taste and adjust for seasoning with salt and pepper.

Tarragon Chicken Salad

Serves 4 to 6

Chicken salad is one of my all-time favorite dishes. It's good mounded in a butter lettuce cup or spread between two slices of whole wheat bread. Many recipes call for poached chicken. Years ago, when trying to replicate the famous chicken salad then sold at Zabar's, the renowned food market on New York's Upper West Side, I tried roasting the chicken at a low temperature on the bone. When meat, any meat, is cooked on the bone, it is more tender and juicy. I still do not know whether this is how Zabar's did it, but it is delicious and wonderfully simple.

4 (8-ounce) bone-in chicken breast halves, with skin

Coarse salt and freshly ground black pepper

2 tablespoons canola oil

Juice of 1/2 lemon

1 1/2 cups mayonnaise (page 282)

4 tablespoons chopped fresh tarragon

Preheat the oven to 300°F. Season the chicken with salt and pepper on both sides and place in a shallow roasting pan. Drizzle over the oil. Bake until the juices run clear, about 1 hour to $1^1/4$ hours, depending on the size of the breasts. Remove to a rack to cool.

When cool enough to touch, remove the skin from the breasts. Pull the meat from the bone. Cut the meat into 1-inch cubes and place in a bowl. Add the lemon juice, mayonnaise, and tarragon. Taste and adjust for seasoning with salt and pepper.

COQ AU VIN

Serves 4 to 6

This classic French country dish consists of chicken cooked slowly in red wine with onions, mushrooms, bacon, and herbs. When we were young, Mama used to make a similar dish in her slow cooker. Opening the front door on a cold night and welcomed by the inviting smells of stew from a slow cooker can be a dream come true. But winter is not the only time a slow cooker is useful. As it puts out no heat, it makes a cool substitute for a hot oven in the summer, and it uses less electricity. For this dish, a slow cooker is fine, as is a Dutch oven set on the cooktop. If using a slow cooker, don't skip the step of browning the chicken, or you will have a flabby, tasteless mess.

This is a l-o-o-ng recipe, requiring many steps to create its layers of flavor, which may seem daunting to some cooks, but it's not a difficult one. Consider making this dish ahead and refrigerating it overnight so the flavors will marry and blend: simply reheat it the next day. **Note:** A wooden spoon is perfect for telling you when your sauce is finished. The sauce will coat the back of the spoon when it has reached the proper coating consistency (*napper* in classic French cooking).

1 (5- to 6-pound) chicken, cut into 8 pieces (see page 99)

1 onion, preferably Vidalia, coarsely chopped

1 carrot, coarsely chopped

1 stalk celery, coarsely chopped

1 clove garlic, peeled and crushed, plus 2 cloves garlic, chopped

1 teaspoon whole black peppercorns

1 (750-ml) bottle red wine, preferably Pinot Noir

6 slices thick-cut bacon, cut into lardons (see page 179)

2 tablespoons canola oil

Coarse salt and freshly ground black pepper

2 shallots, chopped

1/4 cup all-purpose flour

2 cups chicken stock (page 227) or low-fat, reduced-sodium chicken broth, plus more if needed

Bouquet garni (3 sprigs of thyme, 3 sprigs of flat-leaf parsley, and 1 bay leaf, preferably fresh, tied together in cheesecloth)

1 tablespoon unsalted butter

Place the chicken pieces in a large nonreactive bowl. Add the onion, carrot, celery, crushed garlic, peppercorns, and wine. Cover and let the chicken marinate in the refrigerator for at least several hours or overnight.

Preheat the oven to 350°F. Line a baking sheet and a plate with paper towels.

Transfer the chicken pieces from the marinade to the baking sheet. Pat them dry with additional paper towels. Strain and reserve the marinade liquid, reserving the vegetables separately.

To prepare the chicken, heat a large, heavy-bottomed Dutch oven over medium-high heat. Add the bacon and cook until the fat is rendered and the bacon is crisp, about 5 minutes. Remove the bacon with a slotted spoon to the prepared plate. Pour off and discard all but 1 tablespoon of the bacon fat. Decrease the heat to medium, and add 1 tablespoon of the canola oil and heat until shimmering.

Season the chicken with salt and pepper. Add the chicken pieces to the pan, skin side down, and cook over medium heat until a rich, golden brown, 3 to 5 minutes per side. Remove the browned chicken to the baking sheet; set aside.

Add the drained vegetables from the marinade to the pan, and cook until they start to color, 5 to 7 minutes. Add the chopped garlic and shallots and cook until fragrant, 45 to 60 seconds. Sprinkle on the flour and toss again to lightly coat. Cook, stirring constantly, until the flour turns brown, 2 to 3 minutes. Return the chicken to the Dutch oven. Add the reserved marinade liquid and enough stock so that the chicken is barely covered. Add the bouquet garni and

1 sprig of thyme, for seasoning

1 sprig of flat-leaf parsley, for seasoning

1 bay leaf, preferably fresh, for seasoning

10 white button mushrooms, cleaned and trimmed, halved or quartered if large

16 to 24 pearl onions (4 for each person you plan to serve), trimmed and peeled

bring to a boil over medium-high heat on top of the stove. Cover and transfer to the oven.

Bake until the chicken pieces are tender and fall apart easily when pierced with a knife, 45 minutes to 1 hour.

Or, to cook on top of the stove, bring to a boil, decrease the heat to very low and simmer until the chicken pieces are tender and fall apart easily when pierced with a knife, 45 minutes to 1 hour.

To cook the vegetables, in a skillet, heat the remaining 1 tablespoon of oil and the butter over medium heat. Add the sprig of thyme, sprig of parsley, bay leaf, mushrooms, and onions. Season with salt and pepper. Saute until lightly browned and tender, 5 to 7 minutes. Set aside and keep warm. Add the reserved bacon and toss to combine. Remove and discard the sprigs of thyme and parsley and the bay leaf. Set aside and keep warm.

To finish the sauce, once the chicken is tender and fully cooked, transfer the pan from the oven to the cooktop. Remove the chicken pieces to a bowl, cover, and keep warm.

Remove and discard the bouquet garni. In the Dutch oven, using an immersion blender, puree the sauce and vegetables until smooth. Or, once the chicken is removed, ladle the sauce and vegetables into a blender and puree a little at a time until smooth.

Cook over medium-high heat until the sauce coats the back of a wooden spoon; thin with more stock, if needed, to achieve this consistency. Taste and adjust for seasoning with salt and pepper. Lift the spoon out of the sauce and run your finger across the back of the pan; if the line holds, the sauce is done.

Return the chicken to the sauce and turn to coat. Add the reserved mushrooms and onions. Bring to a simmer over medium heat and cook until warm and the flavors marry and blend, 5 to 7 minutes. Taste and adjust for seasoning with salt and pepper. Serve immediately.

VARIATION: You can make this recipe with boneless, skinless breasts instead of bone-in pieces. Simmer the breasts as directed on top of the stove along with the other ingredients, but just until the juices run clear, only 8 to 10 additional minutes. Remove the breasts to a warm plate and cover with aluminum foil. Let the sauce continue to simmer until the vegetables are tender and the sauce is thick enough to coat a spoon. Return the breasts to the sauce and finish as directed.

HERB ROAST CHICKEN WITH PAN SAUCE

Meme washed her chickens inside and out before cooking them, removing every last bit of fat, overlooked feathers, and any bruises, blemishes, or blood spots. She said if you didn't, it tasted too "chickeny." That bird was sanitized—or so she thought. I would never argue with Meme, but according to the USDA, washing chicken is not necessary. If the bird is contaminated, dangerous bacteria are not going to be affected by cold tap water. Washing the chicken actually increases the chance of cross-contamination; water that has touched raw chicken and splashed into the sink can potentially contaminate other food.

This recipe relies on a classic French preparation: stuffing the bird with aromatics, roasting it to perfection, and using the pan juices plus added shallots, wine, and stock to make a light sauce. There's not a lot to cloud the plate or palate or mask a mistake. I will often order chicken, seemingly the most boring dish on the menu, when trying a new restaurant. Simple roast chicken is the test of a good cook.

1 (4- to 5-pound) chicken

1 teaspoon dried herbes de Provence

3 bay leaves, preferably fresh

Coarse salt and freshly ground black pepper

1 large lemon, quartered

3 tablespoons unsalted butter, at room temperature

1 large carrot, chopped

1 onion, preferably Vidalia, chopped

2 shallots, finely chopped

1/2 cup dry white wine

1 1/2 cups chicken stock (page 227) or low-fat, reduced-sodium chicken broth

1 tablespoon unsalted butter, cut into bits (optional)

Preheat the oven to 425°F. To prepare the chicken, trim the excess fat from inside of the chicken cavity. Season the cavity with the herbes de Provence, bay leaves, salt, and pepper. Squeeze lemon juice into the cavity and then insert the used lemon quarters. Rub butter over the skin and season with salt and pepper. Tie the ends of the drumsticks together with kitchen twine. Set the chicken in a roasting pan, on a rack if you have one.

Roast the chicken for 15 minutes, then decrease the heat to 350°F. Roast for an additional 15 minutes, then add the carrot and onion to the pan. Continue roasting, basting occasionally, until the juices run clear when the thickest part of the thigh is pierced with a knife, an additional 30 to 45 minutes. Remove the chicken to a cutting board and tent loosely with aluminum foil to keep warm. Using a slotted spoon, remove the vegetables to a warm platter and tent loosely with aluminum foil to keep warm.

To make the sauce, remove all but several tablespoons of the fat from the roasting pan and place the pan over medium heat. Add the shallots and saute, stirring frequently, until softened, about 2 minutes. Add the wine and cook until it is reduced by half, 3 to 5 minutes. Add the chicken stock and increase the heat to high, scraping the skillet with a wooden spoon to loosen the browned bits.

Cook until the sauce is slightly reduced, about 5 minutes more. Carve the chicken and pour any accumulated chicken juices from the cutting board into the roasting pan. Decrease the heat to medium. Whisk in the butter. Taste and adjust for seasoning with salt and pepper. Serve the chicken with the sauce on the side.

CHICKEN AND TASSO JAMBALAYA

Serves 4 to 6

We moved from Georgia to Louisiana when I was a child and our family's diet changed. Mama armed herself with spiral-bound copies of *River Road Recipes* (Junior League of Baton Rouge, 1959) and *Talk about Good* (Junior League of Lafayette, 1967) and started cooking. Soon, the cuisine of Louisiana—Mama's Red Beans and Rice (page 160), Mama's Shrimp Creole (page 131), and dishes similar to this jambalaya— quickly became as familiar and comfortable as Meme's Old-fashioned Butter Beans (page 179) and her fried chicken (page 106).

According to *Louisiana Entertains* (another regional cookbook), jambalaya is a descendent of paella, brought to New Orleans by the Spanish. The name derives from *jamón*, or ham, but colloquially, the term means "clean up the kitchen." The dish is a delicious way to use leftovers so they don't go to waste. I have seen both shrimp and chicken versions, but all jambalayas contain ham. Tasso, often referred to as Cajun ham, is smoked and very spicy with a peppery crust. This version uses boneless, skinless chicken breasts for a very simple and quick preparation. I also suggest using thighs, which are not as lean, but are less likely to dry out.

1 tablespoon canola oil

1 tablespoon unsalted butter

1/2 pound chopped tasso or other smoked ham

2 (8-ounce) boneless, skinless chicken breasts, or 3 boneless, skinless thighs, cut into 2-inch pieces

1 tablespoon Homemade Creole Seasoning (page 287)

1 onion, preferably Vidalia, chopped

1 stalk celery, chopped

1/2 green bell pepper, cored, seeded and chopped

1 clove garlic, very finely chopped

1 1/2 cups long-grain rice

1 (4-ounce) can tomato sauce

2 1/2 cups chicken stock (page 227) or low-fat, reduced-sodium chicken broth

Coarse salt and freshly ground black pepper

In a large, ovenproof skillet, heat the oil and butter over high heat until shimmering. Add the tasso and cook until the meat starts to brown and render fat, about 3 minutes. Add the chicken and sprinkle over the Creole seasoning. (If using tasso, go easy on the spice, otherwise it may be too hot.) Continue cooking over high heat until the chicken is just beginning to color, about 3 minutes. Remove the meat to a plate.

Add the onion, celery, and bell pepper to the residual oil in the skillet. Cook until the vegetables start to color, stirring occasionally, 5 to 7 minutes. Add the garlic and cook until fragrant, 45 to 60 seconds. Add the rice and stir to coat. Stir in the tomato sauce and chicken stock and bring to a boil. Transfer to the oven and bake, uncovered, stirring once, until the rice is tender, 40 to 45 minutes. Remove from the oven to a rack to cool slightly. Taste and adjust for seasoning with salt and pepper. Serve immediately.

CHICKEN SALTIMBOCCA WITH COUNTRY HAM

Serves 4 to 6

This dish is inspired by a traditional Roman dish made with veal and proscuitto. Translated literally from Italian, saltimbocca means "jump mouth" or "hop in the mouth," perhaps implying that the dish is so good the flavors jump in your mouth. It's best to pound your own chicken breasts, for this or any recipe that calls for cutlets, also known in French cooking as paillards. Chicken sold as cutlets in the grocery store aren't actually pounded, but are horizontally sliced to resemble a cutlet. The meat contracts irregularly in the hot pan, making it tough.

When pounding the chicken, I protect it with a heavy-duty freezer bag that I've cut apart into two thick sheets. I place the breast between the sheets and pound it with a flat meat pounder or the bottom of a heavy skillet. The idea is to create an evenly thin piece of meat, not to pound it into oblivion. This technique works equally well with turkey, pork, or veal.

If necessary, you can substitute white wine or sherry for the Marsala or port. Whatever you do, cook only with what you would drink. Never, ever use anything labeled "cooking wine" or "cooking sherry," which is full of salt and absolute garbage. Herbes de Provence, used here, is a mixture of dried herbs that typically contains some of the following: basil, cracked fennel, rosemary, sage, thyme, marjoram, lavender, and savory.

---

4 to 6 (8-ounce) boneless, skinless chicken breasts

16 to 24 fresh sage leaves, plus more for garnish

8 to 12 paper-thin slices country ham, prosciutto, or Serrano ham (about 6 to 8 ounces total)

$1/4$ cup all-purpose flour

Freshly ground black pepper

2 tablespoons canola oil, plus more if needed

$1/4$ cup dry white wine

$1/4$ cup Marsala or port

$3/4$ cup chicken stock (page 227) or low-fat, reduced-sodium chicken broth

Coarse salt

To prepare the cutlets, place a chicken breast between 2 sheets of plastic wrap and pound to slightly over $1/4$ inch thick. Repeat with the remaining chicken. Place 4 fresh sage leaves on each cutlet; top with 1 or 2 slices of ham and press lightly to adhere. Place on a baking sheet and refrigerate to set, at least 10 minutes.

Place the flour in a shallow dish and season with pepper (no salt is necessary because of the salty ham). To cook the cutlets, heat the oil in a large, heavy-bottomed skillet over medium-high heat. Working with 2 pieces at a time, dredge both sides of the chicken in flour, then shake off the excess flour—the chicken should be lightly dusted. Without crowding, add 2 pieces of chicken to the skillet, ham side down first, and saute for 2 to 3 minutes per side. Transfer to a warm platter and cover loosely with aluminum foil. Repeat with the remaining chicken, adding more oil if necessary.

To make the sauce, pour off any excess oil from the skillet. Return the skillet to the heat. Add the wine and Marsala and bring to a boil over medium-high heat, scraping up any browned bits. Add the stock and increase the heat to high. Cook until the sauce is reduced and slightly thickened, 3 to 5 minutes. Taste and adjust for seasoning with salt and pepper. Spoon the sauce over the chicken, garnish with fresh sage, and serve.

CHICKEN PAILLARD WITH SAUTEED MUSHROOMS

Serves 4 to 6

Many years ago, I needed fresh cèpes for a job. When they were delivered, it was obvious there had been some horrible, grievous misunderstanding. I had ordered two pounds and they had delivered twenty! I called and they promised to pick them up the next day. However, my boss at the time was not the sort to take imperfections lightly. This may sound deceitful, but the truth is, it wasn't worth trying to explain. I just needed to make them go away. So I had eighteen pounds and over $600 worth of mushrooms to hide—no easy feat! It was like hiding a skunk, a deliciously intoxicating skunk, but a skunk nonetheless.

1/2 cup all-purpose flour

Coarse salt and freshly ground black pepper

4 to 6 (8-ounce) boneless, skinless chicken breast, pounded to slightly over 1/4 inch thick (see page 112)

2 tablespoons canola oil, plus more if needed

2 tablespoons unsalted butter

1/4 cup dry white wine

1 pound mixed mushrooms (such as cremini, chanterelle, morel, shiitake, or white button), sliced

1 ounce dried cèpes, reconstituted and liquid reserved (see below, optional)

1 tablespoon chopped fresh thyme

2 tablespoons chopped fresh flat-leaf parsley

Place the flour in a shallow dish and season with salt and pepper. Season the chicken on both sides with salt and pepper.

To cook the chicken, in a large skillet, heat 1 tablespoon each of the oil and the butter over medium-high heat until very hot. Working with 2 pieces at a time, dredge both sides of the chicken in flour, then shake off the excess flour. Without crowding, add the 2 pieces to the skillet, and brown on both sides, 2 to 3 minutes per side. Transfer to a warm platter and cover loosely with aluminum foil to keep warm. Repeat with the remaining 1 tablespoon each of oil and butter, and chicken.

To make the sauce, pour all but 1 tablespoon of oil from the skillet. Return the skillet to the heat. Decrease the heat to medium. Add the wine, using a wooden spoon to loosen any browned bits from the bottom of the pan. Add the mushrooms, cèpes and strained liquid, thyme, and parsley. Season with salt and pepper. Cook, stirring occasionally, until the mushrooms are tender, 8 to 10 minutes. Taste and adjust for seasoning with salt and pepper. Spoon the mushrooms over the chicken and serve immediately.

Rehydrating Cèpes

Called cèpes in French, and porcini in Italian, *Boletus edulis* mushrooms are extremely rich, with an earthy, assertive flavor. They are found only in the wild and not commercially farmed; their incredible flavor and limited supply bestow an intoxicating allure similar to that of black truffles. They are available fresh in season, but are available frozen or dried throughout the year. To plump and reconstitute dried mushrooms, place the mushrooms in a heatproof container. Pour over boiling water and let rest until plump and rehydrated, about 15 minutes. Using a slotted spoon, remove the mushrooms to a cutting board. Coarsely chop and set aside for later use. Strain the soaking liquid through a fine mesh sieve or coffee filter and reserve as a very flavorful cooking liquid.

DEDE'S BARBECUED CHICKEN

Serves 4 to 6

In the heat of the summer, there's nothing better for keeping the heat out of the kitchen than firing up the grill. Dede would make his barbecued chicken on the Fourth of July, using a potent vinegar bath on grilled chicken that produced a pungent, meaty odor, sending out billowing clouds of steam and smoke as the chicken cooked on the grill. My sister and I fought to help pack the ice and rock salt in the ice cream machine for homemade peach ice cream. I wasn't nearly as fond at the time of being given the chore of grating the cheese for the pimento cheese.

For many years, my grandparents did not have air-conditioning. Meme would stay up late the night before or wake up very early in the morning and work in the cool, quiet hours of the hot July heat to prepare her portion of the feast. The humming of the fan was often her only company before the house started stirring and the cousins started piling out of bunks and cots.

1/2 cup water

1/2 cup apple cider vinegar

1/4 cup peanut oil, plus more for the grate

2 tablespoons hot sauce (optional)

2 tablespoons Worcestershire sauce

1 tablespoon coarse salt, plus more for seasoning the chicken

1 (4- to 5-pound) chicken, cut into 8 pieces (see page 99)

Freshly ground black pepper

Prepare a charcoal fire using about 6 pounds of charcoal and burn until the coals are completely covered with a thin coating of light gray ash, 20 to 30 minutes. Spread the coals evenly over the grill bottom, position the grill rack above the coals, and heat until medium-hot (when you can hold your hand 5 inches above the grill surface for no longer than 3 or 4 seconds). Or, for a gas grill, turn on all burners to High, close the lid, and heat until very hot, 10 to 15 minutes.

Combine the water, vinegar, peanut oil, hot sauce, Worcestershire sauce, and salt in a squirt bottle. Set aside.

Season the chicken with salt and pepper. Apply some oil to the grill grate. Place the chicken on the grill, leaving plenty of space between each piece. Grill until seared, about 1 to 2 minutes per side for legs and thighs, and 3 or so minutes for breasts. Move the chicken to medium-low heat or reduce the heat to medium; continue to grill, turning occasionally and squirting with the marinade, until the juices run clear when pierced, 12 to 18 minutes. Remove the pieces from the grill as they cook and transfer to a warm platter. Give them a final squirt of sauce for flavor and serve immediately.

MEME'S ROAST TURKEY AND GIBLET GRAVY

Serves 10 to 12

The first time Mama and I brined a turkey, it was a revelation. The bird emerged from the oven glistening and a rich, golden brown, like the glorious totemic beast from the Rockwell painting. Meme didn't brine her bird, so I have taken a little liberty with this recipe. Let's just say it's the spirit of Meme with a dash of revised technique.

We have never stuffed the bird in our family, but if the turkey is stuffed, make sure the temperature reaches 160°F in the center of the stuffing. When the stuffed turkey is done, remove it from the oven and let the turkey with stuffing stand for 15 minutes. This standing time allows the stuffing temperature to climb to 165°F, for an added measure of safety.

ROAST TURKEY

2 gallons water

1 cup Diamond Brand kosher salt (see page 101)

1/2 cup sugar

1 (12- to 14-pound) turkey, neck and giblets reserved for stock

Freshly ground black pepper

1 stalk celery, coarsely chopped

2 sprigs of flat-leaf parsley

2 sprigs of thyme

4 fresh sage leaves

2 sprigs of rosemary

1 bay leaf, preferably fresh

1 onion, preferably Vidalia, peeled

4 tablespoons (1/2 stick) unsalted butter, at room temperature

TURKEY GIBLET STOCK

Neck and giblets from the turkey

5 cups water

1 onion, preferably Vidalia, halved

1 bay leaf, preferably fresh

To brine the turkey, combine the 2 gallons water, salt, and sugar in a large, nonreactive bucket or stockpot, if storing in the refrigerator, or in an insulated cooler, if not. Two gallons of water will be sufficient for most birds; larger birds may require three. Submerge the turkey in the brine and refrigerate for up to 14 hours. If using a cooler, add ice or freezer packs to keep the bird very cold. Remove the bird from the liquid and rinse inside and out with cold water. Discard the brine.

Preheat the oven to 425°F. Position an oven rack in the lowest part of the oven.

To roast the turkey, season the bird inside and out with pepper (no salt is necessary because of the brining). Place the celery, parsley, thyme, sage, rosemary, bay leaf, and onion in the cavity. Working from the cavity end, loosen the skin without tearing by running your fingers between the skin and flesh of the breast. Put 2 tablespoons of the butter under the skin and spread evenly. Tie the drumsticks together with kitchen twine and fold the wings under the body. Transfer the turkey to a rack in a large roasting pan. Rub the remaining 2 tablespoons butter over the skin.

Roast for 30 minutes. Decrease the oven temperature to 350°F. Baste the turkey with pan drippings and continue roasting, basting every 30 minutes, until an instant-read thermometer inserted into a thigh registers 165°F, about 2 to 2 1/2 hours.

Meanwhile, prepare the giblet stock. While the turkey is roasting, place the neck, heart, and gizzard in a medium saucepan. (Do not add the liver now because it will make the stock bitter.) Add the water, onion, and bay leaf. Bring to a boil over medium-high heat. Decrease the heat to low and simmer until tender, 30 to 45 minutes. Strain through a fine mesh sieve into a small saucepan and discard the onion and bay leaf. Finely chop the heart and gizzard and set aside. Using a small paring knife, remove as much of the meat as

GIBLET GRAVY

4 cups Turkey Giblet Stock (page 116)

2 large onions, preferably Vidalia, finely chopped

1 cup dry white wine

4 fresh sage leaves, chopped

1/3 cup all-purpose flour

4 tablespoons (1/2 stick) unsalted butter, at room temperature

2 large eggs, hard-cooked (see page 11) and finely chopped

possible from the neck bone. Set aside with the chopped heart and gizzard. Keep the stock warm.

Transfer the turkey to a rimmed cutting board or warm serving platter. Tent it loosely with aluminum foil and let rest 30 minutes before carving to allow the juices to redistribute.

Meanwhile, prepare the gravy. Remove the rack from the roasting pan and set aside. Pour the juices from the roasting pan into a fat separator and set aside. The fat will rise to the top and the juices and dark drippings will stay at the bottom. If you do not have a fat separator, pour the juices into a glass measuring cup and remove the fat with a metal spoon; reserve the fat and the drippings.

Pour the separated drippings into a large liquid measuring cup. Add enough of the reserved giblet stock to make 4 cups. Set aside.

Place the roasting pan across two burners on the cooktop over medium-high heat. Add 1 tablespoon of the reserved fat and the onions. Cook until clear and translucent, 3 to 5 minutes. Add the wine and deglaze the pan, stirring and scraping up any brown bits on the bottom of the pan. Cook until reduced to $1/2$ cup, about 5 minutes. Add the sage and cook for 1 minute. Add the turkey stock mixture and any turkey juices accumulated on the platter and bring to a boil.

In a small bowl, using a rubber spatula, blend together the flour and butter to make a paste (*beurre manié*, French technique for thickening sauces). Whisk the flour mixture into the gravy, and decrease the heat to low. Finely chop the reserved liver and hard-cooked eggs and add to the gravy. Cook, stirring occasionally, until the mixture is thickened and the liver is cooked, about 10 minutes. Taste and adjust for seasoning with salt and pepper.

To serve, carve the turkey and arrange on a serving platter. Transfer the gravy to a serving boat and pass around with the turkey. Serve with plenty of cornbread dressing and biscuits.

Instant-Read Thermometer

Instant-read thermometers are indispensable when cooking a large piece of meat because, while the doneness of steaks and chicken breasts can often be gauged by touching the meat and feeling for firmness, a large piece of meat needs a thermometer to really see what's inside. The plastic pop-up timers found in many turkeys are unreliable, often resulting in an overcooked bird.

Mama's Quail in Red Wine Sauce

Quail and dove shoots are still serious Southern rituals, and my father always hunted when I was growing up. Quail meat is darker than that of dove, which has a tendency to be dry. While I don't shoot often anymore, I do love to reap the rewards from my friends and relatives who hunt.

I can hardly eat or cook quail without thinking about a dinner party Mama hosted when I was young. She was frying the quail and her hand was splashed with hot grease. Instead of going to the hospital, she sat with her hand in a bowl of ice water in her lap under the table so as not to disturb her guests. Some people might think that was incredibly stupid, but all I can think about is her amazing hospitality and self-lessness. Mama and I have laughed about it in later years, because the unexpected bonus is she has no age spots on that hand.

8 (4- to 6-ounce) quail

Coarse salt and freshly ground black pepper

1 cup all-purpose flour

¼ cup canola oil, plus more if needed

8 sprigs of thyme, plus more for garnish

1 cup dry red wine

1 cup chicken stock (page 227) or low-fat, reduced-sodium chicken broth

2 tablespoons unsalted butter

Preheat the oven to 350°F. Tie the legs of the quail together with kitchen twine. Season the quail with salt and pepper. Place the flour in a shallow dish and lightly season with salt and pepper. Coat the quail in the flour, shaking off the excess.

To cook the quail, heat the oil in a large ovenproof skillet over medium-high heat. Add the quail without crowding and sear on both sides until the birds are a dark, golden brown color, about 3 minutes per side. Sprinkle thyme sprigs over the birds and transfer the skillet to the oven. Continue cooking until the quail are cooked through but still pink, an additional 8 to 10 minutes.

Remove the pan from the oven and transfer the quail to a warm platter; cover loosely with aluminum foil to keep them warm.

To make the sauce, pour off the excess oil. Place the skillet on top of the stove over high heat. Add the red wine and stir with a wooden spoon to loosen any brown bits from the bottom. Decrease the heat to medium and simmer, stirring occasionally, until the liquid is well reduced, 8 to 10 minutes. Add the stock and continue to simmer until reduced by half, an additional 5 minutes. Taste and adjust for seasoning with salt and pepper. Whisk in the butter. Return the quail to the sauce and spoon over the sauce to coat. Serve immediately.

MAMA'S ORANGE GLAZED CORNISH GAME HENS

Serves 4 to 6

Cornish game hens (or Rock Cornish hens) are not as large as a chicken, yet larger than a quail. The French call them *poussins*, and they are essentially baby chickens. Mama has always cooked game hens for semi-special occasions since we all love them. They are great for a dinner party, too. Plan ahead, however; many grocery stores only sell them frozen.

The safest way to defrost meat is in the refrigerator overnight or in the sink under cold running water. Bacteria thrive when food is between 41° and 140°F. So, you can imagine how appalled I am recalling how my mother, not knowing any better at the time, would defrost these hens, as well as chicken and hamburger meat, on the windowsill in the bright sunshine. It is amazing we never got sick (she knows better, now). Or maybe the early exposure just built up our resistance to food-borne bacteria.

1/4 cup chopped mixed fresh herbs (such as chives, parsley, and thyme)

3 shallots, very finely chopped

Grated zest and juice of 1 orange

1/4 cup unsalted butter, at room temperature

Coarse salt and freshly ground black pepper

2 Cornish game hens (about 1 1/2 pounds each), spatchcocked (see below)

1/4 cup dry sherry or white wine

1 cup chicken stock (page 227) or low-fat, reduced-sodium chicken broth

Preheat the oven to 450°F. Combine the herbs, shallots, orange zest, and butter in a small bowl. Season with salt and pepper and stir to combine. Loosen the skins of the hens without tearing by running your fingers between the skin and flesh of the breast. Place a little of the herb butter under the skin of each bird and spread evenly. Season the hens with salt and pepper, then rub the skin with the remaining herb butter. Place the hens, skin side up, in a large roasting pan.

Roast until the birds are golden brown and the juices run clear, about 30 minutes. Transfer the hens to a large warm platter and tent loosely with aluminum foil to keep them warm.

Place the roasting pan on the cooktop over medium heat. Add the sherry to deglaze the pan and loosen the brown bits on the bottom. Add the chicken stock and orange juice. Bring to a boil, scraping up the browned bits. Cook until reduced and slightly thickened, about 2 minutes. Taste and adjust for seasoning with salt and pepper. Spoon the sauce over the hens to serve.

Spatchcocking

To spatchcock a Cornish game hen or other small bird, place the bird on a clean cutting board, breast side down. Using poultry shears, make a lengthwise cut on both sides of the backbone from neck to tail. Remove the backbone and save it for stock. Open the bird like a book. Proceed with the recipe. For an especially flat bird, place the bird on a baking sheet, top with a second baking sheet, and weight it down in the refrigerator with a brick or several large cans of tomatoes for several hours or overnight.

CHAPTER 6
FISH AND SHELLFISH

SOUTHERN FOOD USUALLY BRINGS to mind fried chicken, grits, greens, and biscuits. But with the Gulf of Mexico to the south and the Atlantic Ocean to the east, there is also a great deal of fish and shellfish in Southern cooking. Southerners have always relied on fish, shellfish, and even frogs, turtle meat, and alligator from the sea and local lakes, ponds, and rivers to augment their diet.

One of my first memories is of falling into the pond behind our family home when I was about three years old. I remember the terror I felt in the brown murky water and the agitation of the adults who pulled me out. My grandmother's main concern was not the possibility of my drowning, but that snakes might be at the water's edge. The most common admonition heard from her throughout my young life was, "Don't go in the bushes, you might get on a snake!" (Since Georgia is home to all the poisonous snakes found in North America, this is not nearly as paranoid as it may sound.)

There's something extraordinarily satisfying about going fishing and then cooking your fresh catch for dinner (though there can be a fine line between fishing and standing on the shore with an empty bucket wasting time and looking stupid). Dede used to have a cement-block "worm bed" for bait in the shade near the shed. He'd empty vegetable peelings, onion skins, and the like into it every night for the worms to eat and compost. When we were little, we loved to help him look for bait. He'd loosen the soil with his pitchfork and my sister, Jona, and I would quickly gather up the squirming worms and put them in an old coffee can. The three of us would walk down the hill to the pond and set up our poles on the dam. He taught us how to bait a hook and the proper way to tie the tackle. Sometimes he would catch a small frog to use as a lure for bass and we would run away squealing. Inevitably, we would get our lines hung up in a tree, or on each other, and he would patiently untangle them. Those are some of my sweetest memories.

We still keep a small boat at the very same pond. Jona is not as fond of fishing as she was when she was a child, but sometimes Mama and I will talk her into it and we'll all walk down the hill just for an hour or so after supper. The worm bed is long gone and I guess we're too lazy to dig for bait, so we buy it at a store up the road. The only sounds are the birds chirping in the trees, often a whippoorwill calling, and the wind whistling in the tall pines. Waterbugs skate across the water, dragonflies buzz in the tall reeds, and the minnows dart about in the shallows. If we're lucky, a heron lands at the water's edge, hoping for a catch of the day. When the sun hits the water at dusk, the pond turns into a shimmering, sparkling mirror and there's nothing remotely stupid about how that makes me feel. It's as wonderful and magical as when I was a child.

If we're lucky enough to catch a few fish, we take them back up to the makeshift sink in the backyard. Trouble is, when the fishing is good, we stay too long at the pond and get back after dark. Mama goes in to the house and gets the flashlight. I pull over the garden hose and clean and scale the fish. (Jona conveniently makes herself scarce.) We fry them in a light dusting of cornmeal in a cast-iron skillet. Jona and I snack on the crispy tails. It's the perfect end to a perfect evening.

I've had the good fortune of enjoying freshly caught fish all over the world. One of my more memorable experiences occurred in Sicily, when filming a segment for Epicurious television. Our crew pulled into the harbor around 5:30 A.M., just as the fishing boats were coming in. It was barely light. I soon realized there were three women (us) and about five hundred Sicilian fishermen on the docks. We were greeted with wolf whistles and big grins. One older man, with gnarled hands, presented me with a brilliant yellow starfish, as large as a dinner plate. But the tall, dark stranger who truly won my heart gave me a sandwich made of hearty semolina bread, marinated anchovies, and olive oil—a Sicilian fisherman's breakfast. The translator explained that the boats go out at night hung with great lanterns to simulate moonlight and draw the fish into the nets. The men take a few fish from the first catch and remove the bones. Then they place the fillets in a bowl and drizzle over freshly squeezed lemon juice and olive oil, and heartily season the mix with coarse sea salt and pepper. The fish cures during the night much like ceviche or escabèche, and when they return in the morning with their catch, breakfast is ready. Dede would have likely referred to it as bait.

CHOOSING FISH

Fish and shellfish are part of a healthy, well-rounded diet. They are high in protein and low in saturated fats, and contain omega-3 fatty acids that are good for your heart. However, we often don't realize we are making ecological and economic as well as health choices every time we buy seafood (or any other food, for that matter). Many popular fish and shellfish species are overfished so badly that the future of the fishery or even of the species is in danger. Programs such as the Monterey Bay Aquarium's Seafood Watch inform people about which seafood to buy and why based on whether species are "abundant, well-managed, and caught or farmed in environmentally friendly ways."

And nearly all fish and shellfish contain traces of methylmercury and other toxic chemicals. They take in the chemicals as they feed; in general, smaller and younger fish have less mercury than larger, older ones. Some species of farmed fish and shellfish may also be more contaminated or ecologically unsound than wild-caught fish; for example, I recommend buying wild American shrimp rather than pond-raised imports for just this reason. The group Oceans Alive, for one, also keeps a list of fish that are more likely or less likely to be highly contaminated with methylmercury and PCBs. The species on these consumer advisory lists change as conditions change.

FISH SUBSTITUTIONS

If the fish in your recipe is unavailable or you want to make a different choice, simply mix and match within the three types of delicate, medium, and firm fish. These categories reflect how fish respond to cooking methods and which substitutions work. Examples of delicate fish include sole, flounder, turbot, plaice, and fluke. Treat delicate fish carefully when you cook them. These fish are traditionally sold as fillets, and they are best prepared by poaching, broiling, pan-frying, or baking. Medium fish include Arctic char, trout, catfish, salmon, mahi-mahi, grouper, snapper, walleye, tilapia, pike, and tilefish. These fish have more resistance than delicate fish, and are firmer when cooked. They are incredibly versatile and best prepared by baking, broiling, pan-frying, or grilling. Examples of firm fish include pompano, amberjack, tuna, shark, and swordfish. These fish have a meaty texture. They are best prepared with high-heat cooking methods such as grilling, pan-frying, or sauteing.

BUYING TIPS AND SERVING AMOUNTS

How much to buy? Here are some rules of thumb: for whole fish, count on 12 ounces per person; for dressed or cleaned fish, count on 4 to 6 ounces per person; for fillets or steaks, count on 5 ounces per person.

How do you know it's fresh? Ask when the fish arrived at the store. Very often fresh fish come into markets on Wednesday and Friday. Sniff the fish if possible. There should be no strong odor. Fresh fish smells sweet and clean. Look for a moist surface and firm flesh. Splits or cracks in fillets are signs of drying. The fish should be moist, but there is a difference between moist and slimy. Press the fish gently. The indentation should spring back. If it doesn't, that means the flesh is starting to break down; don't buy it. It's easiest to check for freshness when buying a whole fish: look for ones with clear eyes, not clouded or sunken eyes. It should have reddish or slightly reddish brown gills. Brown gills indicate the fish is old.

Keep fish as fresh as possible by burying it in ice: cover the bottom of a shallow container with crushed ice or ice cubes. Place the fish on the bed of ice and cover with more ice. Cook within a day of purchase.

LOUISIANA CRAWFISH BOIL

Serves 4 to 6

When I was young, we spent many weekends at the Indian Creek Recreation Area, about ten miles south of Alexandria, Louisiana. In the spring, at the height of crawfish season, several families would get together and have a crawfish boil. I remember a huge pot practically the size of a bathtub filled with bright red crawfish, halved ears of yellow corn, sweet onions, whole new potatoes in the skin, and thick links of sausage, all bubbling in broth. The picnic tables were covered with newspapers and one of the men would dump a steaming basket of the potent mixture into the center of each. We'd gather around and eat, peeling the meat from the tails and sucking on the heads to get every last bit of the peppery juice.

Crawfish are also known as mudbugs, crawdads, and crayfish. These freshwater crustaceans, in season from December to May, range in size from three to six inches and weigh from two to eight ounces. This recipe would be equally delicious made with blue or Dungeness crabs.

2 (3-ounce) bags Zatarain's Dry Crawfish, Crab, and Shrimp Boil (see Sources, page 301)

2 gallons water

3/4 cup coarse salt

12 fingerling potatoes (about 3/4 pound total)

4 onions, preferably Vidalia, halved

4 lemons, halved

4 whole heads garlic

4 ears fresh sweet corn, shucked and silks removed, halved crosswise

2 pounds kielbasa sausage, cut into 2-inch pieces

6 pounds live crawfish (see Sources, page 301)

Fill a large stockpot with the seafood boil, the water, and the salt. Bring to a boil over medium-high heat, cover, decrease the heat to medium, and simmer for 15 minutes.

Add the potatoes, onions, lemons, and garlic. Cover, increase the heat to medium-high, and return to a boil; cook an additional 10 minutes. Add the corn, sausage, and crawfish. Cover and return to a boil; cook until the crawfish are bright red and cooked through, about 10 minutes. Serve immediately.

FRIED CATFISH FINGERS WITH COUNTRY RÉMOULADE

Serves 4 to 6

The fish fry is right up on the list of orchestrated Southern feasts, along with the "pig pull" and "dinner on the grounds." It's a great party and wildly different from throwing a few burgers on the grill. And fried fish are just flat-out good.

My grandparents met at a fish fry in 1930 and were inseparable through almost 65 years of marriage. They were a great team but there was no doubt who was the boss. For as long as I can remember, they had a motor home. They drove as far south as the Yucatan Peninsula in Mexico and to Fairbanks at the far end of the Alaska Highway, where they caught a small plane to the North Pole. I was able to take several long trips with them when I was young. Once the three of us drove north, through Detroit into Canada, east to Nova Scotia, where we caught the ferry to Newfoundland. We were on the one main road in Newfoundland to St. John's and were about halfway across the island when Meme looked at my grandfather and said, "Sam, pull over in that gas station. I'm ready to go home." He did, and we did.

1 cup whole-grain Dijon mustard

1 large egg white, lightly beaten

1 tablespoon hot sauce

1 pound catfish fillets, cut into strips

1/2 cup white or yellow cornmeal

1/2 cup all-purpose flour

Coarse salt and freshly ground black pepper

4 cups peanut oil, for frying

Country Rémoulade (page 286), for accompaniment

Line a plate with paper towels and set by the cooktop.

In a large bowl, stir together the mustard, egg white, and hot sauce. Add the fish and toss to coat well. Cover and marinate in the refrigerator for 1 hour.

In a shallow dish, combine the cornmeal and flour and season with salt and pepper. Pour the oil into a heavy-bottomed saucepan, deep fryer, or Dutch oven, filling it no more than one-third full. Heat the oil over medium heat until it reaches 350°F.

Remove the fish from the marinade and season with salt and pepper. Dredge the fish in the cornmeal mixture to coat both sides and shake off the excess. Carefully add the fish to the oil, a few pieces at a time. Cook until golden brown and crispy, about 2 minutes. Remove with a slotted spoon to the prepared plate. Taste and adjust for seasoning with salt and pepper. Serve with the rémoulade.

Mustard

Dijon mustard is a puree made from husked brown mustard seed blended with white wine, vinegar, salt, and spices. It is straw yellow, and varies from mild to very hot. Dijon mustard is a necessary ingredient for creamy emulsified vinaigrettes and dressings. It is also an absolute must-have condiment for Pot au Feu (page 240). Try a dollop on grilled meats or fish when you don't have time to prepare a sauce for a burst of flavor. **Whole-grain mustard**, also called grainy mustard, coarse mustard, or *ancienne*, is whole mustard seed blended with some mustard puree. It adds great texture to sauces and marinades. **Creole mustard** is a variation of whole-grain mustard with seeds that are slightly crushed rather than completely ground or left whole. It goes well with fish and shellfish, and is traditionally served on a po' boy sandwich. All mustard should be stored in the refrigerator and replaced frequently.

MAMA'S CRAWFISH ÉTOUFFÉE

A Cajun specialty, étouffée is a succulent, tangy, tomato sauce usually made with crawfish or shrimp. The word *étouffée* comes from the French *étouffer* (to smother), and that's it exactly: rich and tender crawfish tails smothered in a spicy blanket of flavorful sauce.

"First, you make a roux" is the start of many Creole and Cajun recipes (it's also the title of a popular cookbook from Louisiana published by the Lafayette Museum in the early 1960s). Roux is a cooked mixture of fat (butter) and starch (flour) used to thicken many sauces in classic French cooking. A Creole roux is not the classic French butter-flour mixture, but sometimes combines flour with an oil like peanut oil that can hold a high temperature. Unlike a French roux, which can be white to pale golden, Creole and Cajun roux are typically, at the very least, the color of peanut butter and progress to deep, dark brown. This process can take 45 minutes or so of constant stirring. It is dangerous stuff. If any splatters on you, it will be perfectly clear why this fiery, sticky combination of oil and flour is often referred to as "Cajun napalm"!

1/2 cup (1 stick) unsalted butter, at room temperature

1/4 cup all-purpose flour

1 onion, preferably Vidalia, chopped

2 stalks celery, chopped

1/2 green bell pepper, cored, seeded and chopped

1/4 cup chopped fresh flat-leaf parsley

5 green onions, green part only, chopped

2 cloves garlic, very finely chopped

2 cups fish or shrimp stock (see page 132) or water

2 pounds crawfish tails, cooked

Hot sauce, for seasoning

Coarse salt and freshly ground black pepper

$20,000 Rice Pilaf (page 158), for accompaniment

In a heavy-bottomed pot or Dutch oven, melt the butter over medium heat. Add the flour, stirring slowly and constantly, and cook to a medium-brown roux, about 30 minutes.

Add the onion, celery, and bell pepper and cook, stirring constantly, until the vegetables are wilted and lightly golden, about 5 minutes. Add the parsley and green onion tops and stir to combine. Add the garlic and cook until fragrant, 45 to 60 seconds. Add the fish stock and stir to combine. Bring to a boil over high heat.

Decrease the heat to low, and simmer, stirring occasionally, until thickened and reduced, about 20 minutes. Add the crawfish and stir to combine. Cook until heated through, 5 to 7 minutes. Season with hot sauce. Taste and adjust for seasoning with salt and pepper. Serve with rice pilaf.

MAMA'S SHRIMP CREOLE

We moved to Louisiana from Evans, Georgia, when I was three years old. I remember the feeling of the winter's morning we left; it was cold, and still dark outside. Up to that point I had spent every day of my short life with Meme and Dede, and I think our leaving broke my grandfather's heart, at least for a little while. One benefit of the big move was that Mama started experimenting with Cajun and Creole cooking. This recipe became a family favorite, and one Dede particularly enjoyed when they came to visit.

When buying shrimp, look for firm shrimp with a mild, almost sweet scent. If there is any scent of ammonia, it is a sign that the shrimp is no longer fresh.

1½ pounds large shrimp (21/25 count), peeled and deveined

Coarse salt and freshly ground black pepper

½ cup canola oil

1 onion, preferably Vidalia, chopped

3 stalks celery, chopped

4 cloves garlic, very finely chopped

1 (6-ounce) can tomato paste

1 (8-ounce) can tomato sauce

1 teaspoon sugar

2 cups water, plus more if needed

Pinch of cayenne pepper

4 green onions, white and green parts, chopped, for garnish

$20,000 Rice Pilaf (page 158), for accompaniment

Place the shrimp in a bowl and season with salt and pepper. Cover with plastic wrap and refrigerate to marinate while you prepare the vegetables.

In a heavy-bottomed skillet, heat the oil over medium heat. Add the onion and celery and cook until soft and translucent, 3 to 5 minutes. Add the garlic and cook until fragrant, 45 to 60 seconds. Add the tomato paste and cook, stirring constantly, an additional 5 minutes. Add the tomato sauce, sugar, water, and cayenne pepper. Bring to a boil over medium-high heat, then decrease the heat to low. Simmer until the oil rises to the surface, stirring occasionally, about 40 minutes. (Use more water if the sauce gets too thick.) Add the shrimp and cook until pink, 3 to 5 minutes. Taste and adjust for seasoning with salt and pepper. Garnish with the green onions. Serve with rice pilaf.

Mama's Seafood Gumbo

Serves 6 to 8

To quote the regional cookbook *Louisiana Entertains*, "Good gumbos are like good sunsets: no two are exactly alike, and their delight lies in their variety." All gumbos use a roux. However, in addition to a roux, some gumbos flavor and thicken with okra and others call for filé powder. Integral to Creole and Cajun cooking, filé powder is made from the dried leaves of the sassafras tree. It is used not only to thicken gumbo but also to impart its mild, lemon flavor. Filé powder should be stirred into gumbo toward the end of cooking or it will become tough and stringy.

2 tablespoons unsalted butter

3 tablespoons all-purpose flour

1 onion, preferably Vidalia, chopped

1 green bell pepper, cored, seeded and chopped

4 cups water or shrimp stock (see below)

2 (6-ounce) cans tomato paste

Coarse salt and freshly ground black pepper

2 pounds large shrimp (21/25 count), peeled and deveined

1 pound jumbo lump or lump crabmeat, picked over for cartilage

Hot sauce, for seasoning

1/4 teaspoon filé powder (optional)

Double recipe $20,000 Rice Pilaf (page 158), for accompaniment

In a heavy-bottomed pot or Dutch oven, melt the butter over medium heat. Add the flour, stirring slowly and constantly, and cook to a medium-brown roux, about 30 minutes.

Add the onion and bell pepper and stir to combine. Cook until the vegetables have wilted and are lightly golden, about 5 minutes. Add the water and tomato paste and stir to combine. Season with salt and pepper. Bring to a boil over high heat. Decrease the heat to low and cover. Simmer, stirring occasionally, until flavorful and thickened, $1^1/2$ to 2 hours.

Add the shrimp and crabmeat and stir to combine. Continue cooking over very low heat until the shrimp are cooked through, an additional 10 minutes. Season with hot sauce and stir in the filé powder, if using. Taste and adjust for seasoning with salt and pepper. Serve with rice pilaf.

Shrimp Stock and Fish Stock

Seafood soup, stew, and gumbo all taste better when prepared with homemade stock as opposed to bottled clam juice, the favorite stand-in to freshly made stock. When you peel the shrimp, save the shells (heads also, if you are fortunate enough to have them), and rinse with cold running water. Place the shells in a pot and add enough water to cover. Add a few fresh bay leaves, sprigs of parsley and thyme, a quartered onion, chopped carrot, and chopped celery, and bring to a boil. Decrease the heat to low and simmer until fragrant and flavorful, about 30 minutes. Strain the stock in a strainer layered with cheesecloth, discarding the solids. If I don't need to make shrimp stock every time I peel shrimp, I save the shells for later in a sealable plastic bag in the freezer. For fish stock, it's the same principle, but use bones instead of shells. Do not use oily or heavy fish such as mackerel, skate, mullet, or salmon; their flavor is too strong and heavy. Use approximately 4 pounds of fish bones to 10 cups of water to make 8 cups of stock.

Stuffed Flounder for Mama

Serves 4 to 6

Mama always loved to order this dish when we went to the beach. But many cooks now avoid serving it since the harvesting methods are not considered ecologically friendly. In many instances, the fish are caught using a trawling method. Imagine a bulldozer scraping along the ocean floor, indiscriminately catching intended as well as unintended species.

Even though flounder also suffers from overfishing (it seems too many people appreciate one of the best fish in the Gulf): I am calling for flounder here for old times' sake. But you can substitute flat fish like English or Dover sole and turbot, which get better ecological marks and whose flavors are similar to that of flounder.

1 tablespoon canola oil, plus more for the baking dish

1 onion, preferably Vidalia, finely chopped

1/2 stalk celery, very finely chopped

1 clove garlic, very finely chopped

1 cup fresh or panko (Japanese) breadcrumbs

2 large eggs, lightly beaten

2 tablespoons chopped fresh flat-leaf parsley

1/4 teaspoon sweet Hungarian paprika

Pinch of cayenne pepper

Coarse salt and freshly ground black pepper

1 pound jumbo lump or lump crabmeat, picked over for cartilage

4 to 6 (5-ounce) flounder, sole, or turbot fillets

4 to 6 tablespoons unsalted butter (optional)

Preheat the oven to 350°F. Brush a large baking dish with oil.

Heat the 1 tablespoon oil in a large skillet over medium heat. Add the onion and celery and cook until clear and translucent, 3 to 5 minutes. Add the garlic and cook until fragrant, 45 to 60 seconds. Remove from the heat and transfer the mixture to a large bowl to cool slightly. Add the breadcrumbs, eggs, parsley, paprika, and cayenne. Season with salt and pepper. Using a large spatula, fold in the crabmeat, taking care not to break the lumps.

Season both sides of the fish fillets with salt and pepper. Place the fillets in the prepared baking dish and top each with an equal amount of crabmeat mixture, patting to a uniform thickness. Top each fillet with a piece of butter. Bake until the fish are cooked through, 15 to 20 minutes. Serve immediately.

CORNMEAL-CRUSTED GROUPER

Serves 4 to 6

Cornmeal-coated fried fish is a product of modest country living: fish were free and cornmeal was cheap. You will not feel poor at all if you try these crusty fillets with Grits with Corn and Vidalia Onion (page 156) for a satisfying supper. This fried grouper also makes an excellent fish sandwich accompanied by homemade mayonnaise (page 282), lettuce, and tomato. Or you can dress it up by serving the fish on a bed of vegetable slaw (page 38). Fried fish with grits is another Southern classic that is good for breakfast, lunch, and dinner. If grouper is unavailable (which is likely, since it is overfished), or you would like to use a more sustainable fish, try mahi-mahi, wild striped bass, or wreckfish.

3/4 cup fresh or panko (Japanese) breadcrumbs

3/4 cup white or yellow cornmeal

1/4 teaspoon cayenne

Coarse salt and freshly ground black pepper

2 large eggs, lightly beaten

4 to 6 (6-ounce) grouper fillets (about 3/4 inch thick)

6 tablespoons canola oil

Lemon wedges, for garnish

Preheat the oven to 500°F. Position an oven rack in the upper third of the oven.

Combine the breadcrumbs, cornmeal, cayenne, 1/4 teaspoon of salt, and 1/4 teaspoon of pepper in a large sealable plastic bag, and shake to mix. Place the beaten eggs in a shallow dish.

Season the fish with salt and pepper on both sides. Working with one fillet at a time, place the fish in the bag and shake to coat well with crumbs. Dip the fish into the eggs, then shake in the crumbs again to coat. Transfer the fish to a plate.

In a large, heavy-bottomed, ovenproof skillet (preferably cast iron), heat 3 tablespoons of the oil over high heat until hot, but not smoking. Fry the fillets until the undersides are golden brown, about 1 minute. Turn, add the remaining 3 tablespoons oil, and cook 1 minute more. Put the skillet in the upper third of the oven and bake until the fish are just cooked through, about 5 minutes. Remove from the oven and serve immediately with lemon wedges.

GULF COAST OYSTER PO' BOYS

Serves 4 to 6

Po' boy sandwiches are found all along the Gulf Coast and are a New Orleans tradition. There are various tales about the origin of the name: that it's a slang version of "poor boy" and the sandwich used to be an inexpensive, yet filling meal; that the sandwich was given out to streetcar workers on strike, who were essentially poor boys; or that it is a bastardized version of the French "pour boire." This last theory holds that the sandwich was a sort of olive branch that men would bring home after a night of drinking and carousing around town. Whatever the name's origin, it is an excellent sandwich.

Although one can find roast beef and gravy po' boys or fried potato and gravy po' boys, possibly the most popular version of this iconic Louisiana treat is fried seafood po' boys made with shrimp and oysters from the Gulf. The key to light and crispy fried food is to use the right oil. Peanut oil is a great choice for frying: it has a mild, pleasant flavor; does not take on the tastes of foods as readily as other oils do; and has a smoke point of about 450°F, meaning you can safely heat it to a very high temperature.

1/3 cup mayonnaise (page 282)

2 teaspoons hot sauce

Juice of 1/2 lemon

Coarse salt and freshly ground black pepper

6 cups peanut oil, for frying

1 large egg

1/4 cup milk

1 1/2 cups white or yellow cornmeal

2 pints shucked oysters, drained (about 60 small oysters)

1 baguette, halved horizontally

2 tablespoons Creole mustard

1 head romaine lettuce, shredded

1 large, ripe tomato, cored and sliced

Line a plate with paper towels and set by the cooktop.

In a small bowl, combine the mayonnaise, hot sauce, and lemon juice. Season with salt and pepper and set aside. Heat the oil in a deep, heavy-bottomed pot over high heat until it reaches 375°F on a deep-fat thermometer.

Meanwhile, combine the egg, milk, and 1 teaspoon of salt in a bowl. Combine the cornmeal, 1 1/2 teaspoons of salt, and pepper to taste in a second bowl.

Working in batches, and being sure to return the oil to 375°F for each batch, add the oysters to the egg mixture, remove with a slotted spoon, letting any excess drip off, and transfer to the cornmeal mixture, tossing to coat well. Carefully transfer the oysters to the oil and fry, turning occasionally, until golden and just cooked through, 1 to 2 minutes. Using a slotted spoon, transfer to the prepared plate to drain. Season with salt and pepper.

To serve, spread the cut sides of the baguette with the seasoned mayonnaise and Creole mustard. Arrange the fried oysters, lettuce, and tomato on the bottom half of the bread and cover with the top half. Using a serrated knife, slice the sandwich into 4 to 6 portions and serve immediately.

NATHALIE'S OYSTER CASSEROLE

Serves 4 to 6

This recipe, a marriage of a recipe I learned while an apprentice to Nathalie Dupree and Meme's version of traditional oyster dressing, is an excellent side dish for a Thanksgiving feast. The myth about buying oysters only in the months with an R is not quite true, but not completely false either. However, it is best to buy oysters during the fall and winter when they are at their prime. Oysters spawn during the summer months and become soft, milky, and bland rather than firm and sweet. It is true that in the South when the water becomes too warm, the oysters are inferior. I only buy oysters to shuck if I am serving them on the half shell. You can generally find pints of shucked oysters in better grocery stores and seafood markets.

2 tablespoons unsalted butter, at room temperature, plus more for the dish

1 tablespoon canola oil

2 green onions, white and green parts, chopped

1/2 red bell pepper, cored, seeded, and finely chopped

1/2 pound white button mushrooms, thinly sliced

Coarse salt and freshly ground black pepper

2 pints shucked oysters, drained (about 60 small oysters)

1/4 cup all-purpose flour

1 cup milk, warmed

1/4 cup grated Parmigiano-Reggiano cheese (about 1 ounce)

2 tablespoons chopped fresh flat-leaf parsley

1/4 teaspoon sweet Hungarian paprika

Pinch of cayenne pepper

1/2 cup fresh or panko (Japanese) breadcrumbs

Place the oven rack 6 inches below the broiler and preheat the broiler. Brush a gratin dish with butter.

In a large skillet, heat the oil over medium-high heat. Add the green onions, bell pepper, and mushrooms and season with salt and pepper. Saute until the vegetables are soft, about 5 minutes. Add the oysters and stir to combine. Decrease the heat to low and cook until the oysters are firm, an additional 5 minutes. Remove from the heat and keep warm.

In a medium saucepan, melt the 2 tablespoons butter over medium heat. Stir in the flour and cook until foamy, about 2 minutes. Add the milk and bring to a boil over medium-high heat, stirring constantly until thickened, 3 to 5 minutes. Add the cheese and stir to combine.

Pour the cheese sauce over the oyster mixture and stir to combine. Add the parsley, paprika, and cayenne. Taste and adjust for seasoning with salt and pepper.

Pour the mixture into the prepared gratin dish and top with the breadcrumbs. Broil until browned and bubbling, about 10 minutes.

SHRIMP WITH PARMIGIANO-REGGIANO GRITS AND TOMATOES

Serves 4 to 6

This is one of those dishes that is just perfect for breakfast, Sunday dinner, or a weeknight supper. I usually peel and devein the shrimp, but leave on the tails. My dear friend Gena Berry grew up on St. Simons Island, Georgia, in the heart of the fishing and shrimping community. One day, we were in the kitchen getting ready for a party. She jumped in, helpful as always, and offered to peel the shrimp. When she saw my technique of leaving the tails on, she raised her eyebrows perilously high (as only Gena can do), and informed me that coast folks don't peel shrimp like that. I still think it looks better.

I use wild American shrimp, not pond-raised imports, because I am supporting those very shrimpers Gena grew up with. Save the shrimp shells to make shrimp stock (pictured opposite; recipe on page 132).

3 cups water

3 cups milk

1 tablespoon unsalted butter

Coarse salt and freshly ground black pepper

1 1/2 cups coarse-ground grits

2 tablespoons canola oil, plus more if needed

1 onion, preferably Vidalia, coarsely chopped

3 cloves garlic, finely chopped

1/4 cup dry white wine

4 bay leaves, preferably fresh

1 (28-ounce) can whole tomatoes, coarsely chopped, with juice

Pinch of cayenne pepper

1/4 cup loosely packed mixed fresh herbs (such as parsley, oregano, and thyme), coarsely chopped

24 large shrimp (21/25 count), peeled and deveined

1/4 cup heavy cream (optional)

2 tablespoons grated Parmigiano-Reggiano cheese, plus shaved cheese, for garnish

To prepare the grits, in a saucepan, over medium-high heat, bring the water, milk, butter, and 1 teaspoon of the salt to a gentle boil. Whisk in the grits. Decrease the heat to low and simmer, stirring often with a wooden spoon, until the mixture is smooth and thick and falls easily from the spoon, 30 to 45 minutes.

Meanwhile, prepare the tomatoes. Heat 1 tablespoon of the oil in a large skillet over medium-high heat. Add the onion and saute until the onion is soft and translucent, 2 to 3 minutes. Add the garlic and cook until fragrant, 45 to 60 seconds. Add the white wine, and cook until it evaporates, 2 to 3 minutes. Add the bay leaves, then stir in the tomatoes and reserved juice. Season with cayenne pepper. Decrease the heat to low, and simmer until the mixture is slightly thickened, about 10 minutes. When the tomatoes are ready, remove the skillet from the heat, and stir in the chopped herbs. Set aside and keep warm.

To prepare the shrimp, heat the remaining 1 tablespoon of oil in a second skillet over medium-high heat to sizzling. Add the shrimp; season with salt and pepper, and saute to sear on both sides until firm and pink, about 2 minutes per side.

When the grits are thickened, stir in the heavy cream and cheese.

To serve, put a heaping spoonful of grits onto individual serving plates. Top with an equal amount of the tomatoes, and top with equal amounts of the shrimp. Garnish with shavings of Parmigiano-Reggiano.

Shrimp Stock (page 132)

Mountain Trout with Lemons and Capers

Serves 2 to 4

Capers are the preserved unopened flower buds of a prickly shrub native to the Mediterranean. The shrubs thrive on rocky cliffs of arid regions, including southern France and Sicily, where they are farmed as a cash crop. Salted capers are hand-harvested then cured and aged in sea salt. This process preserves the intense floral tones, herbal flavor, and firm texture of the buds. Brined capers are soaked in saltwater, then packed in brine or a mixture of brine and vinegar, which dulls the flavor. The salted capers tend to be a little more expensive, but are hand-harvested and worth every penny.

While working for Epicurious television, I was able to travel to Italy to do a story on salted capers. Standing on the rocky hillside of an island, looking out over the sun-drenched Mediterranean, watching the peasant women harvesting the capers by hand while chattering in their local dialect, was pure poetry.

When I returned to the States, I was reviewing the rough cut, which is a very basic edit of footage, a visual rough draft. A colleague who spoke Italian interrupted, "Wait a minute, play that back." Turned out the pleasant chatter was not as idyllic as the scenery. One of the women was talking about her son-in-law, whom she called a worthless bastard and car thief. We decided to replace their conversation with a little music.

1/2 cup all-purpose flour

Coarse salt and freshly ground black pepper

2 (12-ounce) trout, butterflied (have your fishmonger do this)

2 tablespoons canola oil

2 tablespoons unsalted butter

Juice of 1 lemon

2 teaspoons salted capers, rinsed

Place the flour in a shallow dish. Add 1 teaspoon of the salt and 1/2 teaspoon of the black pepper; stir with a fork to combine. Lightly season the trout with salt and pepper. (If you prefer not to have your dinner looking at you while you eat it, snip off the fish heads with a pair of kitchen shears.) Dredge both sides of the trout in flour, shaking gently to remove the excess.

Heat the oil and 1 tablespoon of the butter in a large skillet over medium-high heat. Add the trout to the skillet, skin side up. Cook until pale golden, about 3 minutes. Turn and continue cooking until the fish is firm, an additional 3 to 4 minutes.

Remove the trout to a warm serving platter and tent loosely with aluminum foil to keep warm.

Remove the skillet from the heat. Add the remaining 1 tablespoon of butter, the lemon juice, and capers. Return to the heat if necessary to brown the butter, stirring with a wooden spoon to release the brown bits in the bottom of the skillet, 1 to 2 minutes. Pour the pan sauce over the trout and serve immediately.

HALIBUT PROVENÇAL WITH TOMATOES AND ZUCCHINI

Serves 4 to 6

Halibut caught in the Pacific Ocean, in the northern areas near Alaska, and in the Bering Sea are caught by long-lining, which uses a central fishing line with smaller lines of baited hooks attached. This method is far less destructive to the marine habitat than the trawling methods used in the Atlantic. So, try to find Pacific halibut; alternatives include mako shark or farm-raised sturgeon. This recipe would also work well with a thick fillet of wild salmon.

It's important to cook the vegetables first to evaporate their moisture and concentrate their flavors. While cooking, the fish makes a lovely, fragrant broth, perfect to serve over grits, rice, or instant couscous in a shallow bowl.

3 tablespoons olive oil, plus more for the pan

1 onion, preferably Vidalia, chopped

3 large cloves garlic, finely chopped

1 tablespoon chopped fresh thyme, plus thyme sprigs for garnish

2 small zucchini, chopped

2 tomatoes, cored, seeded, and chopped

20 kalamata or other brine-cured black olives, pitted and halved

1 tablespoon red wine vinegar

Coarse salt and freshly ground black pepper

4 (6-ounce) halibut fillets, skinned, or 1 large (24-ounce) fillet, skinned

Preheat the oven to 375°F. Brush a shallow, ovenproof casserole with olive oil.

To make the sauce, heat the 3 tablespoons oil in a large skillet over medium-high heat. Add the onion and cook until soft and translucent, 2 to 3 minutes. Add the garlic and chopped thyme and cook until fragrant, 45 to 60 seconds. Add the zucchini and tomatoes and sauté until soft, 5 to 7 minutes. Remove from the heat. Add the olives and vinegar. Taste and adjust for seasoning with salt and pepper.

To cook the fish, place the halibut in the prepared casserole and turn in the oil to lightly coat; season with salt and pepper. Spoon the vegetable mixture over the fillets. Bake until just opaque in the center, about 10 minutes. Garnish with additional sprigs of thyme.

APALACHICOLA OYSTERS WITH SAUCE MIGNONETTE

Makes 12 and
serves 1 to 2
as a first course

Most oysters are farmed, but Apalachicola oysters are harvested from some of the only wild oyster beds left in American waters, near Apalachicola, Florida. This area of the Gulf of Mexico is known as Florida's "Forgotten Coast." For generations, residents of the Florida panhandle have made their livelihood working the Apalachicola Bay and surrounding waters. The area's real claim to fame may be oysters, but every Southerner should raise a chilled glass of sweet tea to Dr. John Gorrie. The kind doctor thought Apalachicola summers were too hot for his patients and was a pioneer in the invention of the artificial manufacture of ice, refrigeration, and air-conditioning (he was granted a patent in 1851 for the first ice maker).

This simple, peppery, vinegar sauce is a classic French accompaniment to freshly shucked oysters.

½ cup best-quality white or red wine vinegar

1 small shallot, very finely chopped

1 teaspoon freshly ground white pepper

Grated zest of 1 lemon

Sea salt

12 fresh oysters

In a bowl, combine the vinegar, shallot, pepper, lemon zest, and a pinch of salt; set aside.

To shuck the oysters, using a towel, hold an oyster flat on the work surface, flat shell up. Insert the tip of an oyster knife into the hinge and twist to open it. Slide the knife along the inside of the upper shell to free the oyster from the shell; discard the upper shell. Slide the knife under the oyster to free it from the lower shell, but leave it in the shell.

Arrange the shucked oysters on two serving plates, preferably oyster plates with wells. If you are using regular plates, cover them with rock salt or fresh seaweed, sometimes available at the fishmonger, to create a nest for the oysters so they don't tip over. Spoon a teaspoon of sauce over each oyster and serve immediately.

  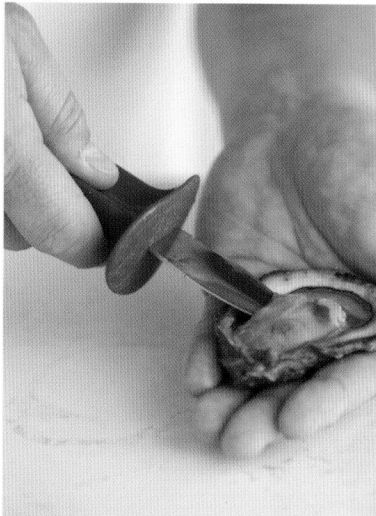

SAVANNAH-STYLE MARINATED SHRIMP

Serves 4 to 6

In Atlanta, people ask you, "What's your business?" In Augusta, they ask, "What's your mother's maiden name?" In Macon, they ask, "Where do you go to church?" In Savannah, they ask, "What would you like to drink?" That generous hospitality and sense of fun is typical of Savannah style; this dish is very likely to be served at one of Savannah's legendary cocktail parties.

As Georgia's most valuable seafood crop, between $4^{1}/_{2}$ million and $9^{1}/_{2}$ million pounds of heads-on shrimp are harvested annually by a fleet of more than five hundred boats, the majority owner-operated and based within an hour or so of Savannah. It is common to find fishermen whose families have fished the same grounds for generations.

Preserving and pickling seafood in citrus juice, vinegar, and brine is a technique used all over the world—in Spanish ceviche, for example. This combination of ingredients acts as a cooking agent, denaturing the proteins and rendering the raw seafood cooked. Many recipes state shrimp pickled by this technique may be stored for up to ten days, tightly covered in the refrigerator, but I disagree. Even if you weren't concerned about food-borne illness, why bother? The acid would continue working and you'd wind up with bouncy balls of shrimp-flavored pink rubber. Up to two days in the refrigerator is fine. Serve on a bed of lettuce for a nice cold salad, or as a delightful nibble on a buffet.

$2^{1}/_{2}$ pounds large shrimp (21/25 count), peeled and deveined

3 onions, preferably Vidalia, very thinly sliced

$^{1}/_{2}$ red bell pepper, cored, seeded, and very thinly sliced

4 bay leaves, preferably fresh

2 cloves garlic, very finely chopped

1 tablespoon whole black peppercorns

1 teaspoon red pepper flakes

Coarse salt and freshly ground black pepper

1 cup apple cider vinegar

$^{1}/_{2}$ cup canola oil

Grated zest and juice of 1 lemon

In a large, nonreactive bowl, layer some of the shrimp, onions, bell pepper, bay leaf, garlic, peppercorns, red pepper flakes, and freshly ground black pepper. Create several layers of these ingredients until the remaining amount is used. Set aside.

In a large liquid measuring cup, combine the vinegar, oil, and lemon zest and juice. Pour this marinade over the shrimp mixture. Cover tightly with plastic wrap and refrigerate, stirring occasionally, until the shrimp is pink and opaque, at least 4 hours and up to 8 hours. Taste and adjust for seasoning with salt and pepper before serving.

CLASSIC CRAB CAKES

Serves 4 to 6 as a main course, or makes 24 bite-size hors d'oeuvres

When vacationing as a child on the Gulf of Mexico or along the Atlantic, we would often spend an afternoon crabbing along a shallow pier or rocky jetty, using crawfish nets whose white-cotton webbing was long-ago colored a muddy red-brown. We would tie a bony chicken neck in the center of the net, toss it out into the shallow waters, and wait.

Being a child and waiting patiently to pull in the nets do not go hand in hand. Until one of our parents intervened, we would pull in the nets to check them so often that the crabs didn't have a chance to find them, much less saddle in for a good gnaw on the chicken. When we did catch them, it was important to release the females to help maintain the crab population. I always had a hard time telling them apart until one crusty Maryland crabber explained to me years later, "The male looks like the Washington Monument and the female looks like the Capitol." Indeed, the underbelly flap of the male is decidedly pointed and long and the female's is round with a nubbin of a tip.

I like crab cakes, not crab-and-bread cakes—there needs to be just enough binder to hold the crab together. Use jumbo lump or lump crabmeat, be sure to keep the crab very cold since it spoils easily, and carefully pick through the meat to remove any bits of shell.

1/3 cup fresh or panko (Japanese) breadcrumbs

1 pound jumbo lump or lump crabmeat, picked over for cartilage

1 large egg, lightly beaten

2 tablespoons mayonnaise (page 282)

Zest of 1 lemon

1 1/2 teaspoons Worcestershire sauce

Dash of hot sauce

Coarse salt and freshly ground black pepper

1/4 cup peanut oil, plus more if needed

4 lemons, cut into wedges, for garnish

Line a plate with paper towels and set near the cooktop.

In a bowl, combine the breadcrumbs, crab, egg, mayonnaise, lemon zest, Worcestershire sauce, hot sauce, salt, and pepper. The mixture will be slightly wet. Form into cakes: use about 1/4 cup for large cakes and 1 tablespoon or so for hors d'oeuvres. Place on a baking sheet and refrigerate to chill and set, about 30 minutes.

Heat the peanut oil in a large skillet over medium heat. Using an offset spatula, gently slip the chilled cakes, in batches, into the oil. Cook until the crab cakes are golden brown, about 5 minutes on each side for large patties, or 1 to 2 minutes per side for small hors d'oeuvres. Remove from the skillet, and transfer to the prepared plate to drain. Serve hot with lemon wedges.

CLASSIC SOFT-SHELL CRABS

Serve 4 to 6

Soft-shell crab season starts the night of the first full moon in May and lasts through September. A soft-shell crab is a blue crab fortuitously interrupted (for us, not the crab) in the middle of a growth spurt. A blue crab emerges from the muddy waters to shed its outer covering (exoskeleton). A soft-shell crab is a blue crab before its new shell hardens.

Fishermen use baskets to catch crabs known as "peelers," crabs that are beginning to split at the ends and are about to molt. They bring them onshore and hold them in water tanks until they complete the molting process. Once the peelers are in the tanks, they are watched closely to catch them within one hour of shedding. Soft-shell crabs that are newly shed and not pulled from the tanks are in danger, since they are immobile and basically dinner to other crabs in the water tank. Another reason to harvest them soon after shedding: if the new shell gets too hard, the fishermen have lost their harvest.

2 cups whole milk

Coarse salt and freshly ground white pepper

4 to 6 soft-shell crabs, cleaned and patted dry (see page 147)

1 cup all-purpose flour

2 tablespoons canola oil, plus more if needed

2 tablespoons clarified butter (see below)

2 tablespoons unsalted butter, cut into bits

Juice of 1/2 lemon

1/4 cup chopped fresh flat-leaf parsley

Place the milk in a bowl and season with salt and pepper. Add the crabs and let soak for 5 minutes. Place the flour in a shallow dish and season with salt and pepper.

Heat the oil and clarified butter in a large nonstick skillet over high heat. Lift the crabs out of the milk, one at a time, letting the excess drip off, and dredge in the seasoned flour.

Add the crabs, without crowding, to the skillet and saute, in batches, until golden, 3 to 5 minutes per side. Transfer the crabs to a warm platter. Discard the oil from the skillet.

To make the sauce, return the skillet to the heat, add the butter pieces, and cook until golden brown. Add the lemon juice and parsley and remove from the heat. Season the sauce with salt and pepper and drizzle over the crabs.

Clarified Butter

Clarified butter has a higher smoke point than regular butter and can be used to cook at higher temperatures. (The smoke point is the temperature at which oil or fat starts to smoke and break down.) When clarified, butter loses about one fourth of its original volume. To clarify butter, cut unsalted butter into 1-inch pieces and melt over low heat in a heavy-bottomed saucepan. It will begin to sizzle as the water evaporates. When the butter stops sizzling, the water has evaporated. Remove the pan from the heat and let the butter stand for 2 to 3 minutes. Using a spoon, skim the froth off the top and discard. Slowly pour the molten butter into a measuring cup, leaving the milky solids in the bottom of the pan. Discard the milky solids. Pour the clarified butter into an airtight container and store in the refrigerator for up to 1 month.

CORNMEAL-CRUSTED SOFT-SHELL CRAB WITH JALAPEÑO TARTAR SAUCE

Serves 4 to 6

For an over-the-top po' boy, try these crabs in a French loaf dressed with shredded lettuce and sliced tomato, or serve them on a bed of heart-healthy Classic Cole Slaw (page 35) for a new Southern twist on an old favorite.

2 cups buttermilk

2 large eggs, lightly beaten

4 to 6 soft-shell crabs, cleaned and patted dry (see below)

4 cups peanut or canola oil, plus more if needed, for frying

1 cup all-purpose flour

1 cup white or yellow cornmeal

2 teaspoons baking powder

Coarse salt and freshly ground black pepper

1/4 cup microgreens (such as basil, arugula, or beet), for garnish (optional)

Jalapeño Tartar Sauce (page 287), for accompaniment

Combine the buttermilk and eggs in a large bowl. Add the crabs and cover with plastic wrap. Refrigerate to marinate for 1 hour.

Fill a large, heavy-bottomed Dutch oven (preferably cast iron) or pot with at least 2 inches of oil. Make sure there will be at least 2 inches headroom at the top of the pot when you add the crabs. Heat the oil over high heat until it reaches 375°F on a deep-fat thermometer. Line a plate with paper towels and set by the cooktop.

Meanwhile, to coat the crab, combine the flour, cornmeal, baking power, and 1/2 teaspoon of the salt in a shallow baking dish or bowl. Working with one crab at a time, remove it from the buttermilk mixture, shake to remove any excess, and dredge in the flour mixture. Turn to coat, and shake to remove any excess flour. Repeat with a second crab.

Immediately place one crab in the hot oil and then the second crab. Fry the crabs, two at a time, turning over halfway through frying, until golden brown, 3 to 5 minutes. Transfer to the prepared plate to drain. Repeat with the remaining crabs, returning the oil to 375°F after each batch.

While hot, season the crabs with salt and pepper. Garnish with the greens and serve with the tartar sauce.

Cleaning Soft-Shell Crabs

To clean and prepare soft-shell crabs for cooking, hold the crab in one hand and bend back the pointed ends of the shell. Using your fingers, remove the cottony pale gray gills on the sides. Turn the crab over and snip off the small flap (known as the apron) and the head with a pair of scissors. Tomalley is the soft green liver and is considered a delicacy. It is very rich, however, so if you don't like the taste of the tomalley, gently squeeze the crab to remove it. Rinse the entire crab well and pat dry before proceeding with the recipe.

VALDOSTA GRILLED TROUT WITH OLIVE OIL

Serves 4

Several years ago, my girlfriend Becky and I were traveling in the Alps and went through the Saint Bernard Pass from France to Italy, stopping in Valle d'Aosta. We laughed the whole time we were there, as we called it Valdosta, a South Georgia town near the Florida border better known more for pine, pulpwood, and turpentine than Roman ruins and fine cheeses.

The first evening, Becky and I went out for dinner, wandering the ancient, winding cobblestone streets looking for a restaurant that seemed inviting. We found one. Thinking of the wooded forests nearby, I ordered rabbit. I should have been thinking of the crystal clear streams of melted snow. Becky ordered trout. They brought it to the table whole, on the bone. The waiter then proceeded to fillet it at the table. When done, he asked if she would like it drizzled with olive oil. It was a revelation.

Trout is a very user-friendly fish to grill. Not only does its tough, leathery skin help keep the fish from falling apart, but it also insulates the flesh from the direct heat of the grill. This is the time to break out your best extra-virgin olive oil. The smoky, herb-infused fish just needs a little kiss of liquid gold.

---

4 (6- to 8-ounce) whole trout, gutted

Coarse salt and freshly ground black pepper

2 lemons, very thinly sliced, plus 2 lemons, cut into wedges, for garnish

8 sprigs of thyme

8 sprigs of parsley

4 bay leaves, preferably fresh

Best-quality extra-virgin olive oil, for drizzling

Prepare a charcoal fire using about 6 pounds of charcoal and burn until the coals are completely covered with a thin coating of light gray ash, 20 to 30 minutes. Spread the coals evenly over the grill bottom, position the grill rack above the coals, and heat until medium-hot (when you can hold your hand 5 inches above the grill surface for no longer than 3 or 4 seconds). Or for a gas grill, turn on all burners to High, close the lid, and heat until very hot, 10 to 15 minutes.

Meanwhile, place the trout on a clean work surface and season inside and out with salt and pepper. Equally divide the lemon slices, thyme, parsley, and bay leaves among the trout cavities.

Place the stuffed trout on the grill, heads facing in one direction. Grill, covered, until cooked on one side, about 5 minutes.

Uncover the grill, and flip the trout over (simply roll them over with a metal spatula). Cover, and continue cooking until the trout is done on the second side, an additional 3 to 5 minutes.

To serve, remove the trout to a warm platter and drizzle with olive oil. Garnish with the lemon wedges and serve immediately.

CHAPTER 7

GRITS, RICE, PASTA, AND POTATOES

SOUTHERNERS, RICH AND POOR, black and white, have histori-
cally consumed the same basic foods that sustained settlers as far back as
the sixteenth and seventeenth centuries: corn, pork, wild game, and food
gathered in the wild such as cress from the river banks and greens from the
woods. The importance of corn in this scheme cannot be overstated. Corn
was eaten fresh in the summer, and dried and ground into meal for boiling
and baking in the winter. Ground corn in the form of grits is simple country
food, and a touchstone of Southern cooking.

Most Southerners love grits, and I am no exception. My grandmother
made old-fashioned grits with water, simmering them on the stove until
they were thick and rich with the taste of corn. My mother has a bowl of
grits with cheese every morning without fail.

Grits are ground from "dent" or field corn, a type of corn with a low
sugar content and a relatively soft, starchy center that is the premier
Southern milling corn. Somewhere along the way, the term "grist,"
meaning grain for milling, became "grits." Other popular types of corn
include popcorn and sweet corn (both of which are widely known and
loved in the United States), flint corn (the type used for polenta in Italy
and for posole and masa harina in Latin America), and flour corn (about
which Southerners take fierce stands on which color is better, white
or yellow).

Grits are further defined by how they are prepared and ground. There are hominy grits, stone-ground grits, and various grades of commercially ground grits from fine to coarse. Hominy is made from corn kernels soaked in an alkaline solution of water and lye to remove the kernel's outer hull. When hominy is dried and coarsely ground, the result is hominy grits.

Stone-ground grits are made from dried whole corn kernels ground between two stones, just as they were centuries ago, which guarantees their old-fashioned flavor. The germ, in the center of the grain, is very oily, which means these grits have a whole lot of corn flavor. The ground corn is sifted (bolted) to remove the husks. The same stone-ground corn can vary in flavor depending on the size of the ground particles. Because stone-ground grits are not as processed and the larger particles retain the oily germ (removed in commercially processed grits), they are more perishable and should be refrigerated or frozen. They must also be simmered very slowly for at least an hour to coax out their tender, creamy texture.

If you are unable to find stone-ground grits in stores, search out the best-quality commercially ground grits, labeled "coarse" or "old-fashioned." They will take thirty to forty-five minutes to cook, and while they are not as richly flavored with corn, they do have some of the toothsome texture of stone-ground.

In massive commercial operations, the grits are processed in big roller mills. The germ is removed to prevent rancidity and improve the product's shelf life. The grits are finely ground and produce a smooth, bland porridge without a whole lot of corn flavor.

In this chapter, most of the recipes call for stone-ground or coarse-ground grits. I suggest using quick grits if you are in a real pinch, making the appropriate adjustments for cooking time. Don't bother with instant grits that cook in mere minutes. You may as well just heat up some glue and sawdust.

Rice is the other prominent Southern grain, and is second only to wheat as the most widely cultivated cereal in the world. A staple food in many countries, it is divided into long-, medium-, and short-grain categories. In general, the longer the grain, the more likely it is to cook in separate, fluffy grains. Rice was planted in South Carolina as early as 1680 and was a major export crop. The coastal sea islands and swampy coastline of South Carolina and Georgia—the Low Country—is very humid, has abundant rainfall, and long hot summers with mild winters. It's the perfect climate for growing rice.

Throughout the eighteenth century, the economy of South Carolina was dependent on the cultivation of rice, specifically a variety of rice known as Carolina Gold, considered the grande dame of American rice. It was called Carolina Gold for its beautiful golden hue in the fields, but it also made Charleston one of the richest cities in the New World.

The labor-intensive grain, grown in boggy fields, owed its success as a crop primarily to the system of slavery that existed for hundreds of years. The plants were tended by hand, and after the harvest, the rice was hand-pounded by mortar and pestle. Plantation owners paid a premium for slaves from the rice-growing region of West Africa, as they were valued for their skills at rice cultivation.

Rice was prized for its unusually starchy properties that allow it to be creamy like risotto or fluffy individual grains, depending on how it was cooked. The bountiful Southern rice harvest allowed the United States to dominate the world rice market until the Civil War.

After the Civil War, the plantations fell into disrepair, Charleston declined in prominence, and Carolina Gold, the rice that had created an entire cuisine—the Carolina Rice Kitchen—almost faded into history. The same wetlands that made Carolina Gold so popular doomed it after the loss of slave labor.

The rice industry moved west to Arkansas, Louisiana, Texas, Mississippi, and eventually California and Missouri, states that had drier fields that were easier to work. Modern, less labor-intensive, more shelf-stable hybrids replaced Carolina Gold, and eventually, after the Depression, this heirloom grain was sent to a USDA seed repository for preservation. According to the Carolina Gold Rice Foundation, in the mid-1980s, Dr. Richard Schulze, an eye surgeon and landowner from Savannah, collected stores of this heirloom rice from the USDA and started growing it once again in the Carolina Low Country.

The rice that was once grown in coastal fields from northern Florida to Delaware, and was once synonymous in the United States with long-grain rice, is now an upscale, boutique item valued by chefs and devoted foodies who don't mind paying seven dollars a pound for rice. The success of this venture is inherently tied to the hope that more and more people will support artisan food, heirloom varieties, and organic, locally grown, sustainable agriculture.

Recently, pasta and potatoes have made their way into the Southern pantry, but I remember my hurt feelings as a small child when my grandmother conjectured that I must like potatoes so much because my father was from Massachusetts. (A friend in college pointed out that as I am ever the Southerner and concerned about my lineage, I should be thankful that at least he was a real Yankee from New England.)

FUNERAL GRITS

Serves 6 to 8

This simple casserole is a familiar dish in the South. It is an absolute standard at pot-lucks, brunches, weddings, and funerals. Casseroles are the salve that heals a Southerner's wounded soul. I always call this dish "funeral grits" because it's the perfect dish to take to the bereaved after the funeral. It can be treated as a side dish, held for hours in a low oven with few ill effects, and the leftovers reheat wonderfully. Funeral food in the South is a category all to itself. The food should be comforting, not too fancy, and even in this day and age, is best if homemade (not a platter of sliced deli meats from the grocery store). When my godfather, Uncle Raymond, died many years ago, I remember the women swarming in the kitchen, each and every one of them taking on a specific chore. Even though I was a professional cook by this time, I was designated for phone duty. I didn't mind; I may have been a professional cook, but I was still the youngest and lowest on the totem pole.

This dish serves six to eight people, more than most of the recipes in this book. Lord knows, a dish serving less people won't go far at a Southern funeral. Use this recipe as a guide and make it your own. Add more jalapeño to give it some real heat, or switch up the cheeses and try adding freshly grated Parmigiano-Reggiano, Gruyère, or white Cheddar.

2 tablespoons unsalted butter, plus more for the dish

2 cups water

2 cups whole milk

1 cup stone-ground or coarse-ground grits

Coarse salt and freshly ground black pepper

1 1/2 cups grated sharp Cheddar cheese (about 6 ounces)

4 large eggs, lightly beaten

1/4 teaspoon cayenne pepper

1 jalapeño chile, seeded and finely chopped

2 green onions, white and green parts, chopped

Preheat the oven to 350°F. Butter a large casserole.

In a large heavy-bottomed saucepan, combine the water and milk and bring to a boil over medium-high heat. Stir in the grits and return to a boil. Season with salt and pepper. Decrease the heat to low, and simmer until creamy and thick, 45 to 60 minutes. Remove from the heat. Add the cheese and 2 tablespoons butter. Taste and adjust for seasoning with salt and pepper and stir to combine. Add the eggs, cayenne, jalapeño, and green onions and stir until well incorporated. Spoon the mixture into the prepared casserole. Bake until bubbly and golden brown, about 1 hour. Remove to a rack to cool slightly before serving.

CREAMY STONE-GROUND GRITS WITH MUSHROOMS AND COUNTRY HAM

Serves 4 to 6

I once demonstrated this recipe for a fundraiser in my hometown. When I started whisking milk into the grits, rather than stirring in water with a spoon, the influence of French culinary training became obvious. I can pretty much guarantee that Meme never whisked her grits. And years ago, grits were a food of the poor and milk was a luxury reserved for dishes deemed more important than grits. For my family and many Southerners, grits are prepared with water. But, for reasons French or otherwise, I like blending a bit of milk or heavy cream with the water to make them even creamier.

Country ham, the South's version of Spanish Serrano or Italian prosciutto, is brined, smoked, and aged, and can be very salty. In this recipe, it is not necessary to soak the ham to remove the salt; simply add less salt when cooking the mushrooms.

2 cups water

2 cups whole milk

1 cup stone-ground or coarse-ground grits

Coarse salt and freshly ground black pepper

2 tablespoons canola oil

4 ounces country ham, thinly sliced into strips

1½ pounds mixed fresh mushrooms (such as white button, cremini, morel, chanterelle, or portobello), sliced

¼ cup dry white wine

¾ cup grated Parmigiano-Reggiano cheese (about 3 ounces)

¼ cup coarsely chopped fresh flat-leaf parsley

1 tablespoon unsalted butter

In a large, heavy-bottomed saucepan, bring the water and milk to a gentle boil over medium high heat. Slowly add the grits, whisking constantly. Season with salt and pepper. Decrease the heat to low, and simmer, stirring often, until the grits are creamy and thick, 45 to 60 minutes.

Line a plate with paper towels. While the grits are cooking, heat the oil in a large skillet over medium-high heat. Add the ham and cook until lightly browned and some of the fat has rendered, about 3 minutes. Remove the ham from the skillet to the prepared plate and tent loosely with aluminum foil to keep warm.

In the same skillet, using the oil left in the pan, add the mushrooms, season with freshly ground pepper, and saute, stirring, until barely tender, about 2 minutes. (No salt is needed, as the salt from the ham has flavored the cooking oil.) Add the wine and cook, stirring, until the liquid has evaporated and the mushrooms are tender, about 5 more minutes. Taste and adjust for seasoning with salt and pepper. Set aside.

Remove the grits from the heat; whisk in the cheese, parsley, and butter. Taste and adjust for seasoning with salt and pepper. To serve, place a dollop of grits on individual serving plates. Spoon over the sauteed mushrooms and top with the country ham. Serve immediately.

GRITS WITH CORN AND VIDALIA ONION

Serves 4 to 6

Only use fresh corn in season for this recipe. As soon as corn is harvested, the sugar in the kernel begins to convert to starch and the corn begins to lose its sweetness. To store corn, leave on the husks and store it loosely wrapped in damp paper towels inside a paper bag. Refrigerate and use it within twenty-four hours.

My friend, chef Marvin Woods, introduced me to the technique of grating the onion on a box grater instead of finely chopping it. When the onion is grated, it almost melts into the grits, adding a layer of onion flavor without any noticeable onion texture (always present with chopped onion, regardless of how fine the pieces). It also adds a bit more moisture to the grits than chopped onion does.

1 tablespoon canola oil

1 onion, preferably Vidalia, grated

Scraped kernels from 2 ears fresh sweet corn (about 1 cup) (see page 188)

2 cups whole milk

2 cups water

Coarse salt and freshly ground black pepper

1 cup stone-ground or coarse-ground grits

2 tablespoons unsalted butter

3/4 cup grated Parmigiano-Reggiano cheese (about 3 ounces)

1 tablespoon chopped fresh flat-leaf parsley

1 tablespoon chopped fresh chives

In a heavy-bottomed saucepan, heat the oil over medium heat. Add the onion and cook, stirring, until transparent, about 2 minutes. Add the corn and cook, stirring occasionally, until the kernels become soft, about 5 minutes.

Add the milk, water, and 1 teaspoon of the salt. Bring the mixture to a boil over high heat. Whisk in the grits, decrease the heat to low, and simmer, whisking occasionally, until the grits are creamy and thick, 45 to 60 minutes. Stir in the butter, cheese, parsley, and chives. Taste and adjust for seasoning with salt and pepper.

VARIATION: Grits and greens are one of the best possible marriages in Southern cuisine. It's a meal in itself or an incredible bed for Bourbon Baked Ham (page 78). Prepare Tangle of Bitter Greens (page 198), then add the greens to the saucepan of cooked grits as the last step, stirring well to combine. Taste and adjust for seasoning with salt and pepper. Serve immediately.

$20,000 Rice Pilaf

Before I attended culinary school, my attempts at preparing rice were absolutely disastrous. Most often the final results were more like gloppy oatmeal, at best. The pilaf method I learned at L'Academie de Cuisine was my saving grace, which is why I call this recipe $20,000 Rice Pilaf (that was the cost of a year of school at the time).

2 tablespoons unsalted butter

1 small shallot, chopped

2 cups long-grain white rice (such as Carolina Gold, jasmine, or basmati)

Coarse salt and freshly ground black pepper

3 cups chicken stock (page 227) or low-fat, reduced-sodium chicken broth or water

2 tablespoons chopped fresh flat-leaf parsley

Preheat the oven to 350°F. In a large, ovenproof saucepan, heat the butter over medium heat until foaming. Add the shallot and cook until clear and translucent, 2 to 3 minutes.

Add the rice and stir to combine. Cook, stirring constantly, until the rice is coated with butter and lightly toasted. Season with 1 teaspoon of the salt and pepper to taste. Add the stock and stir to combine. Bring to a boil over medium-high heat. Cover with a tight-fitting lid and cook until the liquid is absorbed and the rice is tender, 17 minutes. Remove from the oven and let stand, covered, for 5 minutes before serving. Add the parsley and fluff with a fork just before serving.

LOUISIANA DIRTY RICE

Serves 4 to 6

The name "dirty rice" doesn't sound very appealing, but it is an enjoyable combination of creamy rice, savory vegetables, full-flavored chicken liver, and a heavy hand of intense spice. It's an odd conglomeration of a Cajun stir-fry and soft, comforting rice. This is, like many other country recipes, a way to make a filling meal out of a potpourri of simple, inexpensive ingredients. The chopped liver is what gives it the dark, "dirty" color.

Dirty rice is like many old-school recipes—everyone has a different way to prepare it. However, most versions contain the holy trinity of Cajun cooking: bell pepper, onion, and celery. I am not so fond of green bell peppers. They come back to say "hello" a little too often. I prefer poblano chiles, which are just slightly spicier than a green bell pepper, and I suggest using it here.

1¹/₂ cups water

1¹/₂ cups long-grain white rice

Coarse salt and freshly ground black pepper

1 tablespoon canola oil

¹/₂ red onion, chopped

¹/₂ poblano chile or green bell pepper, cored, seeded, and chopped

1 stalk celery, chopped

1¹/₂ teaspoons prepared or Homemade Creole Seasoning (page 287)

1 cup chicken livers, coarsely chopped

2 cloves garlic, very finely chopped

1 cup chicken stock (page 227) or low-fat, reduced-sodium chicken broth

1 bay leaf, preferably fresh

2 green onions, white and green parts, chopped

To parboil the rice, combine the water and rice in a small saucepan and bring to a boil over high heat. Season with salt and pepper. Cover and decrease the heat to low. Simmer until the rice is just tender, 10 to 12 minutes. Cover and keep warm.

Heat the oil in a large, heavy-bottomed skillet over medium-high heat. Add the onion, chile, and celery. Sprinkle over the Creole seasoning. Cook until the vegetables start to color, stirring occasionally, 5 to 7 minutes. Add the chicken livers and cook, stirring frequently, until the liver turns brown, 6 to 8 minutes. Add the garlic and cook until fragrant, 45 to 60 seconds.

Add the reserved rice, chicken stock, and bay leaf. Stir to combine. Decrease the heat to medium-low and cook, stirring occasionally, until the rice is soft and tender, 10 to 15 minutes. Taste and adjust for seasoning with salt and pepper. Add the green onions and serve immediately.

Cajun and Creole

Two great cuisines, Cajun and Creole, make Louisiana their home. Creole cooking, a blend of French, Spanish, and African influences, is slightly more refined than Cajun. With a greater emphasis on French techniques and ingredients, in dishes such as Mama's Shrimp Creole (page 131), Creole cooking is well represented in New Orleans and the wealthier, more populated cities. The Cajun people were originally from France, but spent nearly 150 years in Canada in Arcadia (modern-day Nova Scotia). When the Arcadians—Cajuns—were exiled from Canada by the British, they migrated to remote bayous along the Louisiana coast and lived off the land. Their cooking style is more provincial and rustic; a classic Cajun dish is Louisiana Dirty Rice (see above).

MAMA'S RED BEANS AND RICE

Serves 6 to 8

This famous New Orleans dish was originally served on Mondays, utilizing the ham bone left over from Sunday supper. Very low maintenance, it simmered on the stove all day while the women washed the family's laundry and hung it out to dry. Although for the most part, Monday wash day is a thing of the past, red beans and rice is still often served as a lunch or dinner special at many New Orleans restaurants. Dishes of rice and beans are part of rustic country cooking in the Caribbean and all over the world. The inexpensive combination of rice and beans supplies essential amino acids not often found in plant proteins, and more readily found in expensive meat proteins.

For the ham bone, traditional recipes now often substitute spicy boudin, smoked sausage, or Cajun andouille. Boudin is a spicy pork sausage with onion, rice, and herbs. Cajun andouille is a highly seasoned smoked sausage made from pork, whereas French andouille is made from the stomach and intestines. The andouille of Guémené, France, is crafted so that the intestines are placed inside one another, giving it the appearance of concentric circles before it is dried and smoked. This is potent stuff. I am always willing to try anything once, including chilled slices of smoked pig's intestines. Let's just put it this way, I'd rather have a heaping bowl of Mama's Red Beans and Rice, and I'm not asking for seconds of French andouille any time soon.

1 pound dried red kidney beans, washed and picked over for stones

1 ham bone, or 2 pounds boudin, smoked sausage, or Cajun andouille, sliced 1 inch thick

1 onion, preferably Vidalia, chopped

2 cloves garlic, very finely chopped

6 cups water

Hot sauce, for seasoning

Coarse salt and freshly ground black pepper

Double recipe $20,000 Rice Pilaf (page 158), for accompaniment

Place the kidney beans in a large bowl and add water to cover. Soak overnight. Or place the beans in a large pot of water and bring to a boil over high heat. Once the beans come to a boil, remove from the heat and set aside for 1 hour. Before cooking, discard any floating beans and drain.

To prepare in a slow cooker, place the drained soaked beans, ham bone, onion, garlic, and the water in the insert of a slow cooker. Cook over low heat until the beans are tender, about 6 hours.

To prepare on the stovetop, combine the soaked beans, ham bone, onion, garlic, and water in a large, heavy-bottomed Dutch oven. Bring to a boil over medium-high heat, then decrease the heat to low. Simmer, covered, until the beans are tender, 4 to 5 hours. Season with hot sauce. Taste and adjust for seasoning with salt and pepper. Serve with rice pilaf.

Mama's Sweet Potato Soufflé

I prefer using fresh sweet potatoes over the canned variety. However, not everyone feels this way. Around the fall holidays, towering mountains of canned yams are constructed in grocery stores throughout the South. Truth is, the contents are not yams at all. What is often labeled and sold as yams are actually sweet potatoes. Botanically speaking, yams are tubers and a member of the lily family; sweet potatoes are the root of a member of the morning glory family. Yams originated in Africa, whereas sweet potatoes are New World plants. There are many varieties of both that differ in size, taste, shape, and color.

When I doubted Mama about the amount of butter and sugar in this dish for a mere four sweet potatoes, she laughed and said, "Y'all always like it this way." Feel free to reduce the amount of sugar and butter in the sweet potato base should your conscience (or waistline) see fit.

1 cup (2 sticks) unsalted butter, plus more for the baking dish, melted

4 sweet potatoes, scrubbed

1/2 cup granulated sugar

2 large eggs, lightly beaten

1/3 cup whole milk

1 teaspoon pure vanilla extract

Coarse salt and freshly ground black pepper

1 cup firmly packed light brown sugar

1 cup all-purpose flour

1 cup chopped pecans

Preheat the oven to 350°F. Brush an ovenproof casserole with some of the melted butter.

Place the sweet potatoes on a baking sheet and roast until very tender, about 1 hour. Cool to room temperature. Peel the potatoes, discarding the skins. Place the potatoes in a large bowl and mash until smooth.

To the sweet potatoes, add $1/2$ cup of the melted butter, the granulated sugar, eggs, milk, and vanilla. Stir to combine. Season with salt and pepper. Spoon the mixture into the prepared casserole. Set aside.

In a small bowl, combine the remaining $1/2$ cup of melted butter, light brown sugar, flour, and pecans. Stir until combined. Sprinkle over the reserved casserole.

Bake until bubbly and heated through, 25 to 30 minutes. Transfer to a rack to cool slightly before serving.

BOURBON SWEET POTATOES

Serves 4 to 6

Only a Southerner, inheritor of the infamous Southern sweet tooth, would add massive quantities of butter and sugar to a dish and still regard it as a vegetable. Add a shot of bourbon? No problem.

4 tablespoons (1/2 stick) unsalted butter, plus more for the baking dish

4 to 6 sweet potatoes, peeled and sliced about 1/2 inch thick

Coarse salt and freshly ground black pepper

1/2 cup firmly packed light brown sugar

1/2 cup bourbon

2 tablespoons sorghum, cane, or maple syrup

Preheat the oven to 350°F. Butter an ovenproof gratin or casserole dish. Arrange the sweet potato slices in the prepared dish and season with salt and pepper.

In a large saucepan, combine the sugar, 4 tablespoons butter, bourbon, and syrup and bring to a boil over medium-high heat. As soon as the sauce is boiling, pour it over the sweet potatoes. Bake the casserole, basting and turning the potatoes occasionally, until the sweet potatoes are soft and tender, 45 to 60 minutes. Taste and adjust for seasoning with salt and pepper.

CELERIAC PUREE

Serves 4 to 6

French-style potato purees are very finely processed, and often incorporate copious amounts of butter, so the resulting puree is silky smooth. In this recipe, the addition of celeriac to the potatoes creates another layer of flavor.

Traditionally, in classic French cooking, white sauces use white pepper instead of black, making the finished dish appear more refined. When we were children and would see pepper in a dish we would complain, often without tasting, that it was "too hot." Sneakily, Mama started using white pepper to pull the wool over our eyes.

2 pounds Yukon gold potatoes, peeled and sliced

1 large bulb celeriac (celery root), peeled and sliced (about 2 pounds)

2 cups milk

Coarse salt and freshly ground white pepper

4 tablespoons (1/2 stick) unsalted butter

In a saucepan, add the potatoes, celeriac, and milk, then fill the pot with enough cold water so the liquid covers the vegetables by about 2 inches. Bring to a boil over high heat; salt generously. Decrease the heat to low, and simmer until the potatoes and celeriac are tender when pierced with a knife, about 20 to 25 minutes.

Drain the vegetables in a colander, discarding the liquid, and return them to the saucepan over medium heat. Cook, stirring constantly, until a floury film forms on the bottom of the pan, 1 to 2 minutes.

Mash the vegetables in the saucepan until smooth with a ricer, food mill, or potato masher. Add the butter, stirring vigorously, until well combined. Taste and adjust for seasoning with salt and pepper. Serve immediately.

CORN SPOON BREAD

Spoon bread is more like custard than bread, and less like a casserole than a soufflé. As the name suggests, it's soft enough to eat with a spoon. Spoon bread is more common in Virginia, Maryland, and Kentucky. Berea, Kentucky, in the south central portion of the state, actually boasts a spoon bread festival.

The key to this recipe is using very fine cornmeal for a smooth, creamy texture. If you are unable to find fine meal in the supermarket, try Mexican or South American groceries. Also, adding a bit of fresh corn when in season really makes this spoon bread delicious. Some recipes call for baking powder for lift, but in this recipe, with a nod to my French training, I use beaten egg whites.

2 tablespoons unsalted butter, melted, plus more for the pan

2 cups whole milk

1 cup very fine yellow cornmeal

Coarse salt and freshly ground black pepper

Scraped kernels from 2 ears fresh sweet corn (about 1 cup) (see page 188)

2 tablespoons chopped fresh chives

2 large eggs, separated

Preheat the oven to 375°F. Butter an ovenproof casserole or round 2-quart soufflé mold.

To prepare the batter, in a medium saucepan, combine the milk and cornmeal over medium-high heat. Bring to a boil, whisking rapidly and constantly, until very, very thick, about 5 minutes. Season with salt and pepper.

Transfer the mixture to a large bowl. Add the corn kernels, chives, and the 2 tablespoons melted butter. Season with salt and pepper and stir to combine. Add the egg yolks, one at a time, stirring after each addition.

To beat the egg whites, in a separate bowl, using a handheld mixer, beat the egg whites with a pinch of salt on high speed until stiff peaks form. Gently fold the egg whites into the warm cornmeal mixture.

Transfer the lightened cornmeal mixture to the prepared pan; smooth the surface with a spatula. Bake until puffed and risen and the inside is firm, but moist, and the top is golden brown, 35 to 40 minutes. Serve immediately while puffed and risen.

Aunt Lee's Macaroni and Cheese

Serves 4 to 6

Many Northern macaroni-and-cheese recipes use a béchamel sauce to coat tender elbow noodles, but the only time most Southerners put flour in a skillet is to make gravy—certainly not for a white sauce for macaroni. Our recipes are often simple combinations of pasta, eggs, butter, milk, and cheese. My Aunt Lee often prepares this dish. When I asked her about her recipe, she replied, "I just mix it all up in the dish until it looks right." I had to coax a little more instruction out of her to share it with you here.

1 tablespoon unsalted butter

2 cups elbow macaroni

2 cups whole milk

2 large eggs, lightly beaten

8 ounces extra-sharp Cheddar cheese, cut into 1/4-inch cubes (about 2 cups)

Coarse salt and freshly ground black pepper

Preheat the oven to 350°F. Butter an ovenproof casserole dish.

Bring a large pot of salted water to a boil. Add the pasta and cook until tender (a little more than al dente), about 12 minutes. Drain well in a colander.

In a large bowl, combine the drained macaroni, milk, eggs, and cheese. Season with salt and pepper. Transfer to the prepared dish.

Bake until golden brown and bubbly, 25 to 30 minutes, or longer if you like a dark, chewy, cheesy topping. Transfer to a rack to cool slightly before serving.

Horseradish Mashed Potatoes

Serves 4 to 6

Rich, buttery potatoes are the perfect foil for pungent, spicy, freshly grated horseradish, a fiery cousin to kale, cauliflower, and Brussels sprouts. Although bottled horseradish will do in a pinch, there's nothing like the bite of the freshly grated root. For spectacular results, serve Pepper-crusted Beef with Cognac and Golden Raisins (page 93) or Braised Short Ribs (page 87) on a bed of this.

2 pounds Yukon gold potatoes, peeled and quartered

Coarse salt and freshly ground black pepper

1/2 cup heavy cream

1/2 cup milk

1/2 cup (1 stick) unsalted butter, cut into pieces

2 tablespoons grated fresh or well-drained bottled horseradish

In a large, heavy-bottomed saucepan, place the potatoes and cover with cold water. Season with salt, bring to a boil over high heat, then decrease the heat to low. Gently simmer until fork tender, about 25 minutes.

Meanwhile, in a second saucepan, combine the cream, milk, butter, and horseradish over low heat. Cook until the butter is melted; cover and keep warm.

Drain the potatoes in a colander and return them to the saucepan over medium heat. Cook, stirring constantly, until a floury film forms on the bottom of the pan, 1 to 2 minutes. Remove from the heat. Mash the potatoes in the saucepan until smooth with a ricer, food mill, or potato masher. Add the warm cream sauce, stirring vigorously until well combined. Taste and adjust for seasoning with salt and pepper. Serve immediately.

MIXED BUTTERMILK MASH

The key to a fluffy mash is to use the right tool: a ricer, a food mill, or an old-fashioned potato masher. A ricer resembles an overgrown garlic press. Cooked vegetables are placed in its hopper and forced through tiny holes with a plunger, producing a texture vaguely like that of rice. A food mill consists of a round metal bowl with a curved blade that turns with a hand crank. Secured to the bottom of the bowl are interchangeable disks with holes from fine to coarse. When you turn the crank, the blade mashes the cooked food through the holes. Both the ricer and the food mill produce exquisite mashes and purees with a smoother texture than the humble old-fashioned potato masher.

These simple tools are the precursors to the efficient food processor. However, they do a better job than a processor or electric mixer for any mixture that contains potatoes, as both food processor and mixer produce a gummy mass instead of a silken puree.

Meme had a ricer she used for years. Mama and I joke, "The Smithsonian called and wants their exhibit back." The truth is, sometimes older is better.

---

2 pounds Yukon gold potatoes, peeled and quartered

Coarse salt and freshly ground black pepper

$1/2$ head cauliflower, separated into florets

2 cloves garlic

1 carrot, chopped

$1/4$ cup buttermilk, plus more if needed

2 tablespoons unsalted butter

1 tablespoon chopped fresh flat-leaf parsley

In a large, heavy-bottomed saucepan, place the potatoes and cover with cold water. Season with salt and bring to a boil over high heat; add the cauliflower, garlic, and carrot. Decrease the heat to low. Simmer gently until the vegetables are fork tender, about 25 minutes.

Meanwhile, heat the buttermilk and butter in a small saucepan over low heat. Cook until the butter is melted; cover and keep warm.

Drain the vegetables in a colander, and return them to the saucepan over medium heat. Cook, stirring constantly, until a floury film forms on the bottom of the pan, 1 to 2 minutes. Remove from the heat.

Mash the vegetables in the saucepan until smooth with a ricer, food mill, or potato masher. Add the warm buttermilk mixture and the parsley, stirring vigorously until well combined. Taste and adjust for seasoning with salt and pepper. Serve immediately.

GRATIN DAUPHINOIS

Serves 6 to 8

At first glance, Anne Willan, the proper, Cambridge-educated grande dame of cuisine, would seem to have little in common with a Mafia don. Looks can be deceiving: those "in the know" are well aware of the "La Varenne Way." The La Varenne Way of recipe testing has evolved with Anne's experience of more than thirty-five years as a teacher, cookbook author, and food writer. As the director of École de Cuisine La Varenne, the cooking school that she founded in Burgundy in 1975, with the encouragement and support of the grand doyenne herself, Julia Child, Willan has shaped and influenced countless professional and amateur cooks all over the world, myself included. La Varenne alumni are called, tongue-in-cheek, the "La Varenne Mafia." No secret society, the list of capos reads like a Who's Who of the culinary world. The invaluable training I acquired in France working with Anne opened countless doors and a world of possibilities. Anne is one of the hardest-working individuals I know, and her drive for perfection has long been an inspiration.

This rich gratin, typical of simple country French cooking, was inspired by a version I learned while at La Varenne.

4 slices thick-cut bacon, cut into lardons (see page 179)

1½ to 2 pounds russet potatoes

1 tablespoon chopped fresh thyme

1 clove garlic, finely chopped

Coarse salt and freshly ground black pepper

1½ cups whole milk, plus more if needed

1 cup heavy cream, plus more if needed

Pinch of freshly grated nutmeg

½ cup grated Gruyère cheese (about 2 ounces)

Preheat the oven to 350°F. Line a plate with paper towels. Line a baking sheet with a silicone baking sheet, parchment paper, or aluminum foil to protect the baking sheet from spills and make for easy cleanup.

Heat a skillet over medium heat and cook the bacon until brown and crispy, 5 to 7 minutes. Remove the bacon to the prepared plate, reserving the rendered fat. Brush an ovenproof gratin dish with some of the rendered bacon fat. Save the remaining fat for another use or discard.

Peel the potatoes and, preferably using a mandoline, slice them 1/8 inch thick. Or, using a chef's knife, carefully slice the potatoes thinly and evenly.

Arrange the potatoes in the dish in overlapping layers, seasoning with the reserved bacon, thyme, garlic, and salt and pepper as you go. Place the gratin on the prepared baking sheet. Combine the milk, heavy cream, and nutmeg in a medium heavy-bottomed pot. Bring to a gentle simmer over medium heat. Pour over the gratin. Sprinkle the cheese over the top.

Bake until the potatoes are tender and deep golden brown, and the edges are bubbling, about 1 hour. (If the gratin starts to brown too deeply, cover with aluminum foil.) Let cool slightly, about 10 minutes, before serving.

YUKON GOLD AND EDAMAME MASH

Serves 4 to 6

Edamame is the Japanese word for soybean. Soybeans are somewhat mild in flavor, a cross between a pea and a fava bean. We're lucky enough to sometimes find them fresh during the summer months, at the farmer's market or a specialty store, but they are widely available frozen, both in the pod and shelled. Adults and children alike love edamame as a snack. Once the soybeans are cooked or reheated, drain them well, and season with coarse salt or sea salt. Squeeze the seeds directly from the pods into your mouth. Think highbrow boiled peanuts. Edamame may be eaten as a snack or a vegetable, and used in soups or stir-fries. I also like to mash them with potatoes, as in this recipe.

1½ pounds Yukon gold potatoes, quartered

Coarse salt and freshly ground black pepper

2 cups shelled edamame beans, thawed if frozen

¼ cup whole milk or buttermilk

3 tablespoons unsalted butter

2 tablespoons chopped fresh chives

In a saucepan, add the potatoes and enough cold water to cover, and bring to a boil over medium-high heat. Season with salt, decrease the heat to medium-low, and simmer until tender, about 20 minutes. Add the edamame and cook until tender, about 5 minutes. Drain well in a colander.

Meanwhile, heat the milk and butter in a small saucepan over low heat. Cook until the butter is melted, then cover and keep warm.

Return the drained vegetables to their saucepan and cook, stirring constantly, over medium heat until a floury film forms on the bottom of the pan, 1 to 2 minutes.

Mash the vegetables in the saucepan until smooth with a ricer, food mill, or potato masher. Add the warm milk mixture and the chives, stirring vigorously until well combined. Taste and adjust for seasoning with salt and pepper. Serve immediately.

BAKER'S POTATOES

Serves 4 to 6

Years ago in France, many homes did not have an oven, so if anything was to be baked, it was taken to the local baker (*boulanger*) to cook in his oven. This recipe, known in France as *pommes boulangère*, is a healthy departure from classic potato recipes that use lots of butter and cream. It really shines with freshly harvested potatoes, when they are at their finest. Serve it with Herb Roast Chicken (page 110) for a warming winter meal.

2 tablespoons olive oil, plus more for the dish

1 onion, preferably Vidalia, very thinly sliced

2 pounds Yukon gold potatoes, peeled

2 cloves garlic, finely chopped

1 tablespoon chopped fresh thyme

Coarse salt and freshly ground black pepper

2 1/2 cups chicken stock (page 227) or low-fat, reduced-sodium chicken broth

Preheat the oven to 350°F. Brush an ovenproof gratin dish with oil. Scatter the onions on the bottom of the dish.

Using a sharp knife, thinly slice each potato, stopping each cut 1/4 inch from the bottom, so the potato is sliced, but still intact.

Place the potatoes in the prepared gratin. Drizzle the 2 tablespoons oil over the potatoes and onions. Sprinkle with the garlic and thyme. Season with salt and pepper.

Pour the stock over the potatoes and bake, basting occasionally, until most of the liquid is absorbed and the potatoes are tender when pierced with the point of a knife, about 45 minutes. Taste and adjust the seasoning with salt and pepper. Serve immediately.

BAY ROASTED POTATOES

Serves 4 to 6

The bay tree at La Varenne is a monster, more than twenty feet tall. There's a niche or cubbyhole on one side, the side that everyone approaches to cut fresh leaves for classes. I implore my students to discard the jars of brown, tasteless dried bay leaves in their pantries: even a semi-fresh bay leaf several weeks old from the fridge will have more flavor.

8 medium red-skinned or Yukon gold potatoes

16 to 20 bay leaves, preferably fresh

1/2 cup olive oil

Coarse salt and freshly ground black pepper

Sea salt, for finishing

Preheat the oven to 350°F. Using a sharp knife, thinly slice each potato, stopping each cut 1/4 inch from the bottom, so the potato is sliced, but still intact. Insert 1 to 2 bay leaves into each potato.

Place the potatoes in a large roasting pan. Drizzle over the oil and toss the potatoes to coat. Season the potatoes with coarse salt and pepper.

Roast the potatoes until tender when pierced with the point of a knife, about 1 hour. Season with sea salt and additional freshly ground black pepper. Serve hot.

CHAPTER 8

VEGETABLES

MY GRANDPARENTS ALWAYS HAD a garden, and I remember shelling peas and shucking corn on hot summer evenings (there is simply nothing better on this earth than fresh sweet corn). Of course, they grew vegetables for "putting up"—canning and freezing. Meme cooked her vegetables with bacon grease or fatback. Although Mama now uses olive or canola oil, she still likes her green beans well cooked and often suggests mine need to "sweat a little more."

With its fertile soils and hot climate, the South is a nearly year-round cornucopia of gorgeous produce—this has always been a land people could live off of. All across the region from spring to late fall, produce stands pop up in the corners of shopping center parking lots, at intersections of various main roads, and at the roadside in the country.

The South is also full of diners and restaurants offering a "meat and three," or Blue Plate Special, meaning a choice of meat and three sides, often served with a biscuit or cornbread. When the produce is really good, many people think it is best to leave off the meat and have a vegetable plate.

In recent years, there has been an increased interest in fresh and locally grown produce. We are going back to the foods of our ancestors. Farmer's markets are now appearing all over the South, and stores are listening to customers' requests to eat seasonally and buy locally.

The French emphasis on fresh and seasonal has never flagged, so it requires no renaissance. Shopping daily, or every other day or so, is still very much the rule in France, especially for produce. There's no backing the SUV up to the warehouse store and buying enough for the bunker. When selling fruit to a customer, a good French shop clerk will ask whether it is for today or tomorrow. And the folks who sell the cheese will go so far as to ask whether the cheese is for lunch or dinner. The food is so alive, such a part of every last shopping decision.

There are three main types of markets in France. The *marchés découverts*, or open-air markets, are sometimes referred to as *marchés volants* (roving markets). The old-fashioned *marchés couverts*, or covered markets, are usually in the town center and are open once or twice a week. Both types of market are packed up by lunchtime, so it's essential to visit them in the morning. Even the smallest markets carry a good selection of fresh vegetables and fruits, local cheeses, fresh meat and seafood, paté and *saucisson*, breads and pastries, and homemade preserves, honey, and nuts.

At these markets elderly women, as wrinkled as dried apples, sell heads of fresh lettuce and radishes; plump, red-faced butchers call out to passersby, enticing them to take a look at their offerings; and men with an ever present Gaulois cigarette between their lips insist they have the best price on wild mushrooms. The markets are the heart and soul of the town, and are amazing places to people-watch. When I lived and worked in Burgundy, I bought fresh vegetables, fruit, cheese, and meat several times a week at the *marchés couverts* in Joigny and the larger one in Sens, in the shadow of the town's grand cathedral. These markets are absolutely picture perfect, veritable postcards of rural France.

The French also have *hypermarchés*, grandiose mothership stores such as Carrefour and Intermarché, which seem very American, but have a gourmet French twist, with cafeteria-size cans of *confit de canard* and blocks of truffled foie gras. Fresh vegetables are often sold prepackaged in the hypermarchés, which is decidedly un-French. These hulking stores, made of metal siding and plastic, are always on the outskirts of town near the *zone industrielle*, as if shunned by the centuries-old shops in town.

Although the big box stores carry organic produce and various products labeled *biologique*, organic produce is not as prominent in France. It may not even be labeled as such at the markets, chiefly because produce has always been raised there without the extensive use of chemicals.

Dede didn't use pesticides in his garden, not that he planned organic produce; he just farmed the old-fashioned way: he planted by the *Farmer's Almanac* and used techniques like planting marigolds near his tomatoes to keep away the insects.

The hot topic with produce right now across the United States is whether to buy organic, regardless of where it comes from, or non-organic, but locally grown. Organic produce grown in California and shipped to Georgia doesn't seem to be very environmentally responsible. Organic used to mean small, often family, farms, but now some organic farming is industrialized. Becoming organically certified is time-consuming and expensive. Many small farmers don't have the time, energy, or resources to do so. It's also difficult for these small farmers to enter the distribution systems of the larger grocery stores. Whole Foods, for example, makes a major commitment to support local growers, but sometimes there's just not enough produce available to enter the system.

For the most part, I think that local is better. I feel a real joy in knowing where my food comes from, and I think it's important to support my local economy as well as my friends and neighbors. However, I live in a state with a ten-month growing season. Not everyone does. Supporting organic farming sends a message to agribusiness that consumers do not want unbridled chemical usage. Buying the occasional bag of imported organic carrots from across the country is a reasonable compromise. The bottom line is that fresh tastes best.

MEME'S CREAMED CORN

Serves 4 to 6

Meme always had a tin of bacon drippings adjacent to the stovetop, a sight less and less common in Southern kitchens. It varies from brand to brand, but it takes four to six slices of bacon to produce about two tablespoons of grease. The salty, smoky taste of the bacon complements the sweetness of the corn, which, in a fit of glorious, wretched excess, is finished with a hefty hand of butter.

1 tablespoon bacon fat or canola oil

Scraped kernels from 6 ears fresh sweet corn (about 3 cups) (see page 188)

Coarse salt and freshly ground black pepper

4 tablespoons (1/2 stick) unsalted butter

In a large skillet, heat the bacon fat over medium heat until sizzling. Add the corn and season with salt and pepper. Cook until tender, about 15 minutes. Add the butter and stir to combine. Taste and adjust for seasoning with salt and pepper. Serve immediately.

MEME'S BRAISED CABBAGE

Serves 4 to 6

This is another example of simple country cooking that would be equally at home cooked in a cast-iron skillet in the South or simmered in a *cocotte* on *grandmère's* stovetop in France. Cabbage is an inexpensive vegetable, and if stored properly, will keep for weeks in the refrigerator. Once again, bacon drippings was Meme's fat of choice, but you can substitute butter. Other oils do not give the dish the richness it needs. (Before you make any comments about Meme's arteries, she lived to be ninety-two!)

Try this dish with Meme's Fried Fatback (page 84) and her Cornmeal Griddle Cakes (page 216). You will be glad you did.

2 tablespoons bacon fat or unsalted butter

1 medium head green cabbage, cored and thinly sliced (about 8 cups)

1/2 cup chicken stock (page 227) or low-fat, reduced-sodium chicken broth

1 sprig of thyme

Coarse salt and freshly ground black pepper

In a large skillet, heat the bacon fat over medium-high heat until sizzling. Add the cabbage and saute until the cabbage starts to wilt, 3 to 5 minutes. Add the chicken stock and thyme. Season with salt and pepper.

Decrease the heat to medium, and simmer until the cabbage is meltingly tender, 15 to 20 minutes. Remove the sprig of thyme and taste and adjust for seasoning with salt and pepper. Serve immediately.

A classic meat and three: Meme's Fried Okra (page 181), Tangle of Bitter Greens (page 198), Meme's Creamed Corn (this page), and Meme's Fried Chicken (page 106)

Meme's Fried Green Tomatoes

Every week or so, it seems that the movie *Fried Green Tomatoes* airs on one of the myriad cable television stations. I watch it every time. It's a sweet story, and unlike most "Southern movies," the accents are not too bad. One of my favorite scenes is when the Kathy Bates character, Evelyn Couch, takes a plate of fried green tomatoes to Ninny Threadgoode, played by the incomparable Jessica Tandy, for her birthday. I like the way she thinks!

Don't make the mistake of coating too many tomatoes at a time. The coating won't stick and the tomatoes will become soggy. Set up a workstation with the eggs and dry ingredients leading to the skillet of oil. Your tomatoes will taste better and it will help with cleanup.

2 large eggs, lightly beaten

Coarse salt and freshly ground black pepper

3/4 cup fine white or yellow cornmeal or a combination of both

3/4 cup all-purpose flour

1 cup peanut or canola oil

4 to 6 medium firm green tomatoes, cored and sliced 1/4 inch thick

Break the eggs into a shallow bowl and season with salt and pepper. Combine the cornmeal and flour in a second shallow bowl and season with salt and pepper.

Line a plate with paper towels and set near the cooktop.

Heat the oil in a large skillet over medium heat. Working a few at a time, season the tomato slices lightly on both sides with salt and pepper. Dip the tomato slices into the egg mixture and shake off the excess. Place the dipped slices in the cornmeal mixture, sprinkle breading over, and press to adhere. Turn over and repeat to coat on both sides. Gently shake off the excess and place without crowding in the heated skillet.

Fry the tomato slices until they are golden on one side, about 3 minutes, then gently turn them with an offset spatula or metal turner and continue cooking until golden on the other side. Remove them to the prepared plate. Season with salt and pepper and serve immediately.

Dinner

Not so long ago, dinner was served at noon all across the South. Midday dinner seems confined to Sundays now, but within the past generation, it was the main meal of the day. This was not a soup-and-salad combination or a sandwich with a bag of chips. Dinner was a full meal of meat, vegetables, and cornbread or biscuits. The women did the cooking in the cool morning before the day became too hot, and dinner was served when farmers needed to escape the hot sun.

MEME'S OLD-FASHIONED BUTTER BEANS

Serves 4 to 6

Butter beans are my favorite summer vegetable. Slowly simmered with a bit of fat for flavor, they produce a rich, soothing broth. We would often have them freshly shelled in the summer as part of the large Sunday dinner. Meme would serve a simple slice of white bread or leftover biscuits bathed in the salty broth for a light supper.

There is a raging controversy over whether butter beans are the same as lima beans. The University of Georgia Cooperative Extension states that lima beans and butter beans are interchangeable terms, and there is little difference in the varieties. I hate to besmirch the name of my alma mater, and the gardeners may think they have it all sorted out, but you can't tell me—or many Southern cooks—that flat, tender, petite, green butter beans are the same as the larger, yellow, starchy lima pods. The difference is that some butter bean varieties are grown to harvest when young and immature and some are grown to harvest when older and more mature for drying.

More often than not, I enjoy butter beans as pure, simple, and unadulterated by other flavors as possible, using canola oil and possibly finishing with just a pat of butter. If I am feeling particularly racy, I will add several tablespoons or so of freshly chopped herbs such as basil, parsley, or lemon balm.

6 cups water, plus more if needed

2 slices thick-cut bacon, cut into lardons (see below); 1 ounce fatback; or 2 tablespoons canola oil

4 cups freshly shelled butter beans (about 3 pounds unshelled) or frozen butter beans, not thawed

Coarse salt and freshly ground black pepper

1 tablespoon unsalted butter (optional)

Bring the water and bacon to a boil in a saucepan over high heat. Add the butter beans and season with salt and pepper. Decrease the heat to low and simmer until the beans are tender, 30 to 45 minutes, less for frozen beans. Add the butter and taste and adjust for seasoning with salt and pepper. Spoon into shallow bowls with a little of the rich broth and serve immediately.

Bacon Lardons

Fat is the reason bacon tastes so good—it has long veins of fat running parallel to the rind—and fat is also the problem. Along with the salt and carcinogenic smoke from the cure, it is enough to make the folks at the American Heart Association have, well, a heart attack. For those occasions when you do go "whole hog," make sure you are getting your money's worth. Buy premium quality bacon with a good balance of meat, salt, and smoke. A matchstick-size piece of bacon is called a

lardon, though strictly speaking, a lardon is a long strip of fat sewn into lean meat, with a larding needle (*lardoire*), to keep the meat moist and flavorful during cooking.

OKRA AND TOMATOES

Serves 4 to 6

People love okra, or they hate it. Those who hate it think it is slimy. There are a couple of techniques that prevent okra from becoming too slimy. First and foremost, don't overcook it. When okra is cooked to just tender, it is fresh and crisp, not "ropy." The other technique is to cook okra with an acid. This recipe uses both tomato and a bit of red wine.

3 tablespoons canola oil

1 onion, preferably Vidalia, chopped

2 cloves garlic, finely chopped

1/2 cup dry red wine

1 1/2 pounds okra, stems trimmed, cut into 1/2-inch pieces

4 large tomatoes, cored, seeded, and chopped

3 sprigs of thyme

2 bay leaves, preferably fresh

Coarse salt and freshly ground black pepper

In a saute pan, heat the oil over medium heat. Add the onion and cook, stirring, until soft and translucent, about 5 minutes. Add the garlic and cook until fragrant, 45 to 60 seconds. Add the red wine, and cook until reduced by half, 3 to 5 minutes. Add the okra, tomatoes, thyme, and bay leaves. Season with salt and pepper. Cover, decrease the heat to low, and simmer, stirring occasionally, until the vegetables are just tender, about 15 minutes. Taste and adjust for seasoning with salt and pepper. Serve immediately.

SARA'S CORNMEAL-CRUSTED OKRA

Serves 4 to 6

My mother-in-law is a wonderful woman, very sweet, kind, and generous. Her late husband was the cook in the family, and even she admits she is not much of a cook. She experienced a little culinary serendipity when sauteing okra one night. She put a little too much oil in the pan, so she added a bit of cornmeal to soak up the excess oil. It was wonderful, a modified version of fried okra that is not only somewhat healthier than deep-fried okra, but also less labor-intensive. Maybe she is just bluffing about not being a cook, after all.

6 tablespoons olive oil

2 pounds okra, sliced into 1/2-inch pieces, stems trimmed

Coarse salt and freshly ground black pepper

1/3 cup fine yellow cornmeal

In a large skillet, preferably nonstick, heat 3 tablespoons of the oil over medium-high heat. Add the okra and stir to coat. Cover and cook until bright green, 12 to 15 minutes. Season with salt and pepper. Add the cornmeal and stir to coat. Drizzle over the remaining 3 tablespoons of oil and continue cooking, stirring occasionally, until the okra is tender, browned, and crispy, about 15 minutes. Taste and adjust for seasoning with salt and pepper. Serve immediately.

MEME'S FRIED OKRA

Serves 4 to 6

Dede always grew okra, and I usually have a few plants every summer. Once, I grew them in container boxes on the roof of my apartment in New Jersey, framed by the Manhattan skyline. Guests were astonished at the sight when we would go out on the deck. The plants are beautiful, sometimes growing to five feet tall with pale yellow blossoms similar to hibiscus. When I was working in France for Anne Willan, we once needed okra for a recipe test. It was nowhere to be found in the local markets, so we ordered a case from Rungis, the French wholesale market on the outskirts of Paris, only to use less than a pound! The gumbo was a disappointment, falling short of Anne's strict standards. Since we had almost a full case to use, I made this fried okra, which Anne called "popcorn fried okra." It was a huge hit. I can pretty much guarantee that this was the only time in history fried okra was enjoyed as a snack with apéritifs before dinner. I called Meme every week to tell her about my work and what I had learned. When I told her about the "popcorn fried okra," she giggled like a schoolgirl.

1 pound okra, stems trimmed, cut into 1/2-inch pieces

1 cup buttermilk

1 cup white or yellow cornmeal

1 cup all-purpose flour

3 cups peanut or canola oil, plus more if needed

Coarse salt and freshly ground black pepper

Line a plate with paper towels and set by the cooktop. Combine the okra and buttermilk in a bowl. Combine the cornmeal and flour in a second bowl. Using a slotted spoon, remove the okra from the liquid, letting the excess buttermilk run back into the bowl. Place the okra in the flour mixture and toss to coat.

Heat the oil in a large cast-iron skillet over medium-high heat until it reaches 350°F on deep-fat thermometer. (You can also test the heat by sprinkling a bit of flour into the hot oil to see whether it bubbles.) When the oil is hot, add a large spoonful of okra to the skillet. (Don't add too much at once or the oil will cool down and the okra won't cook properly.)

Cook until brown and crisp, 3 to 5 minutes. Using a slotted spoon, transfer the cooked okra to the prepared plate. Repeat with the remaining okra. Season with salt and pepper. Serve immediately.

Deep Frying

Frying can be messy, but not if you are prepared. Set up a frying center in the kitchen (chefs call it a station) that lets you easily move from marinating the fish to the dry ingredients to the hot oil. Line a plate or baking sheet with paper towels and place it by the pot to receive the fried fish, a clean and efficient system. Only dredge what you can fry at a time: don't coat all the fish and then start frying; the coating will become dense and gummy.

MAMA'S BAKED PECAN AND ACORN SQUASH

Serves 4 to 6

Pecans—all nuts—will go rancid if not stored properly. To stay fresh, pecans should be refrigerated or frozen in an airtight container; they will keep for up to two years without loss of flavor or texture. In the fall, when pecans are in season, buy enough for the year and freeze them. You'll taste the difference.

The flavor of this dish takes me back to childhood. I loved so much when Mama made this dish of tender acorn squash with their centers filled with melted butter and sugar. You can keep the pumpkin pie. Instead, serve me a helping of this dish!

2 or 3 medium acorn squash, halved crosswise and seeded

3 tablespoons unsalted butter, melted

Coarse salt and freshly ground black pepper

2/3 cup pecan halves, chopped

2 tablespoons sorghum, cane, or maple syrup, plus more for drizzling

1 teaspoon chopped fresh thyme

Preheat the oven to 375°F. Brush the inside of the squash halves with butter and season with salt and pepper. Turn them upside down on a baking sheet and bake until just tender when pierced with the point of a knife, 30 to 45 minutes.

Combine the pecans, syrup, and thyme in a small bowl. Turn the squash upright on the baking sheet. Place an equal amount of the pecan mixture in the cavities of the halved squash. Return to the oven and bake until the squash are very tender and the syrup is bubbly, an additional 10 to 15 minutes. Serve immediately.

Southern Syrups

Sorghum is a cane-like grass related to millet. When crushed, the juice is boiled down to produce sorghum syrup or sorghum. The grain is now widely used as an animal crop in the United States, but it is very nutritious and is the world's third-largest food grain. Sorghum is rich with iron, calcium, and potassium. Cane syrup is the boiled-down juice from sugar cane, similar to the way maple syrup is boiled down to make maple syrup. Cane syrup is thicker than sorghum syrup, with more viscosity, and tends to have a fuller, sweeter taste. It is delicious. Molasses is a by-product of sugar refining. There are three grades: light, dark, and blackstrap. Blackstrap, from the Dutch word *stroop*, meaning syrup, is very dark in color and slightly bitter in flavor as a result of repeated boiling. Molasses is available as unsulphured, made from the concentrated juice of sun-ripened cane, and sulphured, made from cane that is harvested when slightly green—the latter is generally considered less desirable. This syrup is best used as an ingredient, since it can be overwhelming on foods when raw.

BUTTERNUT SQUASH PUREE

Serves 4 to 6

Sweet, nutty butternut squash is one of fall's most delicious vegetables. It is wonderful roasted, in a soup, or as a creamy puree. A touch of brown sugar brings out its natural sweetness. For a great change of pace, try this as a side dish instead of mashed potatoes.

1 tablespoon unsalted butter

1 shallot, finely chopped

3 pounds butternut squash, peeled, seeded, and cut into 1/2-inch cubes (see below)

1 teaspoon firmly packed dark brown sugar

Pinch of freshly grated nutmeg

3 cups chicken stock (page 227) or low-fat, reduced-sodium chicken broth

Coarse salt and freshly ground black pepper

2 tablespoons heavy cream (optional)

4 fresh sage leaves, chopped, for garnish

To cook the squash, in a large saucepan, melt the butter over medium-low heat until foamy. Add the shallot and cook until translucent, about 3 minutes.

Add the squash cubes, brown sugar, and nutmeg. Add enough chicken stock to not quite cover the squash, and season with salt and pepper. (Reserve any remaining stock for another use.) Bring to a boil over high heat, then decrease the heat to low. Simmer until the squash is tender, about 30 minutes.

To make the puree, using a slotted spoon, transfer the squash mixture to the work bowl of a food processor fitted with the metal blade. Process until a smooth puree. If the mixture is too thick, add some of the cooking liquid, if necessary. If too thin, transfer to a clean saucepan and cook over low heat to evaporate some of the moisture, then proceed with the recipe. Add the heavy cream; taste and adjust for seasoning with salt and pepper. Garnish with the sage leaves and serve immediately.

Cutting Up Butternut Squash

The large bell-shaped squash may seem a bit daunting to chop at first, but it's actually one of the easiest squash to handle. Using a large chef's knife, slice a bit off the ends to create flat surfaces. Halve the squash crosswise between its narrow and bulbous ends. Stand the slender, solid neck piece on one flat end and remove the tough outer peel by slicing from top to bottom with a chef's knife. Use a vegetable peeler to pare off the skin from the round section. Halve this section and remove the seeds from the cavities with a metal spoon and discard. Cut the squash into uniform 1/2-inch cubes.

BUTTERY BRAISED ENDIVE

Serves 4 to 6

Endive is a slightly bitter lettuce, but bitter isn't necessarily bad; just consider it a vegetable for grown-ups. Our palate senses sour, salty, bitter, sweet, and umami (for more on umami, see page 239). When these flavors come together in balance, we perceive a dish to be delicious. Most Americans think of lettuce as a vegetable to be eaten raw. Europeans, however, prepare lettuce soups, as well as sauteed and braised lettuce. Step out of the box (or the salad bowl) and give this French version a try.

2 tablespoons unsalted butter, plus more for the baking dish and parchment

4 to 6 Belgian endives, root ends intact, halved lengthwise

Juice of 1 lemon

1 teaspoon sugar

1/2 cup chicken stock (page 227) or low-fat, reduced-sodium chicken broth

Coarse salt and freshly ground black pepper

1/2 cup finely grated Gruyère cheese (about 2 ounces)

1 cup fresh or panko (Japanese) breadcrumbs

Butter a shallow baking dish just large enough to hold the endive in a single layer. Cut a round of parchment paper the same diameter as a large skillet: fold a rectangular sheet of parchment paper in half lengthwise. Fold the paper in half, widthwise, so that it is in quarters. Then fold the paper again three more times, creating a slender triangle. Align the tip of the triangle with the center of the skillet. Cut off the back of the paper triangle where it meets the rim of the skillet and discard. Butter one side of the parchment round.

To cook the endive, place the halves, cut sides down, in the large skillet. Add the lemon juice, 2 tablespoons butter, sugar, and chicken stock. Season with salt and pepper. Bring to a boil over high heat, then decrease the heat to low. Cover with the buttered parchment round, gently tucking and pressing it around the ingredients. Cover the pan with a tight-fitting lid. Simmer until tender when pierced with the point of a knife, 20 to 25 minutes.

For the topping, preheat the broiler. Using a slotted spoon, transfer the cooked endive, cut sides down, to the prepared baking dish. Combine the cheese and breadcrumbs in a small bowl. Sprinkle the mixture evenly over the endive, and broil about 4 inches from the heat until golden and the cheese is melted, about 3 minutes. Serve immediately.

SPICY OKRA AND TOMATOES

San Marzano tomatoes are grown in the shadow of Mount Vesuvius, southeast of Naples. The highly fertile volcanic soil of the San Marzano Valley, coupled with lots of sunshine and a benevolent Mediterranean climate, adds up to tomato heaven. The San Marzano tomato is a long, thin, plum-shaped variety known for its low acidity and earthy, intense tomato flavor.

Except during summer, when fresh tomatoes are at their best, a good canned variety is a better choice. Canned San Marzano tomatoes are one of the few canned products that chefs otherwise fixated on local, fresh produce will use.

1/4 cup canola oil

1 pound small to medium okra, whole if small, or cut into 1/2-inch pieces, stems trimmed

1 onion, preferably Vidalia, chopped

2 cloves garlic, very finely chopped

1 tablespoon finely chopped fresh ginger

2 teaspoons ground cumin

2 teaspoons ground coriander

1/4 teaspoon cayenne pepper

1/4 teaspoon ground turmeric

1 (28-ounce) can tomatoes (preferably San Marzano), chopped, with juices

Coarse salt and freshly ground black pepper

2 tablespoons chopped fresh cilantro, for garnish

Line a plate with paper towels. In a large skillet, heat the oil over medium-high heat. Add the okra and cook until lightly browned, about 4 minutes. Transfer with a slotted spoon to the prepared plate. Set aside.

Add the onion to the residual oil in the skillet and cook, stirring occasionally, until golden, about 10 minutes. Add the garlic and ginger and cook until fragrant, 45 to 60 seconds. Add the cumin, coriander, cayenne, and turmeric and stir to combine. Add the tomatoes with juices, and stir to combine.

Cook until slightly thickened, about 5 minutes. Add the reserved okra and stir to combine. Decrease the heat to medium-low and cook until the okra is tender, about 10 minutes. Taste and adjust for seasoning with salt and pepper. Garnish with cilantro and serve immediately.

GREEN BEANS WITH TOMATOES

Serves 4 to 6

I think Dede, who loved green beans, would have choked if I had suggested serving them with olives and feta cheese. He was more inclined to enjoy beans simmered until very soft and laced with transparent bits of fatback, swimming in a deliciously salty broth. More often than not, before cooking, green beans only need their tough, unsightly stems removed. I guess we are getting lazy about everything, including green beans. I like to leave them whole, curly "tail" attached, instead of snapping them.

1½ pounds fresh green beans, trimmed

2 tablespoons olive oil

2 cloves garlic, very finely chopped

½ cup kalamata or other brine-cured black olives, pitted and halved

2 tomatoes, cored, seeded, and chopped

1 tablespoon fresh chopped oregano

4 ounces crumbled sheep's milk feta cheese

Coarse salt and freshly ground black pepper

Make an ice-water bath by filling a large bowl with ice and water. Line a plate with paper towels.

To cook the beans, bring a large pot of salted water to a rolling boil over high heat. Add the beans and cook until crisp-tender, about 3 minutes. Drain well in a colander, then set the colander with beans in the ice-water bath (to set the color and stop the cooking), making sure the beans are submerged. Once chilled, remove the beans to the prepared plate.

In the same pot, heat the oil over medium heat. Add the garlic and cook until fragrant, 45 to 60 seconds. Add the cooked green beans, olives, tomatoes, oregano, and feta, and toss to coat. Cook until just heated through, 2 to 4 minutes. Taste and adjust for seasoning with salt and pepper. Serve hot, warm, or cold.

Olive Oil

Olive oil gets its flavor from the growing environment of the olive tree—the soil and the climate. In general, extra-virgin olive oils from Spain, France, northern Italy, Sicily, and Crete are milder than oils from Greece and central Italy. California has several hundred olive-oil producers and more than a hundred olive varietals, so its extra-virgin olive oil ranges in taste from sweet and mild to peppery and aggressive. Extra-virgin is the highest-quality olive oil. It is cold pressed, using pressure only, with no heat or chemicals. It's fairly unrefined and has a moderately low smoke point; it is best used for dipping, drizzling, and dressings. Olive oil, often labeled "pure olive oil," has been more refined and has a higher smoke point. Olive oil is appropriate for cooking when its flavor complements the dish.

FRESH SUMMER VEGETABLE SUCCOTASH WITH BASIL

Serves 6 to 8

This recipe is a multi-pot process, not my usual modus operandi of simply executed recipes involving as few dishes as possible. (I like to cook, not do dishes.) It's also a bit larger than many of my vegetable dishes—it makes for delicious leftovers.

Succotash has many versions, but all contain corn and beans. If butter beans are not available, I often substitute shelled edamame or black-eyed peas. Small farm stands, local and state farmer's markets, and even the Whole Foods in my area usually carry shelled peas and butter beans in the summer. They are both doubly precious—extremely delicious and fairly expensive, the result of the luxury of not having to shell your own.

2 cups shelled fresh butter beans (about 1½ pounds unshelled) or frozen butter beans

Coarse salt and freshly ground black pepper

½ pound small Yukon gold potatoes, halved

2 tablespoons canola oil

2 tablespoons unsalted butter

1 onion, preferably Vidalia, chopped

Scraped kernels from 4 ears fresh sweet corn (about 2 cups) (see sidebar)

1 small yellow squash, chopped

1 small zucchini, chopped

1 cup grape, cherry, or teardrop tomatoes, halved

¼ cup chopped fresh basil

To cook the beans, place them in a pot and cover with cold water. Bring to a boil over high heat and season the water with salt and pepper; decrease the heat to low. Simmer until tender, about 30 minutes for fresh beans, less for frozen. Drain well and set aside.

To cook the potatoes, place them in a second saucepan and cover by 1 inch with cold water; season with salt. Bring to a boil over high heat, then decrease the heat to low and simmer until the potatoes are just tender, about 20 minutes. Drain in a colander and set aside.

In a large, heavy-bottomed skillet, heat 1 tablespoon of the oil and 1 tablespoon of the butter over high heat until the foam subsides. Add the drained potatoes and season with salt and pepper. Cook the potatoes, stirring infrequently, until nicely crusted, 8 to 10 minutes. Transfer to a serving bowl.

In the same skillet, heat the remaining 1 tablespoon each oil and butter over medium-high heat; add the onion, corn, squash, and zucchini and cook, stirring, until crisp-tender, about 5 minutes. Stir in the reserved butter beans and cook, stirring, until heated through. Add to the potatoes along with the tomatoes and fresh basil, stirring to combine. Taste and adjust for seasoning with salt and pepper. Serve hot, warm, or cold.

Cutting Corn off the Cob

There are gadgets to cut the corn kernels off the cob, but a sharp knife will do the job well. Most people stand the corn vertical to a cutting board and the kernels go everywhere. Instead, set the ear of corn on its side and, using a chef's knife, slice away the kernels on four "sides," squaring off the round ear. The kernels will fall away, but not  having far to go, will not scatter. Then, stand the ear on one end and cut away the "corners" of the cob. Finally, scrape the milky remainder into a bowl with the back of the knife.

Green Beans Provençal

Serves 4 to 6

My grandparents had a garden each summer and fall. To keep the soil rich and fertile, Dede would alternate between the fields in front of the house and behind it and the property down at the river. He planted by the moon and used time-honored wisdom as his guide. Meme would drive the tractor and Dede would follow behind with the plow. Dede loved green beans and would plant rows and rows. When he passed away, Mama tucked a handful in his suit pocket as he lay in his coffin so he wouldn't miss them.

These green beans are fresh and flavorful—a favorite Southern vegetable made with a classic French technique. This dish is excellent served hot, at room temperature, or chilled. If making it ahead, do not add the vinegar until the last moment or it will cause the beans to look mottled and green like hunter's camouflage.

1½ pounds haricots verts or other thin green beans, trimmed

1 tablespoon olive oil

1 clove garlic, very finely chopped

2 tomatoes, cored, seeded, and chopped

30 niçoise or other brine-cured black olives, pitted, or 15 kalamata olives, pitted and halved

2 to 3 tablespoons mixed chopped fresh herbs (such as parsley, tarragon, and basil)

1 tablespoon red wine vinegar

Coarse salt and freshly ground black pepper

Prepare an ice-water bath by filling a large bowl with ice and water.

Bring a large pot of salted water to a rolling boil over high heat. Add the beans and cook until crisp-tender, about 3 minutes. Drain well in a colander, then set the colander with beans in the ice-water bath (to set the color and stop the cooking), making sure the beans are submerged.

In the same pot, heat the oil over low heat. Add the garlic and heat until fragrant, 45 to 60 seconds. Drain the beans, shaking off the excess water. Return the beans to the pot along with the tomatoes. Add the olives and herbs and toss to combine. Drizzle over the vinegar and toss to coat. Taste and adjust for seasoning with salt and pepper. Serve hot, warm, or cold.

Bush Beans and Pole Beans

Green beans grow as either bush beans or pole beans (the beans grow on a vine that travels up a pole). Typically, pole beans are bigger, thicker, and tougher than bush beans. They can be substituted for their thinner counterparts, but will take longer to cook until tender. Pole beans are still fairly old-school and are most often simmered with fat until they are soft and tender, not crisp. Haricots verts are especially thin and tender French green beans that are better when briefly cooked to showcase their flavor.

MISS SHIRLEY'S ASPARAGUS

Serves 4 to 6

Shirley Corriher is a world-renowned food scientist who happens to live in Atlanta, Georgia. Everyone from the elves at the cookie company to the late Julia Child has called her to ask, "why?" Her detailed explanations help cooks understand why certain things happen in the kitchen, which liberates the cook from the recipe (to a certain extent).

Shirley shows in this recipe how green vegetables remain bright green if not overcooked (see page 196). She also demonstrates how lemon zest will give a fresh lemon taste without the acidity of the lemon juice, which will turn cooked green vegetables, as she says, "yucky army drab."

1 pound thin asparagus, ends trimmed

2 tablespoons canola oil

Coarse salt and freshly ground black pepper

Grated zest of 1 lemon

Preheat the broiler. Spread out the asparagus spears in a single layer on a rimmed baking sheet. Drizzle with oil and shake the pan to evenly coat the spears. Season with salt and pepper.

Broil until the spears are just tender, 4 minutes for thin and up to 10 minutes for thick asparagus.

Add the lemon zest and toss to coat. Taste and adjust for seasoning with salt and pepper.

TOASTED-PECAN GREEN BEANS

Serves 4 to 6

The aroma of the basil when combined with the green beans is vibrant and intoxicating. This dish is almost like a deconstructed pesto without the cheese, or a Southern version of green beans amandine, a once-elegant side dish, that in the 1970s became a sad image of itself, banished to cafeterias and dining halls.

1 1/2 pounds haricots verts or other thin green beans, trimmed

1/4 cup olive oil

1/2 cup chopped pecans

1 clove garlic, very finely chopped

1 tablespoon chopped fresh basil

Coarse salt and freshly ground black pepper

Prepare an ice-water bath by filling a large bowl with ice and water.

Bring a large pot of salted water to a rolling boil over high heat. Add the beans and cook until crisp-tender, about 3 minutes. Drain well in a colander, then set the colander with beans in the ice-water bath (to set the color and stop the cooking), making sure the beans are submerged.

In the same pot, heat the olive oil over medium-low heat. Add the pecans and cook until toasted, about 5 minutes. Add the garlic and basil; cook until fragrant, 45 to 60 seconds.

Drain the beans, shaking off the excess water, and return them to the pot. Toss to combine with the pecan mixture. Taste and adjust for seasoning with salt and pepper. Serve immediately.

SARA'S SQUASH CASSEROLE

Serves 4 to 6

Summer squash is a tender vegetable that differs from winter squash in that it is harvested before the rind hardens. It grows on bush-type plants, not vines that spread. There are many varieties, including yellow crookneck and straightneck, scallop, patty-pan, and zucchini, that all cook in the same amount of time. When preparing summer squash dishes, I like to mix the varieties for an interesting contrast of color.

When there is a family gathering or buffet, my mother-in-law, Sara, is always asked to bring her squash casserole.

4 tablespoons (1/2 stick) unsalted butter, plus more for the dish

3 yellow squash, sliced 1/4 inch thick (about 1 pound)

1/2 onion, preferably Vidalia, chopped

3 zucchini, sliced 1/4 inch thick (about 1 pound)

2 to 3 tablespoons firmly packed light brown sugar

2 large eggs, lightly beaten

Scant 1/2 cup half-and-half

3 slices whole wheat bread, torn, (about 2 1/2 cups, loosely packed)

1 cup grated Cheddar cheese (about 3 1/2 ounces)

Coarse salt and freshly ground black pepper

Preheat the oven to 350°F. Brush an ovenproof casserole dish with butter.

Bring a pot of salted water to a rolling boil over high heat. Place the yellow squash and onion in a steamer basket and set over the boiling water; steam until the squash is just tender. Repeat with the zucchini and steam until just tender. Transfer the yellow and zucchini squash and onion to a bowl. Add the brown sugar, eggs, the 4 tablespoons butter, half-and-half, bread, and cheese. Season with salt and pepper and stir to combine. Transfer to the prepared casserole and bake until firm and brown on top, 30 to 45 minutes. Remove to a rack to cool slightly before serving.

SLOW-ROASTED TOMATO CONFIT

Makes 24

This recipe uses slow-cooking technique to intensify the tomatoes' flavor. It is a wonderful technique to remember in the heat of the summer during tomato season.

This is an excellent alternative to the fresh tomato salad for Corn Soup with Tomato Garnish (page 230), but take a cue from fine French kitchens and fold the confit into scrambled eggs, toss it with salad greens or pasta, or place some on top of crisp grilled bread with chopped fresh herbs for a tasty hors d'oeuvre.

12 Roma or plum tomatoes, cored

1/2 cup extra-virgin olive oil

2 cloves garlic, thinly sliced

2 sprigs of thyme

Coarse sea salt and freshly ground black pepper

Preheat the oven to 200°F. Prepare an ice-water bath by filling a large bowl with ice and water. Line a rimmed baking sheet with a silicone baking sheet.

Bring a large pot of water to a boil over high heat. Score an X in the blossom ends of the tomatoes. Drop the tomatoes into the boiling water and blanch for 30 seconds. Transfer immediately to the ice-water bath. When the tomatoes are cool enough to handle, peel off the skin using a paring knife. Halve the tomatoes lengthwise, stem to blossom ends, and use your fingers to remove the seeds.

In a bowl, combine the seeded tomato halves, oil, garlic, and thyme; season with salt and pepper.

Place the tomatoes in a single layer on the prepared baking sheet. Bake, rotating once, until soft but not caramelized, about 4 hours. Transfer to a bowl and pour over the leftover oil-garlic mixture. To store, refrigerate, covered with oil, in an airtight container for up to $1^1/2$ weeks.

CORN ON THE COB WITH PARMIGIANO-REGGIANO

Serves 4 to 6

Long hot Southern summers produce delicious corn, but some of the best corn I ever had in my life was from New Jersey. The farmer had a stand on the side of the road in front of his cornfield. He would ask how many you wanted, and march back into the green, rustling stalks to pick your order. Freshness is important, since the moment corn is picked, the sugars begin converting into starch. Straight from the row to a pot of boiling water is an indulgent luxury.

Some folks may look twice when they see that this recipe instructs you to coat the corn in mayonnaise. It's a Southern take on Mexican corn that is coated in crema, a soft sour cream–like cheese. You cannot get more Southern than mayonnaise. If you don't care for mayonnaise, use soft unsalted butter instead.

4 to 6 ears fresh sweet corn, unshucked

Coarse salt and freshly ground black pepper

1/2 cup grated Parmigiano-Reggiano cheese (about 2 ounces)

Pinch of cayenne pepper

1/4 cup mayonnaise (page 282) or unsalted butter

Preheat the oven to 350°F. Place the unshucked corn in the sink and add water to cover. Weight down the corn with a heavy pot or plate to keep it submerged. Let the corn soak for about 30 minutes. Remove the corn from the water, pull back the husks, and strip away the silk. Season the corn with salt and black pepper. Pull the husks back over the corn and place in the oven, directly on the rack. Roast until the corn is tender, 40 to 45 minutes.

Meanwhile, combine the cheese and cayenne in a shallow plate. Set aside.

Remove the corn from the oven and shuck while warm. Using a pastry brush, coat the hot ears of corn with mayonnaise. Roll the ears in the cheese mixture to coat. Serve immediately.

Spinach with Shallots, Pine Nuts, and Golden Raisins

Serves 4 to 6

Classic French cooking technique dictates that spinach should be blanched before sauteing. I learned the science behind the method when I produced a DVD with Shirley Corriher called *Kitchen Secrets Revealed!*

Fresh fruits and vegetables are made from living cells. When heated, these cells die and fall apart. All vegetables are slightly acidic, and as the cells deteriorate and continue cooking, the acids leak out and turn the chlorophyll present in green vegetables brown. Miss Shirley (see page 191) calls this "mass death and destruction." The French technique of blanching vegetables first in a large pot of boiling water dilutes the acids as they leak out, minimizing the amount of acid in contact with chlorophyll. Steaming is another excellent cooking method because as soon as the acids are released from the vegetables they wash away in the steam, limiting the amount of damaging contact with chlorophyll. Finally, stir-frying is a quick cooking and open technique, letting those acids evaporate, and limiting the time for the chlorophyll to lose color.

If you don't want to blanch spinach (or dandelion or chard) and still have it bright green, the trick is too cook it very, very quickly over high heat.

1/2 cup golden raisins

1/2 cup chicken stock (page 227) or low-fat, reduced-sodium chicken broth, heated

1/2 cup pine nuts

2 tablespoons olive oil

2 shallots, chopped

2 pounds spinach, dandelion, or chard, tough stems removed

Coarse salt and freshly ground black pepper

Place the raisins in a small bowl. Pour over the heated chicken stock. Let rest to plump and rehydrate, 10 to 15 minutes.

Meanwhile, place the pine nuts in a large heavy-duty skillet over medium heat. Toast, stirring frequently, until golden brown, about 8 minutes. Remove to a bowl and set aside.

Heat the olive oil in the same skillet over medium-low heat. Add the shallots and cook until translucent, 3 to 5 minutes. Increase the heat to high, add the spinach, and stir-fry until wilted, 1 to 2 minutes. Drain the golden raisins, discarding the liquid or reserving for another use. Add the drained raisins and toasted pine nuts. Taste and adjust for seasoning with salt and pepper. Serve immediately.

Toasting Nuts

Toasting nuts really brings out their flavor. Toast nuts in a dry skillet over medium-high heat until fragrant, 5 to 7 minutes. Or place them on a baking sheet and toast in the oven at 350°F until brown and toasted, about 10 minutes.

SMOKY COLLARD GREENS

Serves 4 to 6

You simply won't believe your mouth when you taste these greens. They smell like bacon, and taste a lot like bacon, but there is no bacon. The flavor comes from smoked salt. In its pure state, salt is a simple chemical compound, sodium chloride. There are many types of salt from all over the world that contain different elements and minerals. But things get really "fired up" when salt is smoked. The best ones are slowly smoked over a natural fire, often made of used oak barrels recycled from making wine. The smoke permeates the salt crystals, infusing them with a rich, distinct smoked taste, and transforms their color from a light toasty brown to deep amber. This ingredient adds a unique flavor to a wide range of dishes, including beef, pork, duck, chicken, and fish. I use it most often in Southern-style vegetables, to replicate that smoky taste evocative of hog jowl or bacon without the fat, and it is great for vegetarians.

Other favorites that I prepare with smoked salt are black-eyed peas and butter beans. If you can't find smoked salt (available online and at specialty markets), you have permission to use bacon.

2 tablespoons canola oil

1 onion, preferably Vidalia, chopped

1 clove garlic, finely chopped

1 medium bunch collard greens (about 1½ pounds), cleaned (see page 198), tough stems removed and discarded, and leaves very thinly sliced in chiffonade (see sidebar)

4 cups water

1 tablespoon smoked salt

2 teaspoons apple cider vinegar

Freshly ground black pepper

Hot Pepper Vinegar (page 284) for accompaniment

Heat the oil in a large pot over medium heat. Add the onion and saute until soft and translucent, 3 to 5 minutes. Add the garlic and cook until fragrant, 45 to 60 seconds. Add the greens, water, smoked salt, and apple cider vinegar. Season the mixture with pepper. Increase the heat to medium-high and bring to a boil. Decrease the heat to medium-low, cover, and cook until the greens are tender, 20 to 25 minutes. Taste and adjust for seasoning with smoked salt and pepper. Serve immediately with the hot pepper vinegar on the side.

Chiffonade

Chiffonade is a classic French technique that means thinly slicing an herb, such as basil, or a leafy vegetable, into strands or ribbons. To make chiffonade, stack the leaves one on top of the other, and roll them tightly into a cylinder. Using a chef's knife, slice the cylinder crosswise into thin strips.

TANGLE OF BITTER GREENS

Serves 4 to 6

Kale, collards, turnip greens, and mustard greens are dark leafy winter greens that are nutritional powerhouses and familiar friends on the Southern table. Look for brightly colored greens free of brown spots, yellowing edges, or limp leaves. Try flavorful seasonings such as smoked turkey or ham hock for the meat eaters and smoked salt or chipotle chiles for the vegetarians.

I once demonstrated this recipe on a local morning TV show. Aunt Louise was watching and told Mama later, "She took those greens out of that pan just like they were done!" You won't believe how fast they cook, either.

The best way to clean greens is to fill a clean sink with cold water, add the greens, and swish them around. The dirt will fall to the bottom of the sink. Lift the greens out, drain the sink, and repeat until the water is clear and the greens are free of dirt and grit.

2 tablespoons canola oil

3 medium cloves garlic, mashed into a paste (see sidebar)

1 medium bunch kale, collards, turnip greens, or mustard greens (about 1½ pounds), cleaned, tough stems removed and discarded, and leaves very thinly sliced in chiffonade (see page 197)

Coarse salt and freshly ground black pepper

In a skillet, heat the oil over medium-high heat. Add the garlic and slightly damp ribbons of greens; season with salt and pepper. Cook until the greens are bright green and slightly wilted, 3 to 4 minutes. Taste and adjust for seasoning with salt and pepper. Serve immediately.

Garlic Paste

To prepare garlic paste, place the broad side of an unpeeled clove of garlic on a clean work surface and give it a whack with the flat side of a chef's knife. Remove the papery skin and trim away the tough basal plane at the top of the clove. Halve the garlic lengthwise and remove any of the green shoot, if present, as it is bitter. Coarsely chop the garlic, then sprinkle it with coarse salt. (The salt acts as an abrasive and helps chop the garlic.) Then, using the flat side

of a chef's knife like an artist's palette knife, press firmly on the garlic, crushing a little at a time. Repeat until the garlic is a fine paste.

SUMMER SQUASH AND TURKEY SAUSAGE GRATIN

Serves 6 to 8

Southerners love a casserole. They are church supper staples, great to take to the new neighbor, and equally welcome to a new mom. Cheddar, sometimes called "rat cheese" in the South, ranges in flavor from mild, nutty, and creamy to extra-sharp, rich, and robust. Gruyère is a low-moisture cow's milk cheese from eastern France and western Switzerland. It has a sweet, rich, almost nutty flavor and is excellent for a cheese sauce. Cheddar cheese is more Southern, though, if you wanted to stay truer to those roots.

Turkey sausage is much lower in fat than sausage made from pork and other kinds of meat. Use country-style or coarse-ground sausage, and if purchased in links, remove it from the casing before cooking.

3 tablespoons unsalted butter, at room temperature

2 cups whole or low-fat milk

3 sprigs of flat-leaf parsley

2 sprigs of thyme

10 whole black peppercorns

2 tablespoons canola oil

3/4 pound Italian turkey sausage

4 green onions, white and green parts, sliced

4 medium yellow squash (about 1 1/4 pounds), cut into 1/4-inch-thick slices

4 medium zucchini squash (about 1 1/4 pounds), cut into 1/4-inch-thick slices

Coarse salt and freshly ground black pepper

1 clove garlic, very finely chopped

1 teaspoon chopped fresh thyme

2 tablespoons all-purpose flour

1 cup grated sharp Cheddar or Gruyère cheese (about 4 ounces)

3 large eggs, lightly beaten

Pinch of cayenne pepper

1 cup fresh or panko (Japanese) breadcrumbs

1/4 cup grated Parmigiano-Reggiano cheese (about 1 ounce)

Preheat the oven to 350°F. Brush a baking dish with 1 tablespoon of the butter.

In a saucepan, heat the milk over medium heat until bubbles form around the edges of the pan. Add the parsley, thyme, and peppercorns. Cover, remove from the heat, and set aside to steep while cooking the sausage and squash.

Heat the oil in a large skillet over high heat. Add the sausage and cook, stirring occasionally, until cooked through, about 5 minutes. Add the green onions and the yellow and zucchini squash, season with salt and pepper, and cook until tender, about 8 minutes. Add the garlic and thyme and cook until fragrant, 30 to 45 seconds. Transfer to a colander to drain.

Meanwhile, to make the sauce, in the same skillet used for the squash, melt the remaining 2 tablespoons of butter. Add the flour and stir until foamy. Strain the heated milk into the flour mixture and stir to combine. Bring to a boil over medium-high heat, and cook until the sauce is thick enough to coat the back of a spoon, about 3 minutes. Remove from the heat. Add the cheese and stir to melt and combine. Add a little bit of the sauce to the beaten eggs; stir to combine, then add the egg mixture back to the sauce and stir to combine. Add a pinch of cayenne and season to taste with salt and pepper.

Combine the breadcrumbs and the grated Parmigiano-Reggiano in a small bowl. Set aside.

Add the well-drained sausage-squash mixture to the sauce and stir to combine. Transfer the mixture to the prepared baking dish. Top with the cheese-breadcrumb mixture. Bake until bubbly and set, about 30 minutes. If necessary, for the last few minutes, broil until the topping is a rich, golden brown, 2 to 3 minutes.

CHAPTER 9

Biscuits, Rolls, and Breads

BREAD IS ONE OF the most basic of foods, and it's a symbol of hospitality: there is no act more social than sharing, or breaking, bread with someone. In many cultures, breaking bread signifies an act of peace. Conversely, riots protesting the cost of bread have occurred in countries all around the world for centuries. Regardless of the type of grain, bread occupies an important place in nearly every civilization, society, and culture on earth.

More than once when munching on a French baguette in Paris or a bagel in New York, my heart and stomach were pining for a light-as-air, buttered Southern biscuit. When Southern prayers go to the heavens requesting daily bread, it is biscuits we have in mind. Meme and Mama most often made rolled biscuits. There are photos of me as young as three years old standing on a stool "helping." I remember we'd roll out the biscuits and Meme would let me make a handprint with the scraps of dough. The tiny fingers on my handprint biscuit would cook very dark in the heat of the oven, taking on a slightly bitter, almost nutty taste. I know that's where my passion for cooking took root, working at her side on her linoleum countertop in the gentle breeze of the oscillating fan.

There is a Southern bread for every meal—breakfast, lunch, and dinner—and soda crackers to munch on in between. These breads are made from wheat, rice, and corn as well as sweet potato, potato, and hominy. Typical Southern breads (other than biscuits) include yeast rolls, batter bread, cornbread, corn cakes, cracklin' bread, and hushpuppies. Hardtack was part of the diets of soldiers fighting on both sides of the Civil War, and hoe cakes take their name from originally being cooked on the flat of a hoe over an open fire.

Until the latter part of the nineteenth century, leaveners—commercial yeast, baking powder, and baking soda—were not widely available. Grains were usually not refined, so the breads were heavy and dense from whole-grain flour. With the introduction of commercial leaveners, bread became lighter and was baked on a daily basis. Milling methods also changed. Grains were milled to remove the fatty germ, which caused the grain to spoil and become rancid. Flour and meal became more shelf-stable.

But the new milling techniques, which reduced the nutritional content of cornmeal, were actually detrimental. Pellagra, a disease caused by deficiencies in niacin and tryptophan, reached epidemic proportions among the rural sharecroppers, farmers, and cotton mill workers of the South. The prevalence of the disease was exacerbated by a lack of variety in people's diet because farmers were using every last row to grow cotton, not food. By World War II, federal legislation mandated that bakeries enrich flour with these essential vitamins and minerals.

The government of France also oversees an aspect of bread baking: the long, slender baguette (from the French word for wand) is so intertwined in French culture that its price is regulated by law, which also specifies its content—only water, flour, yeast, and salt. Because baguettes contain no fat, they go hard and stale very quickly. As they do for produce at the market, the French go once or twice a day to the *boulangerie* for baguettes.

Most of the breads found on our own grocery shelves are mass-produced in large factories. Vitamins are added, as are chemical preservatives that allow the bread to be shipped across the country and stay shelf-stable without refrigeration for days. These breads have no soul. They are the antithesis of breads in France and the traditional breads of the South.

The recipes in this chapter are a small representation of mostly Southern breads (including three kinds of biscuits and a choice of cornbreads), a honey-spice bread I grew to love during my years in Burgundy, and a few of my favorite quick and yeasted breads that are just plain good.

BUTTERMILK ANGEL BISCUITS

Makes about
3 dozen biscuits

Angel biscuits are lighter than traditional buttermilk biscuits because they contain yeast as well as the usual baking powder, baking soda, or both. The yeast gives them an extra push as well as another layer of flavor.

Traditional biscuits can be intimidating to novice bakers, especially if first efforts yielded rock-hard results, not light and tender biscuits. The trio of leaveners protects even the worst of bakers from abject failure. This dough is also appealing because it can be prepared ahead of time and held in the refrigerator for three to five days (baking powder and baking soda alone would have long lost their "oomph"). This holding power lets you pinch off a bit of dough at a time to make a few fresh biscuits during the week. It's also a heck of a lot better than the preservative- and chemical-laden tubes of refrigerated biscuit dough.

1/4 cup warm water (100° to 110°F)

1 package (2 1/4 teaspoons) active dry yeast

1/4 cup sugar

6 cups White Lily or other Southern all-purpose flour (see page 206), plus more for rolling

1 tablespoon baking powder

1 teaspoon baking soda

1 teaspoon fine sea salt

1 cup solid vegetable shortening, preferably Crisco, cut into bits

2 cups buttermilk

3 tablespoons unsalted butter, melted

To proof the yeast, in a liquid measuring cup, combine the warm water, yeast, and 1 tablespoon of the sugar. Set aside to proof. The mixture will become creamy and foamy, about 5 minutes.

To make the dough, in a large bowl, whisk together the flour, the remaining 3 tablespoons of sugar, baking powder, baking soda, and salt. Using a pastry cutter or two knives, cut the shortening into the dry ingredients until the mixture resembles coarse meal and there are no large bits of shortening.

Add the yeast and buttermilk to the dough and stir until the dough just comes together. Turn the dough out onto a lightly floured work surface and knead 5 or 6 times; the dough should be soft and moist. Return the dough to the bowl. Cover the bowl with plastic wrap and refrigerate overnight or up to a week before using.

When ready to bake, preheat the oven to 425°F. Dust a clean work surface with about 1 cup of flour. Turn out the chilled dough and knead about 10 times to punch down. Using a lightly floured rolling pin, roll the dough out to 1/3 inch thick. Using a 2 1/4-inch round cutter, cut out the biscuits as close together as possible. Gather the dough scraps and place one on top of the other. Knead until a cohesive dough forms again and roll the dough out once again. Stamp out as many biscuits as possible from the re-rolled dough. Discard the remaining scraps.

Arrange the biscuits, sides touching, on an ungreased baking sheet. Brush with the melted butter. Set aside to rise in a warm place for about 30 minutes.

Bake until golden brown, 10 to 12 minutes. Transfer to a rack to cool slightly. Serve warm.

MEME'S BISCUITS

Makes about 9
biscuits

Meme most often made rolled biscuits. For large biscuits, she had a special aluminum cutter with a small wooden handle that fit in the palm of her hand. She cut out small biscuits with an empty apple juice can open at both ends. Some purists use lard instead of butter. Although I like biscuits made with lard and understand the tradition and history, Meme and Mama had started using butter by the time I was born.

The perfect biscuit should be golden brown and slightly crisp on the outside, with a light, airy interior. For a flaky, tender biscuit, don't overwork the dough: gently combine the ingredients until just blended. A very hot oven is essential. The steam interacts with the baking powder to create the biscuit's ideal textures inside and out.

2 cups White Lily or other Southern all-purpose flour (see page 206), or cake flour (not self-rising), more for rolling out

1 tablespoon baking powder

1 teaspoon fine sea salt

4 tablespoons (1/2 stick) cold unsalted butter, cut into bits and chilled

3/4 to 1 cup buttermilk

Preheat the oven to 500°F. In a bowl, combine the flour, baking powder, and salt. Using a pastry cutter or two knives, cut the butter into the flour mixture until it resembles coarse meal. Pour in the buttermilk, and gently mix until just combined.

Turn the dough out onto a lightly floured surface. Knead lightly, using the heel of your hand to compress and push the dough away from you, then fold it back over itself. Give the dough a small turn and repeat 8 or so times. (It's not yeast bread; you want to just barely activate the gluten, not overwork it.) Using a lightly floured rolling pin, roll the dough out 1/2 inch thick. Cut out rounds of dough with a 2 1/4-inch round cutter dipped in flour; press the cutter straight down without twisting so the biscuits will rise evenly when baked.

Place the biscuits on an ungreased baking sheet or in an 8- by 2-inch round cake pan. If the biscuits are baked close together the sides will be moist. If the biscuits are baked further apart, the sides will be crisp.

Bake until golden brown, 8 to 10 minutes. Transfer to a rack to cool just slightly. Serve warm.

VARIATION: If I don't feel like rolling out biscuits, or just want a different texture, I tweak the recipe by adding more buttermilk to the dough and make drop biscuits: use 3 cups of flour—2 for the dough and 1 cup placed in a bowl to shape the dough into biscuits. Increase the buttermilk to 2 cups. The dough will be very wet and resemble cottage cheese. To form the biscuits into balls, scoop up some dough with a large ice cream scoop; place the dough balls in the bowl with the 1 cup of flour. Working one at a time, roll the balls to coat in flour, then set in an ungreased 8- by 2-inch round cake pan. The baking time will be the same as for cut biscuits.

MEME'S YEAST ROLLS

Meme may have made the rolls, but it was Dede who did a lot of the work. He beat the dough with a special wooden spoon that had a small ledge on the end for gripping. He'd cradle the big bowl in his arm and beat the wet dough so it slapped "wap, wap, wap" against the bowl. All that "muscle" developed the dough's structure, causing the rolls to rise in the oven light as air, slightly sweet, and richly sour with the scent of yeast. We all thought it was Meme's gentle touch forming the rolls, but it was actually Dede's strong arms that made them taste so good.

When yeast begins to ferment and grow, it converts its food to alcohol and carbon dioxide. The gluten sheets that form when water is stirred into flour trap the carbon dioxide and allow the dough to rise.

3 packages (6¾ teaspoons) active dry yeast

½ cup warm water (100° to 110°F)

2 cups hot water

1 cup dry milk

1 cup sugar

½ cup corn oil, more for brushing

4 large eggs, lightly beaten

4 teaspoons fine sea salt

9 to 10 cups all-purpose flour

To activate the yeast, combine the yeast and warm water in a large bowl. Set aside to proof. The mixture will become creamy and foamy after about 5 minutes.

To make the dough, combine the hot water and dry milk in a liquid measuring cup; let cool slightly. Add the reconstituted milk to the yeast. Stir to combine. Add the sugar, the ½ cup of oil, eggs, salt, and 4 cups of the flour. With a wooden spoon, hand-held electric mixer, or large heavy-duty mixer fitted with the dough hook at medium speed, beat very hard until smooth, 3 to 5 minutes. Gradually add additional flour, 1 cup at a time, beating hard after each addition. When the dough is too firm to stir, using your hand, work enough of the remaining flour into the dough by kneading and turning the dough until it becomes smooth and elastic. Turn the dough out onto a lightly floured surface. Knead, using the heel of your hand to compress and push the dough away from you, then fold it back over itself. Give the dough a small turn and repeat. (The dough is ready if it bounces back when pressed with your fingers.) Return the dough to the bowl.

Cover the bowl with plastic wrap or a dry towel and place in a warm, draft-free spot to rise until doubled in size, about 2 hours.

Lightly grease a baking sheet. Punch down the dough with your hands, then turn out onto a lightly floured surface. Flour your hands and pull off equal pieces of dough about the size of apricots and shape into balls. (If you are using a scale, 3-ounce portions will make 28 large rolls.) Place them on the prepared baking sheet about ¼ inch apart. Brush off any excess flour from the rolls and brush their surfaces with oil. Cover and let rise again in a warm place until doubled in bulk, 1 to 1½ hours.

Preheat the oven to 375°F. Bake until brown, 12 to 15 minutes. Transfer to a rack to cool slightly, then invert the rolls onto a rack so they won't become soggy on the bottom.

MAMA'S MAYONNAISE BISCUITS

Makes 12

Mama made these often when we were growing up. After I attended culinary school, I admittedly became quite snobby about using store-bought ingredients in recipes. I wanted to make the mayonnaise, not buy it. This type of recipe seemed one short step above a baking mix. Now a little older and wiser, I appreciate it for what it is. I understand Mama was putting freshly baked bread on the family table, and that was really important. I now ask for them when I go home to visit and enjoy every sweet bite.

1 tablespoon canola oil, for the tin

2 cups self-rising flour (see below)

3 tablespoons mayonnaise (page 282)

1 cup whole milk

1 teaspoon sugar

Preheat the oven to 350°F. Brush a 12-cup medium muffin tin with oil.

Combine the flour, mayonnaise, milk, and sugar in a bowl. Using a spoon or an ice cream scoop, spoon dough into each muffin cup, filling about half full. Alternatively, drop spoonfuls of the dough onto a greased baking sheet. Bake until golden brown, 15 to 20 minutes. Transfer to a wire rack to cool slightly, then invert the biscuits onto the rack to cool until warm. Serve warm.

Southern Flour

Wheat flour contains two proteins, glutenin and gliadin. When you combine flour with water, the proteins create a strong and elastic sheet called gluten. Flours vary in their protein levels, which affects the texture of baked goods. Gluten gives structure to yeast breads, but is not recommended for tender cakes, biscuits, and quick breads. Southern all-purpose flour is milled from soft red winter wheat that has less gluten-forming protein. It is typically bleached, which makes it whiter, but this does not affect the protein. My family has always used White Lily flour, a staple across the South; another dependable Southern brand is Martha White.

Most national brands of all-purpose flour are a combination of soft winter wheat and higher-protein hard summer wheat. White Lily contains approximately nine grams of protein per cup of flour, whereas national brands can contain eleven or twelve grams of protein per cup of flour. If you live outside the South, White Lily is available online or in some specialty shops in other parts of the country.

For results similar to those of Southern flour, substitute one part all-purpose flour and one part cake flour for the amount of Southern flour in a recipe.

Finally, high-protein flour absorbs more liquid than does low-protein flour; if you attempt to make biscuits with a high-protein flour, you will need to add more liquid.

Self-rising flour is all-purpose flour that is low in protein and contains a leavening agent and salt. It is widely available in the South, but less so in other regions of the country. If you have a recipe that calls for self-rising flour, use the following formula to convert all-purpose into self-rising: to 1 cup of Southern all-purpose flour, add $1\frac{1}{2}$ teaspoons baking powder and $\frac{1}{2}$ teaspoon fine sea salt.

Meme's Biscuits (page 204), Meme's Yeast Rolls (page 205), and Mama's Mayonnaise Biscuits (this page)

MEME'S CORNBREAD DRESSING

Serves 6 to 8

At Thanksgiving Meme always prepared her dressing on the side, as opposed to stuffing her turkey. Although there are exceptions, it seems most Southerners "dress" instead of "stuff." I've taken a few liberties with Meme's recipe, adding brioche and panko. It's okay to use store-bought cornbread, but make sure it is not sweet. Typically, Southern cornbread is savory and rich with the taste of corn, with no sugar added. Sweet cornbread produces a dressing that's just not quite right.

This dish is another in the book that serves more than the four to six people, and is best for larger gatherings of friends and family. It can be halved, or divided into two smaller pans—one to cook now, the other to wrap tightly in plastic and freeze for later use. After thawing to room temperature, cook as directed.

4 tablespoons (1/2 stick) unsalted butter, plus more for the dish

4 cups day-old, crumbled Buttermilk Cornbread (page 211)

1 loaf brioche or egg bread, cut into 1-inch cubes (about 2 cups)

3/4 cup fresh or panko (Japanese) breadcrumbs

3 stalks celery, chopped

1 onion, preferably Vidalia, chopped

2 cups chicken stock (page 227) or low-fat, reduced-sodium chicken broth, plus more if needed

2 large eggs, lightly beaten

1 tablespoon chopped fresh sage

1 teaspoon chopped fresh thyme

Coarse salt and freshly ground black pepper

Preheat the oven to 350°F. Butter an ovenproof gratin or casserole dish.

In a very large bowl, combine the cornbread, brioche, and breadcrumbs in a very large mixing bowl; set aside.

Heat the 4 tablespoons butter in a large skillet over medium heat. Add the celery and onion and cook until soft, 5 to 7 minutes. Transfer the cooked vegetables to the bread mixture. Pour over the stock and add the eggs, sage, and thyme. The mixture should be fairly soupy; if not, add additional stock. Stir well to combine and season with salt and pepper. Transfer to the baking dish. Bake until heated through, puffed, and golden brown, about 45 minutes. Remove from the oven to cool slightly before serving.

CHEDDAR CORNBREAD

One of my favorite possessions is my grandmother's cast-iron skillet. It's more precious to me than the antique bone china that I also inherited. To think of all the fried chicken and cornbread it has held is amazing. Several years ago, I returned home to Georgia after living in New York City, and I carried my treasured skillet in a blanket on my lap practically the whole trip. It is almost like my sacred talisman. No one will dare touch it when we are cleaning up from dinner. If I leave the room, I return to a spotless kitchen with a dirty cast-iron skillet on the stovetop. No one wants the responsibility. It sounds severe, but a little fear is fine with me.

When properly seasoned over time, cast iron develops a virtually nonstick surface that only improves with use. To clean cast-iron cookware, wash with a nonabrasive sponge and warm soapy water. Rinse it well. To prevent rust, make sure the piece is completely dry before you store it. As insurance, I usually place mine in a warm oven for a little while to fully dry out. Cast iron is great for baking cornbread, pan-frying, and sauteing. It is a little slow to heat up, but once it does, it heats evenly and stays hotter longer. Cast iron is inexpensive and can be found at hardware and cookware stores.

4 tablespoons (½ stick) unsalted butter

1 cup all-purpose flour

1 cup white or yellow cornmeal

1½ teaspoons baking powder

1½ teaspoons baking soda

¾ teaspoon fine sea salt

1¼ cups grated extra-sharp Cheddar cheese (about 5 ounces)

1¼ cups buttermilk

2 large eggs, at room temperature

Preheat the oven to 400°F. Place the butter in a 10½-inch cast-iron skillet and heat in the oven for 10 to 15 minutes.

In a bowl, whisk together the flour, cornmeal, baking powder, baking soda, and salt. Stir in 1 cup of the cheese.

Remove the skillet from the oven and pour the melted butter into the flour mixture. Add the buttermilk and eggs and stir to combine. Pour the batter back into the prepared skillet and smooth the top. Bake until a toothpick inserted into the center comes out clean and the bread is golden brown, about 20 minutes.

Just before the cornbread is done, remove from the oven and sprinkle with the remaining ¼ cup of cheese. Bake until the cheese is melted, 3 to 5 minutes. Transfer to a rack to cool slightly before serving.

BUTTERMILK CORNBREAD

Makes one
10 1/2-inch
skillet bread

I could make a meal out of just buttered cornbread. Except perhaps for barbecue, cornbread is as close to religion in the South as any particular food gets. At the top of the list of cornbread sins is adding sugar. You will notice a complete lack of sugar in this cornbread recipe. Sugar is more often found in what is referred to derisively as "Yankee cornbread."

Adherents of white versus yellow cornmeal are like Methodists and Baptists: some think you're going to hell if you follow one path and not the other. I am of the white cornmeal sect. The theory is that white corn was less hybridized and closer to the original grain than yellow. Plain white cornmeal can be surprisingly tricky to find, even in Atlanta; most of what lines the grocery store shelves is a mix or self-rising, which already contains the leavener that makes the cornmeal rise. Although yellow and white cornmeal are interchangeable, plain and self-rising cornmeal are not.

Warming the skillet and bacon grease or butter in the oven prepares the skillet for baking and melts the fat. Most often, I use butter. I like to let it get just barely nutty brown on the edges. The brown flecks give the cornbread extra color and flavor.

2 tablespoons unsalted butter or bacon grease

2 cups white or yellow cornmeal (not cornmeal mix or self-rising cornmeal)

1 teaspoon fine sea salt

1 teaspoon baking soda

2 cups buttermilk

1 large egg, lightly beaten

Preheat the oven to 450°F. Place the butter in a 10 1/2-inch cast-iron skillet or ovenproof baking dish and heat in the oven for 10 to 15 minutes.

Meanwhile, in a bowl, combine the cornmeal, salt, and baking soda. Set aside. In a large measuring cup, combine the buttermilk and egg. Add the wet ingredients to the dry and stir to combine.

Remove the heated skillet from the oven and pour the melted butter into the batter. Stir to combine, then pour the batter back into the hot skillet. Bake until golden brown, 20 to 25 minutes.

VARIATION: Instead of baking in a skillet, this batter may be prepared as muffins. Preheat the oven to 425°F. Melt the butter in a small pan over low heat or in the microwave. Prepare the batter as directed; after mixing with the melted butter, spoon the batter into a 12-cup standard muffin tin, filling each cup no more than two-thirds full. Bake for 25 to 30 minutes.

BANANA NUT BREAD

Quickbreads use baking powder or baking soda or both as leavening agents and therefore require no kneading or rising, as do traditional yeast breads. This quickbread recipe comes from my cousin-in-law Lisa, whose mama passed it on to her. It was originally baked in a loaf pan, as it is here, but I also like to bake it in a 9-inch cake pan. The temperature stays the same, but the cooking time will reduce to 30 to 45 minutes. It's great for breakfast, an afternoon snack, or topped with ice cream for a delicious dessert.

1/2 cup (1 stick) unsalted butter, at room temperature, plus more for the pan

1 1/4 cups all-purpose flour

1 teaspoon fine sea salt

1 teaspoon baking soda

1 cup sugar

2 large eggs, at room temperature

3 ripe bananas, mashed

1/2 cup chopped pecans

Preheat the oven to 350°F. Brush an 8 x 5 x 3-inch loaf pan with butter. In a bowl, whisk together the flour, salt, and baking soda. Set aside.

To make the batter, in the bowl of a heavy-duty mixer fitted with the paddle, cream the 1/2 cup of butter and the sugar on medium speed until light and fluffy. Add the eggs, one at a time, then the mashed bananas. Add the reserved dry ingredients and pecans and stir to combine. Transfer the batter to the prepared pan.

Bake until a rich, golden brown and the cake starts to pull away from the sides of the pan, 1 hour to 1 1/4 hours. Transfer to a rack to cool slightly, then invert onto the rack. Serve warm or at room temperature. Store in an airtight container for up to 3 days.

Measuring Dry Ingredients

Wet and dry measuring cups are not interchangeable. To measure a dry ingredient such as flour or sugar, scoop, level, and scrape; do not pack the ingredient into the cup. Scoop up, tap across the cup with the back of a knife or a straight-edge spatula to settle the ingredient, then level by scraping across the rim of the cup with a straight edge. You can't accomplish this with a liquid measuring cup, as the measure markings stop below the rim and it has a spout, so you can't level off. A dry measure will work for a wet ingredient, but it is more difficult to use, as dry measures do not normally have spouts for pouring.

HUSHPUPPIES

Makes about 15

A fish fry would not be complete without hushpuppies, yet another dish Southerners prepare with corn. Meme always added grated onion to the meal leftover from frying the fish, and then added an egg and enough buttermilk until the consistency looked about right.

My late father-in-law used to host fish fries, cooking up what they'd caught over the weekend at Lake Lanier. Now, I never actually had one of his hushpuppies, but I've spent fifteen years trying to replicate one, based on what his family describes. He used beer instead of buttermilk and, it seems, lots of onion. It doesn't matter how much onion I add, there's never enough onion. I have a sneaking suspicion that a special food memory created on a sunny summer afternoon has bypassed reality and it's actually not about the onion. No worries, I'll keep trying. There are impossible quests that produce far worse results.

4 cups peanut oil, for frying, plus more if needed

2 cups white or yellow cornmeal

2 teaspoons baking powder

Pinch of cayenne pepper

Coarse salt and freshly ground black pepper

1 cup beer, plus more if needed

2 large eggs

1 onion, preferably Vidalia, very finely chopped

In a large cast-iron Dutch oven or heavy-bottomed pot, heat the oil over high heat until it reaches 375°F on a deep-fat thermometer.

To make the batter, in a large bowl, whisk together the cornmeal, baking powder, cayenne pepper, and 1 teaspoon of the salt. In a second bowl or large liquid measuring cup, combine the beer, eggs, and onion. Season with salt and pepper. Whisk until smooth. Stir the wet ingredients into the dry ingredients, using as few strokes as possible. (The mixture should resemble wet sand; add more beer, if needed.)

Line a plate with paper towels and set by the cooktop. To fry the hushpuppies, scoop up batter using a medium ice cream scoop and drop it into the hot oil without crowding. Fry, stirring occasionally with a slotted spoon, until golden brown, 3 to 5 minutes. Remove with a slotted spoon to the prepared plate. Adjust the heat to maintain the proper temperature and repeat with the remaining batter. Serve immediately.

Peanut Oil

The key to light and crispy fried food, not heavy and greasy fried food, is choosing the right oil. Peanut oil is a great oil for frying, because it has a mild, pleasant flavor; does not take on the tastes of foods as readily as other oils do; and has a smoke point of about 450°F, meaning it burns at a very high temperature. (Be warned, however, that Asian peanut oil is completely different. It has the fragrance of freshly roasted peanuts and is not good for frying.) Once the oil is used, strain it through a mesh sieve to remove the larger bits. Then, strain it again, this time through cheesecloth, to remove the finest particles. Store at room temperature for up to 3 months.

CORNMEAL FOCACCIA

Cornmeal gives this bread a subtle crispy crunch. For the best results, use the best-quality extra-virgin olive oil possible. If you really want to "gild the lily," top the warm bread with a few curls of freshly shaved Parmigiano-Reggiano cheese.

2 cups warm water (100° to 110°F)

1 packet (2 1/4 teaspoons) active dry yeast

4 1/2 to 5 cups unbleached all-purpose flour, plus more for kneading

1/3 cup white or yellow cornmeal

2 teaspoons fine sea salt

1/2 teaspoon chopped fresh rosemary, plus 5 to 6 small sprigs

4 tablespoons extra-virgin olive oil

1 tomato, cored and thinly sliced vertically

1/2 onion, preferably Vidalia, very thinly sliced

Coarse salt and freshly ground black pepper

Place the warm water in the bowl of a heavy-duty mixer fitted with the dough hook. Sprinkle the dry yeast over the water; stir. Let stand until the yeast dissolves, bubbles, and proofs, 5 to 7 minutes.

Add 4 cups of the flour, cornmeal, salt, and chopped rosemary and stir on low to combine. Add an additional 1/2 to 1 cup of the remaining flour and knead on medium speed until smooth.

Turn the dough out onto a floured surface and knead by hand until smooth and elastic, 5 to 7 minutes. Form the dough into a ball.

Place 1 tablespoon of the olive oil in a large bowl; add the dough, turning to coat in oil. Cover with plastic wrap and let rise in a warm area until doubled in size, 1 to 1 1/2 hours.

Preheat the oven to 475°F. Brush a 18 x 13-inch rimmed baking sheet with 1 tablespoon of the remaining olive oil. Punch down the dough and transfer to the prepared sheet. Using your fingertips, press out the dough to fit the pan. Drizzle with the remaining 2 tablespoons oil. Let the dough rise, uncovered, in a warm place until puffy, about 30 minutes.

Dimple the dough with your fingertips, forming indentations. Top with the sliced tomatoes and onion and season with salt and pepper. Scatter the rosemary sprigs around and press lightly into the dough. Bake until brown and crusty, 20 to 25 minutes. Serve warm or at room temperature.

Proofing Bread

When proofing bread in a cool, drafty kitchen, I often turn my microwave into a makeshift proofing box. I boil water in a microwave-safe measuring cup for a couple of minutes to heat the microwave and create steam (don't remove the cup of water). I then place my bowl of dough in the microwave and quickly shut the door. This creates a warm, draft-free spot for the bread to rise.

CRUNCHY CORN MUFFINS

Makes 12 muffins

What impresses me the most about all the types of cornbread is how quickly they can be brought to the table. Warm bread for supper makes everything taste better. My version of pantry cooking is to pull a bag of butter beans or black-eyed peas frozen last summer out of the freezer and cook a pot of rice. While the rice is cooking, I can throw together a batch of corn muffins. It's a simple, quick supper ready in less than thirty minutes.

The fallacy that you need to open a can or use a mix is just that—a lie. I find that shortcuts and prepared products actually do not often make things easier, and usually take as long as doing things "right" in the first place.

4 tablespoons (1/2 stick) unsalted butter, melted, plus more for the muffin tin

1 cup all-purpose flour

2/3 cup white or yellow cornmeal

1 1/2 teaspoons baking powder

1/2 teaspoon fine sea salt

1/4 teaspoon baking soda

1/2 cup grated Parmigiano-Reggiano cheese (about 2 ounces)

1/4 teaspoon cayenne pepper

1/2 cup whole milk

1/2 cup sour cream

2 large eggs

Preheat the oven to 425°F. Brush a 12-cup standard muffin tin with some of the butter.

In a large mixing bowl, combine the flour, cornmeal, baking powder, salt, baking soda, cheese, and cayenne; make a well in the center of the mixture.

In a second bowl or large liquid measuring cup, combine the milk, sour cream, eggs, and the remaining 4 tablespoons of butter. Whisk until smooth. Stir the wet ingredients into the dry ingredients, using as few strokes as possible. Place a scoop of dough into each muffin cup, filling no more than two-thirds full.

Bake until golden, about 15 minutes. Transfer to a rack to cool slightly. Turn out of the tin and serve warm.

MEME'S CORNMEAL GRIDDLE CAKES

Makes 12

Cornbread was for many years the basic bread of the rural South, the very poor South. I mentioned earlier that cornbread and barbecue are close to being religion in the South. But, for years, cornbread was the primitive Baptist to the Episcopalian biscuit, the all-night tent revival to the ladies' prayer luncheon. Cornmeal griddle cakes are the most basic of Southern breads. Biscuits require expensive dairy products, while cornmeal griddle cakes, also known as hoe cakes, can be made with little more than meal, a bit of oil, and water.

The batter should be quite soupy, but not watery. When the batter hits the hot oil the edges sizzle and become very crisp. For best results, be sure to cook the cakes until the edges are a deep, rich, golden brown. Meme always served them as a very quick bread on the side. They are especially delicious when used to sop up juices and gravy.

2 cups white or yellow cornmeal

2 teaspoons baking powder

1 teaspoon fine sea salt

1 large egg, lightly beaten

1 cup water, plus more if needed

1/4 cup corn oil, for frying

To prepare the batter, in a large bowl, whisk together the cornmeal, baking powder, and salt. In a second bowl or large liquid measuring cup, combine the egg and the 1 cup water. Whisk until smooth. Stir the wet ingredients into the dry ingredients, using as few strokes as possible.

To fry the griddle cakes, heat the oil in a cast-iron skillet over medium heat. Ladle 1/4 cup of batter onto the heated skillet. Repeat with additional batter, without crowding.

Cook the cakes until the bottoms are brown and bubbles form on the tops and edges, 2 to 3 minutes. Turn and brown the other side, an additional 2 to 3 minutes. Serve immediately.

Storing Dry Ingredients

To avoid insects in flour and cornmeal, transfer the product to a sealable airtight container immediately after purchase. To keep flour and cornmeal absolutely fresh, particularly if they are whole-grain (see page 202), store the sealed container in the refrigerator or freezer. Allow the flour or meal to come to room temperature before using.

TOO-MUCH-ZUCCHINI-IN-THE-GARDEN BREAD

Makes two 8 x 5 x 3-inch loaves

A long hot summer with just the right amount of rain will create a situation of disastrous consequences—too much zucchini in the garden. Zucchini is prolific. You and your family can eat it every night. You can leave bags of zucchini at the front doors of all your neighbors. You can give it away to strangers. But the plants relentlessly continue to produce more and more. At a certain point in midsummer, you will notice your neighbors crossing to the other side of the street when they see you, and the postman conspicuously looking the other way as he deposits your mail. So, when you have too much zucchini in your garden, make a few loaves of this homestyle quickbread. No one can turn away from freshly baked bread.

1 cup canola oil, plus more for the pans

3 cups all-purpose flour

3/4 cup sugar

1 teaspoon fine sea salt

1 teaspoon baking powder

1 teaspoon baking soda

1/2 teaspoon ground cinnamon

3 large eggs, lightly beaten

1 tablespoon pure vanilla extract

4 zucchini, peeled and grated (about 2 cups)

1 cup chopped pecans

Preheat the oven to 350°F. Brush two 8 x 5 x 3-inch loaf pans with oil.

In a bowl, whisk together the flour, sugar, salt, baking powder, baking soda, and cinnamon. Combine the 1 cup of oil, eggs, and vanilla extract in a large liquid measuring cup.

Add the oil mixture to the dry ingredients, stirring until just combined. Add the zucchini and pecans and stir until combined. Divide the batter equally between the prepared pans.

Bake until golden brown, about 1 hour. Transfer to a rack to cool slightly. Store in an airtight container for up to 3 days.

Stout Batter Bread

Makes one 9 x 5 x 3-inch loaf

Other than sharing the quickbread gene, this beer batter bread doesn't have much of a Southern heritage. For minimum effort and maximum results, it's hard to beat. This takes the phrase "dump and stir" to a whole new level. Different beers produce breads with different flavors and textures. This recipe calls for stout, producing a bread somewhat dark in color with a slightly heavy flavor. It goes well with a hearty stew such as Boeuf Bourguignonne (page 91) or Old-fashioned Pot Roast (page 89). Lighter ale produces a lighter loaf and would be more appropriate with milder dishes such as Potato and Cheddar Soup (page 241).

4 tablespoons (1/2 stick) unsalted butter, melted, plus more for the loaf pan

3 cups all-purpose flour

1 tablespoon baking powder

3 tablespoons sugar

1 teaspoon fine sea salt

1 (12-ounce) bottle stout, at room temperature

Preheat the oven to 375°F. Brush one 9 x 5 x 3-inch loaf pan with some of the butter.

In a bowl, combine the flour, baking powder, sugar, and salt. Add the beer and 2 tablespoons of the remaining melted butter, stirring just until combined. (The batter will be somewhat lumpy.)

Pour the batter into the prepared loaf pan and drizzle with the remaining 2 tablespoons of melted butter. Bake until a skewer inserted into the center comes out clean, 35 to 40 minutes. Transfer to a wire rack to cool slightly, then invert onto the rack to cool until warm. Serve warm or at room temperature.

HONEY WHOLE WHEAT BREAD

Makes two 9 x 5 x 3-inch loaves

Whole wheat flour may seem to be the choice of health nuts or diet-conscious shoppers looking for whole grains, neither of which suggests typical Southern bread. This is true for more modern breads, but Antebellum and Colonial grains were not as processed as modern flour is and were closer to what we now consider whole wheat flour. This homey bread also uses honey, a natural sweetener, instead of refined white sugar. I do, however, suggest using a modern fat, canola oil, over bacon fat (but now that I think of it, bacon fat sure sounds good!).

3¼ cups warm water (100° to 110°F)

⅓ cup honey (preferably tupelo, orange blossom, or sweet clover), plus more for accompaniment

2 packets (4½ teaspoons) active dry yeast

Canola oil, for the bowl and pans

4 cups bread flour, plus more for dusting

3 cups whole wheat flour

1 cup wheat germ

2 tablespoons fine sea salt

Unsalted butter, for accompaniment

In a large liquid measuring cup, combine the warm water, ⅓ cup honey, and yeast. Stir until dissolved. Set aside to proof. The mixture will become creamy and foamy, about 5 minutes. Lightly oil a large bowl.

To make the dough, in the bowl of a heavy-duty mixer fitted with the dough hook, combine the bread flour, whole wheat flour, wheat germ, and salt. Pour in the yeast and knead on low speed until well combined.

To shape the dough, turn it out onto a lightly floured surface. Knead the dough by using the heel of your hand to compress and push the dough away from you, and then fold it back over itself. Give the dough a small turn and repeat until the dough is smooth and elastic, 5 to 7 minutes. (The dough is ready if it bounces back when pressed with your fingers.) Place the dough in the oiled bowl. Cover with plastic wrap or a dry towel and let the dough rise in a warm place until doubled in size, about 1 hour.

Brush two 9 x 5 x 3-inch loaf pans with oil.

Turn the dough out onto a clean, lightly floured work surface, and punch down. Halve the dough; flatten one piece into an oval and roll up lengthwise. Place the roll, seam side down, into one of the prepared pans. Repeat with the remaining dough. Cover the loaves with a dry cloth and let rise in a warm place until doubled in size, about 45 minutes.

To bake the loaves, preheat the oven to 400°F. Bake until deep golden brown, about 55 minutes. The loaves will sound hollow when tapped on the top. Transfer the pans to a wire rack, and let cool for 5 minutes. Invert the loaves onto the rack to cool completely. Serve warm with butter and additional honey.

BURGUNDIAN HONEY SPICE BREAD

Makes two 9 x 5 x 3-inch loaves

The wealthy and powerful Dukes of Burgundy controlled the spice trade in the Middle Ages. The windows of the shops and bakeries of Dijon are filed with tightly wrapped loaves of *pain d'épice*, the traditional honey spice bread of the region. It's similar to American-style gingerbread only in that they both contain a variety of spices. The texture of the French bread, however, is denser, as it is traditionally baked at a low temperature for several hours, and the spice combination is slightly different. I've adapted this version to cook in less time at a higher temperature. The texture is not as traditional, but the flavor is still incredible. Ground fennel seed is not widely available; to order it, see Sources (page 301), or simply grind your own in a spice grinder.

While at La Varenne, we served this bread for breakfast for special guests. It's also wonderful with a hot cup of tea on a chilly fall afternoon.

3 tablespoons unsalted butter, at room temperature, for the loaf pans

1¼ cups milk

1 cup firmly packed light brown sugar

1½ cups honey (preferably tupelo, orange blossom, or sweet clover)

4 cups unbleached all-purpose flour

1 teaspoon ground fennel seed

½ teaspoon ground cinnamon

¼ teaspoon ground cloves

¼ teaspoon ground ginger

½ teaspoon fine sea salt

2 tablespoons very finely chopped candied ginger

1 large egg, at room temperature

1 large egg yolk, at room temperature

2 teaspoons baking soda

Preheat the oven to 350°F. Brush two 9 x 5 x 3-inch loaf pans with butter. Cut four strips of parchment: two 15 x 5 inches, and two 14 x 8 inches. Lay the two long pieces of parchment the length of the buttered pan and press to adhere. Brush the parchment with butter. Lay the two wider pieces crosswise on top. Brush the parchment with butter. Everything must be very well buttered or the bread will stick.

Heat the milk, brown sugar, and honey in a small saucepan over medium heat. Stir until the sugar is dissolved. Remove from the heat and set aside until slightly cooled.

To make the batter, in the bowl of a heavy-duty mixer fitted with the paddle, combine the flour, ground fennel, cinnamon, cloves, ginger, and salt. In two batches, add the honey mixture and candied ginger. Scrape down the sides as needed, and blend on low speed until just combined.

In a small liquid measuring cup, combine the egg, egg yolk, and baking soda. Stir to combine. Add the egg mixture to the batter and beat until well blended.

To bake the loaves, pour the batter into the prepared loaf pans, dividing it evenly and not filling the pans more than halfway. Bake, rotating once, until a skewer inserted into the center comes out clean, 45 to 50 minutes. Cover with aluminum foil if the bread starts to become too dark.

Remove the loaves to a rack to cool slightly, about 15 minutes. Turn them out of the pans and immediately remove the parchment paper. Store very tightly wrapped in plastic wrap for up to 1 week.

CHAPTER 10

SOUPS AND STEWS

THE WHOLE SUBSET OF casserole cooking in the South would be lost without the familiar red-and-white can of cream of mushroom soup. But there's so much more to soups and stews than pulling out a can opener. Homemade soups are nourishing, hot ones warming on a cold winter night, chilled versions refreshing on a hot summer day.

Soups made from just a few ingredients may seem simple, but if properly made, they can taste as complex as any dish. Good soup is not the result of throwing a bunch of ingredients in a pot and covering the mixture with water or stock. The fewer the ingredients, the better quality they must be, and the more careful their assembly. It's a multistep process of building layers of flavor.

The first step of many classic French soups and stews is the *mirepoix*, a combination of finely diced onion, celery, and carrots (the term refers to not only the specific combination of ingredients but also the cut). The *mirepoix* is the basis of many recipes—practically everything but ice cream—and especially soup. The next key step is to sweat or saute these vegetables, perhaps allowing them to color a little, but mainly to concentrate their flavors and evaporate any exuded moisture. This step is crucial. The main ingredients are then added, topped with stock, broth, or water and simmered (not boiled) until the flavors have married and the soup is complete. While classic French soups have a *mirepoix*, not all good soups need it. Southern soups typically get their layers of flavors in other ways.

Salt is also crucial to developing flavors, and that is why it is important to taste and season as you go. If all the salt and pepper in a recipe is added at the beginning of cooking, the flavors will not be right, and it will not work if all the seasoning is added at the end. It's important to build layers of flavors, to coax out the flavors as you cook. Always, always taste and adjust for seasoning with salt and pepper before you serve any soup.

In dark times of hunger, soup may be nothing more than a thin watery broth with no attention to technique—just a way of stretching too little food to fill too many bellies. Something as simple as a bowl of soup can represent a massive societal shift: between the Civil War and World War II, more and more Southerners left a predominantly agricultural life and moved to the cities to work in factories. The economy had not truly recovered from the Civil War when the Great Depression of the 1930s hit, and it hit Southerners very hard. In the cities, soup kitchens provided the only meals available to some of the unemployed. In the country, the traditional soups and stews of the South helped keep people alive. They were made from what could be harvested from the land, rivers, and ponds, with an emphasis on vegetables, often flavored with a ham bone or a small amount of meat.

I find the process of making soup almost as rewarding as eating it. Soup was one of the first dishes we learned in culinary school. For all soups, the steps are the same, only the flavors change. I relish the techniques, creating layers of flavors, tasting and adjusting the seasoning as I go. I love how the whole house is perfumed with the aroma and how the kitchen windows bead with condensation as a pot of nourishing goodness simmers on the stovetop.

The soups in this chapter include the most homey and basic, from a Southern-style vegetable soup with tender bits of diced vegetable in a rich tomato-based broth (page 228) to the classic Potato-Leek Soup (page 232) that has nourished many French families for generations. Soups also give the cook an opportunity to stretch, as in the marriage of styles that is Vidalia Onion Soup with Bacon Flan (page 244)—a Southern soup with a French accent.

HOMEMADE STOCKS

Well made stocks are one of the foundations of classic French cuisine. A good stock is redolent with flavor, clear, not cloudy, and rich with the naturally occurring gelatin in the bones. Have you made roast chicken and refrigerated the leftovers? Then, the next day you look at the chicken and the juices have congealed into a kind of meat Jell-O? That's the gelatin that gives stocks—and the soups and sauces made from them—their wonderful flavor.

CHICKEN STOCK

Makes about 10 cups

2 pounds chicken wings or bones

14 cups water

3 stalks celery, coarsely chopped

3 onions, preferably Vidalia, coarsely chopped

3 carrots, coarsely chopped

2 bay leaves, preferably fresh

2 sprigs of parsley

2 springs of thyme

4 to 6 whole black peppercorns

In a large soup pot, combine the chicken wings, water, celery, onions, carrots, bay leaves, parsley, thyme, and peppercorns. Bring the mixture to a boil over high heat. Decrease the heat to low and simmer for $1^1/2$ hours, skimming the foam off the top as it rises. Strain through a colander, reserving the stock and discarding the chicken and vegetables.

Store in an airtight container in the refrigerator for up to 1 week or freeze for up to 3 months. Before using, skim off and discard any fat that has risen to the surface.

BEEF STOCK

Makes 10 cups

6 pounds beef bones

3 carrots, coarsely chopped

3 onions, preferably Vidalia, coarsely chopped

3 stalks celery, coarsely chopped

1 head garlic, halved

1 (6-ounce) can tomato paste

5 quarts water

2 bay leaves, preferably fresh

10 whole black peppercorns

Preheat the oven to 400°F. Place the beef bones in a roasting pan. Roast, turning them occasionally, until they start to brown, about 15 minutes. Add the carrots, onions, celery, garlic, and tomato paste. Continue roasting until the vegetables are brown, an additional 20 to 30 minutes.

Transfer the contents of the roasting pan to a large stock pot and add the water. Add the bay leaves and peppercorns. Bring the mixture to a boil over high heat. Decrease the heat to low and simmer for a minimum of 4 hours and up to 8 hours, skimming the foam off the top as it rises. Strain through a colander, reserving the stock and discarding the beef bones and vegetables.

Store in an airtight container in the refrigerator for up to 1 week or freeze for up to 3 months. Before using, skim off and discard any fat that has risen to the surface.

MEME'S VEGETABLE SOUP

Serves 6 to 8

My grandfather used lots and lots of black pepper, especially to season Meme's vegetable soup. It tasted wonderful, so it wasn't like he was trying to hide the taste. He just loved pepper. We always had vegetable soup in the winter, using the vegetables we had canned or frozen that summer.

This recipe easily doubles or triples. I like to make a large batch and enjoy it a few days in a row. You can prepare this with the traditional ham bone or opt for a vegetarian version. Serve with piping hot biscuits.

1 ham bone, with some meat on it

2 bay leaves, preferably fresh

1 sprig of thyme

6 cups water

1 (15-ounce) can tomato puree

1 (14½-ounce) can whole tomatoes, with juices

2 cups shelled fresh butter beans (about 1½ pounds unshelled) or frozen butter beans, thawed

1 onion, preferably Vidalia, chopped

Coarse salt and freshly ground black pepper

3 carrots, sliced into thin rounds

2 stalks celery, chopped

2 Yukon gold potatoes, cubed

½ pound fresh green beans, trimmed and cut into 1-inch pieces

Scraped kernels from 4 ears fresh sweet corn (about 2 cups) (see page 188)

¼ pound fresh okra, stems trimmed, cut into ½-inch pieces (optional)

Meme's Biscuits (page 204), for accompaniment

In a large pot, place the ham bone, bay leaves, thyme, and water. Bring to a boil over high heat, then decrease the heat to low and simmer until the broth is flavorful and fragrant, about 1 hour.

Add the tomato puree, whole tomatoes with juices, butter beans, and onion. Season with salt and pepper. Continue cooking on low heat until the butter beans are just tender, about 30 minutes. Add the carrots, celery, potatoes, green beans, corn, and okra. Continue cooking until the vegetables are tender, about 30 additional minutes. Remove the bay leaves and thyme. Taste and adjust for seasoning with salt and pepper.

Enjoy with hot biscuits.

CHILLED CANTALOUPE SOUP

Serves 4 to 6

I made this soup for Mama when I was in junior high. She had been going through a tough time and one day when she came home for lunch I had prepared a chilled cantaloupe soup out of *Southern Living* magazine.

Even though I had always enjoyed cooking, I think that this slightly unusual soup caught her off guard. I wanted to make her feel better, and as it often does, home-made food made with love can make a dark day seem brighter.

1 medium cantaloupe, peeled, seeded, and chopped

2 tablespoons sugar

1/4 cup freshly squeezed orange juice

Pinch of coarse salt

Fresh mint leaves, for garnish

In the jar of a blender, combine the cantaloupe, sugar, orange juice, and salt; process until smooth. Transfer to a bowl, cover with plastic wrap, and refrigerate to chill thoroughly, at least 30 minutes. Taste and adjust for seasoning with additional sugar and salt, if needed.

Serve chilled in chilled bowls, garnished with mint.

CORN SOUP WITH TOMATO GARNISH

Serves 4 to 6

Dede always preferred to plant his corn patch in the fruitful black soil at the river's edge. He taught me that when corn is ripe and ready to be picked, the silk at the top of the ear should be dark brown, almost black. It is not unusual to see people peeling back the husks in search of ears with perfect rows of kernels. Just take a peek to make sure the ear is full and free of worms, but keep the husk on to keep the corn moist and sweet.

Do not bother with this recipe unless it is summer and you can make it with fresh corn and the best tomatoes, preferably heirloom. You will only be disappointed. Heirloom tomatoes, varieties passed down through generations by farmers and gardeners the world over, come in all shapes, sizes, colors, and tastes. If you cannot find heirlooms, this garnish would also be delicious with any ripe tomato from your garden or market.

Scraped kernels from 6 ears fresh sweet corn (about 3 cups; see page 188), cobs reserved and cut in half

4 cups chicken stock (page 227) or low-fat, reduced-sodium chicken broth

1 tablespoon corn oil, preferably unrefined

1 onion, preferably Vidalia, chopped

1 clove garlic, very finely chopped

1 russet potato, peeled and finely chopped

1 tablespoon fine yellow cornmeal

Bouquet garni (2 sprigs of flat-leaf parsley, 2 sprigs of thyme, 1 bay leaf, preferably fresh, 6 whole black peppercorns, tied together in cheesecloth)

2 to 3 heirloom tomatoes, cored, seeded, and chopped

1 tablespoon extra-virgin olive oil

1 tablespoon chopped fresh herbs (such as parsley, tarragon, or basil)

Coarse salt and freshly ground black pepper

1/2 cup heavy cream (optional)

To make the corn stock, in a saucepan, combine the corncobs and chicken stock and bring to a boil over medium heat. Decrease the heat to low and simmer until the stock has taken on a light corn flavor, about 10 minutes. Remove the corncobs, strain the stock into a bowl, and set aside.

To prepare the soup, in the same saucepan, heat the oil over medium heat and cook the onion until soft and translucent, about 5 minutes. Add the garlic and cook until fragrant, 45 to 60 seconds. Add the corn kernels, potato, and cornmeal. Add enough of the corncob-infused stock to cover. Add the bouquet garni and bring to a boil over medium-high heat. Decrease the heat to low and simmer until the chopped potato is tender, about 20 minutes.

Meanwhile, to prepare the garnish, combine the tomatoes and any juices, olive oil, and herbs. Season with salt and pepper. Set aside.

To finish the soup, in the saucepan, using an immersion blender, puree the soup. Or ladle the soup into a blender and puree until smooth a little at a time. Leave it coarse and chunky if you prefer a more rustic soup, or puree until smooth for a more elegant soup. Stir in the cream and reheat. Taste and adjust for seasoning with salt and pepper.

To serve, spoon into bowls and top with the tomato garnish. Serve immediately.

POTATO-LEEK SOUP

A French classic, this soup marries humble ingredients and well-executed technique to produce an excellent first course or a warming meal with cornbread on a cold winter night. When chilled, this is the famous vichyssoise, a great soup for a cool day. Omit the cream if you want a lighter soup.

2 tablespoons canola oil

2 tablespoons unsalted butter

2 stalks celery, finely diced

3 leeks, white and pale green parts, well washed (see below), halved and thinly sliced into half-moons

2 shallots, chopped

2 cloves garlic, very finely chopped

2 pounds Yukon gold potatoes, peeled and cut into 1-inch pieces

4 cups chicken stock (page 227) or low-fat, reduced-sodium chicken broth

Bouquet garni (1 bay leaf, preferably fresh, 2 sprigs of rosemary, 2 sprigs of thyme, 2 sprigs of flat-leaf parsley, 6 whole black peppercorns, tied together in cheesecloth)

1/4 cup heavy cream (optional)

Coarse salt and freshly ground white pepper

To prepare the soup, in a stockpot, heat the oil and butter over medium-low heat. Add the celery, leeks, and shallots. Cook until soft, about 4 to 5 minutes, stirring occasionally, but do not brown. Add the garlic and cook until fragrant, 45 to 60 seconds. Add the potatoes, stock, and bouquet garni.

Bring the mixture to a boil over high heat, decrease the heat to low, and simmer until the potatoes are tender, 40 to 45 minutes. Remove the bouquet garni and discard.

To finish the soup, in the stockpot, using an immersion blender, puree the soup. Or, ladle the soup into a blender and puree until smooth a little at a time. Leave it coarse and chunky if you prefer a more rustic soup or puree until smooth for a more elegant soup. Stir in the cream. Taste and adjust for seasoning with salt and pepper. If needed, re-warm the soup over medium-low heat.

Leeks

Leeks grow in sandy soil, are often dirty, and can be difficult to clean without the proper technique. (Chewing on a mouthful of grit is the gastronomical equivalent of nails on a chalkboard.) To clean a leek: using a chef's knife, remove the hairy root end and dark green top. Halve the leek lengthwise, then slice crosswise into half-moons. Separate the half-moons with your fingers and place them in a sink or large bowl filled with cold water. Swish the slices around, letting the dirt fall to the bottom. Using your hands or a fine mesh sieve, scoop the leeks from the water, leaving the dirt at the bottom. Drain, clean, and refill the sink or bowl. Repeat the process until the leeks are clean and free of dirt. This method also works for greens and herbs.

Winter Squash Soup with Sauteed Apples

Serves 4 to 6

I reach for my immersion blender when I prepare pureed soups. If you don't have one, a regular blender is fine, but use it with care: let hot soup cool for about ten minutes before blending, or the steam could force the lid off. Don't fill the blender carafe more than halfway or the whirling soup could force off the lid and spew out. Finally, hold the lid on tightly with a heavy-duty kitchen towel.

You'll find many types of winter squash in your produce department. For this sweet-savory soup, reach past the standard acorn and butternut varieties for something new like carnival, delicata, or kabocha for a different feel and flavor.

2 tablespoons unsalted butter

1 shallot, finely chopped

1 carrot, finely chopped

1 stalk celery, very finely chopped

Bouquet garni (3 sprigs of flat-leaf parsley, 2 sprigs of thyme, 10 whole black peppercorns, tied together in cheesecloth)

3 pounds winter squash, peeled, seeded, and chopped

3 cups chicken stock (page 227) or low-fat, reduced-sodium chicken broth

Coarse salt and freshly ground black pepper

2 Granny Smith apples, peeled, cored, and diced

1 sprig of thyme

1/2 cup heavy cream (optional)

1 teaspoon firmly packed dark brown sugar

Pinch of freshly grated nutmeg

To prepare the soup, in a large, heavy-bottomed Dutch oven, melt 1 tablespoon of the butter over medium-low heat until foaming. Add the shallot, carrot, and celery. Cook, stirring frequently, until soft and translucent, about 3 minutes.

Add the bouquet garni, squash, and chicken stock. Season with salt and pepper. Bring to a boil over high heat, decrease the heat to low, and simmer until the squash is tender, about 30 minutes.

Meanwhile, to cook the apples, in a skillet, heat the remaining 1 tablespoon of butter over medium heat. Add the diced apple and remaining sprig of thyme; season with salt and pepper. Cook, stirring occasionally, until the apple is tender and lightly caramelized, about 5 minutes. Set aside and keep warm.

To finish the soup, remove the bouquet garni and discard. In the Dutch oven, using an immersion blender, puree the soup until smooth. Or ladle the soup into a blender and puree until smooth a little at a time. Leave it coarse and chunky if you prefer a more rustic soup or puree until smooth for a more elegant soup. Add the cream, brown sugar, and nutmeg. Taste and adjust for seasoning with salt and pepper.

To serve, ladle into warm bowls and garnish with the sauteed apples. Serve immediately.

CLASSIC FRENCH ONION SOUP

Serves 4 to 6

Mama loves this soup. What's not to love? It's a hearty bowl of sweet, brown, caramelized onions in a rich beef broth, enriched with a dose of sherry and topped with deliciously nutty, golden brown, melted Gruyère cheese.

Why does Gruyère taste so good? Aged, low-moisture cheeses such as Gruyère and Parmigiano-Reggiano have a stronger protein structure than younger, softer cheeses like fontina or fresh mozzarella, and require higher temperatures to melt. The higher heat, combined with less moisture, causes the protein to actually break down, bringing out their nutty flavor.

4 tablespoons (1/2 stick) unsalted butter

6 onions, preferably Vidalia, sliced

2 leeks, white and pale green parts, well washed (see page 232), halved lengthwise, and thinly sliced into half-moons

1 shallot, chopped

Coarse salt and freshly ground black pepper

1 teaspoon sugar

1 tablespoon all-purpose flour

1/2 cup dry sherry

6 cups beef stock (page 227) or low-fat, reduced-sodium beef broth

1 tablespoon chopped fresh thyme

1 baguette, sliced diagonally 1/2 inch thick

3 cups grated Gruyère cheese (about 12 ounces)

Snipped fresh chives, for garnish

To caramelize the onions, in a large, heavy-bottomed Dutch oven, melt the butter over medium-low heat. Add the onions, leeks, and shallot. Season with salt and pepper, sprinkle with sugar, and cook, stirring as needed to keep the onions from sticking, until the onions are melting and soft, golden brown, and beginning to caramelize, 30 to 45 minutes.

To prepare the soup, sprinkle the flour over the onions, and stir to coat. Add the sherry, stock, and thyme and bring to a boil over high heat. Decrease the heat to low, and simmer, partially covered, for about 30 minutes. Taste and adjust for seasoning with salt and pepper.

Preheat the broiler. To serve, ladle hot soup into 6 ovenproof bowls. Arrange the bowls on a baking sheet. Place 1 or 2 slices of baguette over each bowl of soup. Top each bowl with 1/2 cup grated cheese so it covers the baguette slices. Broil until the cheese is melted and crusty brown around the edges. (Watch carefully so the bread doesn't burn.) Garnish with the chives. Serve immediately.

Sherry

Sherry is a fortified wine from the town of Jerez de la Frontera, in the Andalusia region of Spain. Sherries can range in flavor from sweet to dry, and are served either at room temperature or chilled. Sherry is an excellent apéritif and adds a lively punch in cooking, where it is typically added as a finish for soups.

Gazpacho with Tarragon Crème Fraîche

Gazpacho is essentially a liquid salad. It's best prepared at the height of summer, using fresh, local ingredients—I always use Georgia-grown vegetables when I make this gazpacho. The key is to use the proper amount of salt to draw out the moisture and flavor of the vegetables. There is nothing so simple, yet so vitally essential to cooking, as salt. Without salt even the most elaborate dish would be lifeless and dull. I remember staring incredulously as my chef in culinary school would toss what seemed to be handfuls of salt into food. Now I giggle when my students stare at me when I do the same!

3 tomatoes, cored and coarsely chopped

1 English cucumber, seeded and coarsely chopped

1 red bell pepper, cored, seeded, and coarsely chopped

1 green bell pepper or poblano chile, cored, seeded, and coarsely chopped

1 onion, preferably Vidalia, coarsely chopped

1 carrot, chopped

1 stalk celery, chopped

Juice of 1/2 lemon, plus more if needed

1 teaspoon Worcestershire sauce

1/4 teaspoon cayenne pepper

1 cup tomato juice (optional)

1/2 cup crème fraîche or sour cream

1/4 cup chopped fresh tarragon

Coarse salt and freshly ground black pepper

1/4 cup best-quality extra-virgin olive oil

In the bowl of a food processor or jar of a blender fitted with the metal blade, puree the tomatoes until very smooth. Transfer the tomato puree to a large nonreactive bowl. Puree the cucumber, red and green bell peppers, onion, carrot, and celery. (If your bowl isn't large enough, puree the vegetables in batches.) Add the pureed vegetables to the pureed tomatoes and stir to combine. Add the lemon juice, Worcestershire sauce, and cayenne pepper. If the soup seems too thick, add the tomato juice, if necessary, to achieve the proper consistency. Cover with plastic wrap and chill thoroughly in the refrigerator, at least 30 minutes.

Meanwhile, in a small bowl, combine the crème fraîche and tarragon. Season the mixture with salt and black pepper. Set aside.

To serve, taste the soup and adjust the seasoning with salt, pepper, and lemon juice, if necessary. Ladle the soup into chilled bowls. Drizzle over the olive oil and top each bowl of soup with a small dollop of the seasoned crème fraîche. Serve immediately.

New Southern Chicken and Herb Dumplings

Serves 4 to 6

Several years ago, my sister was involved in a very serious accident and nearly died. It was perhaps the most pure, absolute fear I had ever felt in my entire life. Mama and I were only allowed to see her twice a day. One morning early on, when our grief and worry were still overriding any desire to eat, a group of ladies came to the hospital and set up lunch. The volunteer explained that several of the local churches provided lunch and supper for the families of patients. It was real food, made with love and care. Pimento cheese sandwiches and individual slices of pound cake were hand-wrapped in waxed paper and homemade yeast rolls were delivered while still warm, shiny with butter. There were hunks of meaty pot roast bathed in dark brown gravy and a comforting combination of tender chicken and dumplings. The food was amazing. It was restorative, as much for the delicious taste as the real caring and kindness. It was without a doubt the most rewarding, healing love I have ever felt from absolute strangers.

3 boneless, skinless chicken breasts, cubed (about 2 pounds)

6 cups chicken stock (page 227) or low-fat, reduced-sodium chicken broth

Bouquet garni (3 sprigs of parsley, 2 sprigs of thyme, 1 bay leaf, preferably fresh, 6 black peppercorns, tied together in cheesecloth)

2 cups unbleached all-purpose flour

2 tablespoons finely grated Parmigiano-Reggiano cheese (about 1/2 ounce), plus more for garnish

1 tablespoon baking powder

1 tablespoon chopped fresh flat-leaf parsley

Coarse salt and freshly ground black pepper

1 cup whole milk

3 tablespoons unsalted butter

1 tablespoon canola oil

1 onion, preferably Vidalia, chopped

3 carrots, cut into 1/2-inch rounds

1 large sweet potato, peeled and cut into 1/2-inch cubes

2 cloves garlic, finely chopped

10 ounces fresh baby spinach

1/2 teaspoon red pepper flakes (optional)

To poach the chicken, in a large saucepan, add the breasts and the chicken stock to cover. Add the bouquet garni. Bring to a boil over high heat, then decrease the heat to low. Simmer, skimming off the foam occasionally, until the chicken is tender, 10 to 15 minutes. (If the stock is cloudy, don't worry; it's simply protein clarified from the stock. Just ignore it or strain it out.) Transfer the poached chicken to a warm plate; reserve the stock. Cover with a lid and set aside.

To prepare the dumplings, in a bowl, combine the flour, cheese, baking powder, parsley, and 3/4 teaspoon of the salt. In a small saucepan, bring the milk and butter to a simmer over low heat; season with black pepper. Add the milk mixture to the dry ingredients and stir to combine.

In a second large saucepan, heat the oil over medium heat. Add the onion, carrots, and sweet potato. Cook until the onions are translucent, 3 to 5 minutes. Add the garlic and cook until fragrant, 45 to 60 seconds. Add the reserved stock and bring to a boil over high heat. Decrease the heat to low. Using a small ice cream scoop or tablespoon, drop the dough, about 1 tablespoon at a time, into the simmering stock. Cover and simmer until the dumplings are cooked through and the vegetables are tender, about 20 minutes.

To assemble, add the reserved chicken and cook just until heated through, about 5 minutes. Stir in the spinach; cover and continue cooking for an additional 30 to 45 seconds. Add the red pepper flakes. Taste and adjust for seasoning with salt and pepper.

To serve, ladle into shallow bowls and garnish with additional cheese; serve immediately.

GULF COAST OYSTER CHOWDER

Serves 4 to 6

Chowders are thick soups containing fish or shellfish and vegetables such as potatoes and onions in a milk or tomato base. People most often associate these hearty soups with cold New England winters, but the Gulf of Mexico also has a history with them. Poor people living on the coast were able to supplement a diet of salted, preserved meat and inexpensive potatoes with seafood they caught or harvested.

Meme would prepare this soup in the fall more often, using fatback for salt and flavor instead of bacon. Both meats produce a smoky, salty layer of flavor that is complemented by the sweet oysters. Use canola oil if you prefer a lighter, healthier version.

6 slices thick-cut bacon, cut into lardons (see page 179); 1 ounce fatback; or 2 tablespoons canola oil

2 leeks, white and pale green parts, well washed (see page 232), halved horizontally, and thinly sliced into half-moons

2 tablespoons all-purpose flour

4 cups bottled clam juice

1½ cups milk

1½ cups heavy cream

2 (8-ounce) containers of oysters, drained, juices reserved

2 large russet potatoes, peeled and cut into ½-inch pieces

1 sprig of thyme

1 bay leaf, preferably fresh

2 tablespoons dry sherry

Coarse salt and freshly ground black pepper

In a saucepan, cook the bacon over medium heat until crisp, about 5 minutes. Add the leeks and saute, stirring often, until they begin to soften, 3 to 5 minutes. Sprinkle over the flour and stir to combine. Whisk in the clam juice, milk, cream, and reserved oyster juice. Add the potatoes and bring to a boil over high heat. Decrease the heat to low. Add the thyme and bay leaf, cover, and simmer until the potatoes are tender, about 10 minutes. Add the oysters and simmer, uncovered, until they are heated through and their edges begin to curl, about 3 minutes. Remove the thyme and bay leaf and discard. Add the sherry and stir to combine. Taste and adjust for seasoning with salt and pepper. Serve immediately.

Oysters

Sometimes containers of oysters contain bits of shell or grit. To clean the oysters, strain them in a fine mesh sieve over a bowl, allowing the juice to pass into the bowl. Examine the oysters and remove any bits of shell. Use the strained juice in the chowder for extra oyster flavor.

SOUTHERN MINESTRONE

Serves 4 to 6

Like many recipes of humble country origins, there is no carved-in-stone recipe for minestrone, the iconic Italian vegetable soup. Mamas from both sides of the Atlantic have used fresh seasonal vegetables with a bit of hambone or cheese rind to prepare soulful, satisfying soups. We've long known that this combination tastes good. Now we have a name for why it does: umami. The Japanese term *umami* is now familiar to culinary professionals, chefs, and informed foodies, yet Asian cooks have appreciated the taste for centuries. It is the fifth taste after sour, salty, bitter, and sweet. Scientifically, umami is the distinctive flavor of amino acids, which are the building blocks of protein. Think about classic Caesar salad dressing, a combination of egg protein and salted anchovies. Or old-fashioned greens simmered with ham. Or this soup, in which the rind of the Parmigiano-Reggiano cheese complements the vegetables in the tomato broth.

1 tablespoon olive oil

2 onions, preferably Vidalia, chopped

1 carrot, chopped

1 stalk celery, chopped

2 large cloves garlic, finely chopped

6 cups water, plus more if needed

1/4 medium head green cabbage, chopped

Rind from a piece of Parmigiano-Reggiano cheese

Coarse salt and freshly ground black pepper

1 (14 1/2-ounce) can crushed tomatoes

1/4 pound green beans, trimmed and cut into 1/2-inch pieces

1/4 pound fresh okra, stems trimmed, halved lengthwise

1 yellow squash, chopped

1 zucchini, chopped

2 tablespoons chopped fresh flat-leaf parsley

2 tablespoons chopped fresh basil

1/2 teaspoon red pepper flakes

1/2 cup elbow macaroni

Extra-virgin olive oil, for drizzling

Parmigiano-Reggiano cheese, for garnish

In a large, heavy-bottomed Dutch oven, heat the oil over medium heat. Add the onions, carrot, and celery and cook until the onions are golden, 10 to 12 minutes. Add the garlic and cook until fragrant, 45 to 60 seconds. Add 4 cups of the water, the cabbage, and the cheese rind. Season the mixture with salt and pepper. Bring to a boil over high heat, and then decrease the heat to low. Simmer until the mixture is flavorful and well combined, about 30 minutes.

Add the tomatoes, green beans, okra, yellow squash, zucchini, parsley, basil, and red pepper flakes. Add more of the remaining water to cover by about 1 inch. Continue to simmer slowly over very low heat until the vegetables are just tender, an additional 20 minutes. Add the pasta, and more water, if needed. Simmer until the pasta is tender, an additional 10 to 15 minutes. Taste and adjust for seasoning with salt and pepper.

To serve, ladle the soup into warmed bowls. Drizzle with extra-virgin olive oil and sprinkle with grated cheese.

Parmigiano-Reggiano

Parmigiano-Reggiano is a hard, dry cheese made from cow's milk. The rind is golden tan and the interior is creamy yellow. True Parmigiano-Reggiano from Italy is aged eighteen to thirty-six months and is sharp and rich in flavor with a salty kick. While other countries make Parmesan cheese, real Italian Parmigiano-Reggiano is more expensive and is well worth every dime. Look for "Parmigiano-Reggiano" stenciled on the rind to authenticate the origin.

QUICK POT AU FEU

Serves 4 to 6

This French dish, which translates to "pot on the fire," consists of meat and vegetables slowly cooked in water or stock. The broth is traditionally served with croutons as a first course, followed by an entrée of the meat and vegetables. The combination of meat and vegetables varies according to the region. It's traditionally a slow-cooking dish that takes hours. This version makes use of more tender cuts of meat and therefore cooks much more quickly.

8 cups beef stock (page 227) or low-fat, reduced-sodium beef broth

Bouquet garni (8 sprigs of flat-leaf parsley, 6 sprigs of thyme, 2 bay leaves, preferably fresh, 10 whole black peppercorns, tied together in cheesecloth)

Coarse salt and freshly ground black pepper

2 leeks, white part only, quartered to the root, well washed (see page 232), and tied

8 small red or Yukon gold potatoes

1 small head green cabbage, quartered

2 stalks celery, halved crosswise

4 cloves garlic, halved

1 pound boneless, skinless chicken breasts or thighs

1 pound boneless beef rib-eye

8 small carrots, peeled

1 pound haricots verts or young, tender green beans, trimmed

GARNISHES

1 baguette, sliced diagonally 1/2 inch thick

Dijon mustard

Cornichons

Freshly grated horseradish

Coarse salt and freshly ground black pepper

In a large stockpot, add the stock and bouquet garni. Season with salt and pepper. Add the leeks, potatoes, cabbage, celery, and garlic. Bring to a boil over high heat, cover, and decrease the heat to low. Simmer until the vegetables are almost tender, 10 to 12 minutes.

Season the chicken and beef with salt and pepper and add to the pot along with the carrots. (Use tongs to move all the ingredients around so the raw ingredients are fully submerged in the stock.) Continue to simmer, partially covered, until the chicken and beef are almost cooked through, about 5 minutes. Add the haricot verts and continue cooking until the beans are tender and the chicken and beef are completely cooked through, an additional 5 to 7 minutes.

To serve, remove the leeks and untie them. Divide the leeks and vegetables among shallow serving bowls, followed by the chicken and beef. Taste and adjust the seasoning of the broth with salt and pepper. Ladle some of the broth over the meat and vegetables. Serve with baguette slices, mustard, cornichons, horseradish, and salt and black pepper.

POTATO AND CHEDDAR SOUP

Serves 6

Since this soup is the liquid version of a baked potato, calories and all, you can use low-fat milk with no detrimental effect on flavor, if it gives you any comfort. But don't do anything silly, like use low-fat cheese, which melts poorly and tastes worse. It's important to add the cheese a little at a time, so it incorporates and doesn't become an oily mess.

2 tablespoons canola oil

1 onion, preferably Vidalia, chopped

1 carrot, chopped

1 stalk celery, chopped

2 cloves garlic, finely chopped

1 teaspoon chopped fresh thyme

Coarse salt and freshly ground black pepper

3 tablespoons all-purpose flour

4 cups chicken stock (page 227) or low-fat, reduced-sodium chicken broth

3 cups (whole or lowfat) milk

4 russet potatoes, peeled and cubed (about 1¾ pounds)

3 cups packed grated sharp Cheddar cheese (about 12 ounces)

Snipped fresh chives, for garnish

Bacon Croutons (recipe follows), for garnish (optional)

In a large, heavy-bottomed Dutch oven, heat the oil over medium heat. Add the onion, carrot, celery, garlic, and thyme. Season with salt and pepper. Cook, stirring occasionally, until the vegetables begin to soften, 5 to 7 minutes. Sprinkle the flour over and cook, stirring, for 2 minutes. Gradually whisk in the stock, and then the milk. Add the potatoes and bring the soup to a boil over high heat. Decrease the heat to low and simmer until the potatoes are tender, about 20 minutes.

Add the cheese, about $1/3$ cup at a time, stirring until melted and smooth after each addition. Taste and adjust for seasoning with salt and pepper.

To serve, ladle the soup into warmed bowls. Sprinkle with chives and croutons and serve immediately.

BACON CROUTONS

Makes 2 cups

4 ounces country-style bread, cut into ½-inch cubes (about 3 cups)

6 slices thick-cut bacon, cut into lardons (see page 179)

1 tablespoon canola oil

Freshly ground black pepper

Position an oven rack in the center of the oven and preheat the oven to 350°F. In a large bowl, combine the bread, bacon, oil, and pepper. Toss to coat. Transfer to a rimmed baking sheet. Bake, stirring occasionally, until the bacon is crisp and the croutons are golden, about 20 minutes.

SAVANNAH RIVER CATFISH STEW

Serves 4 to 6

The Savannah River is one of Georgia's longest and largest rivers and defines most of the boundary between Georgia and South Carolina. I've seen photos of my grandfather and his brother with catfish almost as big as a man that they caught in the Savannah River. Wild catfish that live in rivers, lakes, and ponds are bottom dwellers, and the flesh picks up a distinctively earthy flavor. For years, there were catfish in our pond even though the pond was solely stocked with bass and bream. Dede explained to me when I was young that the catfish eggs would be transported on the wings and feet of the water birds.

So, it was something special when we would catch them. We'd catch these monsters, and they terrified me, with their flat black mouths and whiskers popping as they flailed on the shore. The whiskers are scary, but they are not what hurts. Dede had a few special tools in his tackle box to deal with catfish. The fish have sharp spines on their fins, and he would fearlessly grab them behind the head and clip off the fins with pliers. Catfish also differ in that they don't have scales. But their skin is tough and they have to be skinned before they are eaten. He'd hammer a nail through their head into the tree and, using the same pliers, peel the skin off the fish like taking off a sock from your foot.

If you are not catching your own, make a point to buy American farm-raised catfish, which are fed a diet of high-protein pellets made from soybean meal, corn, and rice that give the flesh a consistent, sweet, mild flavor. You just don't know what you are getting if you buy imported fish.

4 slices thick-cut bacon, cut into lardons (see page 179); 1 ounce fatback; or 2 tablespoons canola oil

1 onion, preferably Vidalia, chopped

2 large russet potatoes, peeled and cut into 1/4-inch pieces

2 tablespoons all-purpose flour

3 cups water

3 cups milk

1 sprig of thyme

1 bay leaf, preferably fresh

1/2 teaspoon Cajun seasoning, cayenne pepper, or Creole Seasoning (page 287)

2 pounds catfish fillets, cut into strips

2 tablespoons chopped fresh flat-leaf parsley

Coarse salt and freshly ground black pepper

Line a plate with paper towels. In a saucepan, cook the bacon over medium heat until crisp, about 5 minutes. Using a slotted spoon, remove the bacon to the prepared plate to drain. Pour off all but 1 tablespoon of the grease (reserve the excess fat for another use or dispose). Add the onion and potatoes to the saucepan and cook, stirring often, until golden, 5 to 7 minutes. Sprinkle over the flour and stir to coat and combine. Stir in the water and milk. Add the thyme, bay leaf, and Cajun seasoning. Bring to a boil over high heat. Decrease the heat to low and simmer until the potatoes are just tender, about 15 minutes.

Add the catfish and simmer, uncovered, until the fish is falling apart, an additional 15 to 20 minutes. Remove the thyme and bay leaf and discard. Add the parsley and stir to combine. Taste and adjust for seasoning with salt and pepper. Ladle into warmed bowls and garnish with the reserved bacon.

BLACK-EYED PEA AND HAM HOCK SOUP

Serves 6

In the summer, we'd sit on the porch shelling the black-eyed peas that Dede had picked that morning. The purple hulls dyed our fingers smoky violet. I've used frozen black-eyed peas to prepare this soup, but don't use canned, as they are too soft. If using frozen peas, reduce the cooking time according to the package instructions or until the peas are tender. Note that the dried peas must soak overnight or have a quick soak. Don't skip the essential step of simmering the ham hocks in the chicken stock. The flavor and aroma are what makes this soup extraordinary.

2 cups dried black-eyed peas, washed and picked over for stones

4 to 6 cups chicken stock (page 227) or low-fat, reduced-sodium chicken broth, plus more if necessary

2 smoked ham hocks

1 tablespoon canola oil

1 onion, preferably Vidalia, chopped

2 carrots, chopped

2 stalks celery, chopped

2 cloves garlic, very finely chopped

1 teaspoon red pepper flakes

1 bunch collards, tough stems removed and discarded, leaves very thinly sliced in chiffonade (see page 197)

Coarse salt and freshly ground black pepper

Place the peas in a large bowl and add water to cover. Soak overnight. Or place the peas in a large pot of water and bring to a boil over high heat, then remove from the heat and set aside for 1 hour. Discard any floating peas and drain before cooking.

In a pot, bring the stock and the ham hocks to a boil over high heat. Decrease the heat to low and simmer until the flavors have married, at least 30 minutes.

Meanwhile, in a large, heavy-bottomed Dutch oven, heat the oil over medium heat. Add the onion, carrots, and celery and cook until soft and translucent, 3 to 5 minutes. Add the garlic and cook until fragrant, 45 to 60 seconds. Drain the peas and add to the pot. Add the red pepper flakes and ham hocks with stock to cover. Bring to a boil over high heat, decrease the heat to low, and simmer until the peas are tender, 2 to 2 1/2 hours.

Just before serving, bring the soup to a boil over high heat. Add the collards and stir to combine. Cook until wilted, about 5 minutes. Taste and adjust the seasoning with salt and pepper. Ladle into warmed bowls and serve immediately.

VIDALIA ONION SOUP WITH BACON FLAN

This soup is decidedly uptown and was inspired by one I had at the Ritz-Carlton dining room in Atlanta. It's a perfect marriage of Southern ingredients and French techniques that clearly states, *bon appétit, y'all!* I like to serve it in mason jars or French glass yogurt cups so you can see the layering.

SOUP

4 tablespoons (1/2 stick) unsalted butter

8 onions, preferably Vidalia, sliced

Coarse salt and freshly ground black pepper

1 teaspoon firmly packed brown sugar

1 tablespoon all-purpose flour

Bouquet garni (3 sprigs of flat-leaf parsley, 3 sprigs of thyme, 1 bay leaf, preferably fresh, 10 whole black peppercorns, tied together in cheesecloth)

1/2 cup dry sherry

6 cups beef stock (page 227) or low-fat, reduced-sodium beef broth

FLAN

6 slices thick-cut bacon, cut into lardons (see page 179)

3 shallots, chopped

1 1/2 cups whole milk

3 large eggs, lightly beaten

Coarse salt and freshly ground black pepper

To prepare the soup, melt the butter in a large, heavy-bottomed Dutch oven over medium-low heat. Add the onions and season with salt and pepper. Sprinkle with the brown sugar and cook, stirring just enough to keep the onions from sticking, until they are melting and soft, golden brown, and beginning to caramelize, 30 to 45 minutes.

Sprinkle the flour over the onions, stirring to coat. Add the bouquet garni, sherry, and stock. Bring to a boil over high heat. Decrease the heat to low and simmer, partially covered, for about 30 minutes. Taste and adjust for seasoning with salt and pepper.

To prepare the flan, line a plate with paper towels. Lightly butter six 4-ounce ramekins or small glass jars. Preheat the oven to 350°F.

In a skillet, cook the bacon over medium heat until crisp, 5 to 7 minutes. Remove the bacon with a slotted spoon to the prepared plate to drain. Pour off all but 1 tablespoon of the grease (reserve the excess fat for another use or dispose). Add the shallots, decrease the heat to medium-low, and cook until translucent, about 3 minutes. In the jar of a blender, combine the bacon, shallots, milk, and eggs. Puree until smooth. Season with salt and pepper.

Divide the custard among the prepared ramekins so that it fills each about 1/2 inch. Cover each ramekin with aluminum foil and place in a roasting pan. Pour enough hot water around the ramekins in the roasting pan so that the water comes halfway up the sides of the ramekins, creating a bain-marie (water bath). Bake until just set, but still wiggly and slightly soft in the center, about 30 minutes. Using a metal spatula or tongs, remove the ramekins from the bain-marie to a rack to cool. Run the blade of a thin metal spatula around the edge of the flan to loosen. Set aside.

When ready to serve, unmold the flans into the centers of warmed, shallow soup bowls and ladle the soup over. Alternatively, ladle the soup into the glass jars, if using, to see the layers of flan and soup. Serve immediately.

CHAPTER 11
DESSERTS

SEVERAL YEARS AGO I spent a Thanksgiving evening walking the beautiful Champs-Élysées in Paris. I was working in France at the time, and, aside from the magical twinkling lights in the trees, what I remember most is feeling like it was not Thanksgiving at all. An American in Paris? No, I was a pitiful, homesick Southerner. I wanted, in this order, Mama, the smell of roast turkey in my grandmother's kitchen, and a buttery wedge of Meme's pound cake with a little piece of Mama's pecan pie on the side.

Notice the prominence of dessert in my longings—the Southern sweet tooth is a powerful force. Sugar is more than an ingredient in the South. It falls somewhere between condiment and food group. We have desserts at birthday parties, holidays, and special occasions. Like lonely me walking the streets of Paris in a reverie, people want to experience those memories again and relive their pasts through dessert. Mamas calm crying babies with sugar. (Mama dipped my sister's pacifier in Karo syrup; she finally put a stop to it when Jona was old enough to reach the bottle on the dresser herself.) We drink tea so sweet it will make your teeth hurt, slather jam and jelly on biscuits, eat ham cured in sugar and salt, often put a pinch of sugar in slow-cooked greens, and finish up the meal with a sweet wedge of pie.

Some food historians claim that the Southern fascination with sugar is a practical one. In the hot, humid South, sugar was originally a means of preservation. That's why we have sugar-cured ham and bacon, sweet pickles, and boiled icing to protect cakes. Another reason for sugar's importance is that the crop was tied to slavery. Sugar production is undeniably back-breaking work and very labor-intensive. Sugar cane followed the movement of African slaves through the islands of the Caribbean and into the plantations of the South where it was grown. The mothers and sisters of the men working hard in the fields were in the kitchen, making the food that eventually evolved into Southern cuisine.

When transportation of goods depended upon horses and wagons on iffy roads, it could take months for sugar to travel from the sugar-growing state of Louisiana to hill and mountain country. Sugar was a precious commodity then, kept under lock and key, and Southern craftsmen created a specialized piece of furniture known as the sugar chest to store it. These strong, decorative boxes were built throughout the South, most notably in Kentucky and Tennessee. Finally, with the advent of steamboats and improved shipping, sugar prices fell in the nineteenth century and sugar became more widely available throughout the region.

In the South of living memory, the pièce de résistance of all holidays and special occasions is the sideboard laden with an immense dessert buffet. Imagine a profusion of tender layer cakes, golden pecan pies, pumpkin pies the color of burnt sienna, amber peanut brittle, sugared pecans, and bubbling cobblers. I feel the presence of my grandmother with every crumb—the toasted buttery smell of the cakes coming out of their pans instantly reminds me of Meme.

Choosing a balanced representation of recipes to include in this chapter was a daunting task. The list of Southern desserts is a lengthy one. I've included the desserts of my childhood, faithful friends and tried-and-true recipes we still enjoy, such as Meme's Pound Cake (page 266) and Aunt Julia's Chocolate Pie (256). (I calculated that it was entirely possible my grandmother made her pound cake more than one thousand times in the course of her lifetime!)

The litany of classic and country desserts I learned in the pastry kitchen in France made selection of French desserts no less of a challenge. I remember the joy I had when visiting home and making my newly learned treats for my family and friends, how much Meme loved crème brulée (page 259) and Chocolate Pots de Crème (page 255). It suddenly was not so difficult after all. Life is undeniably sweet on both sides of the Atlantic.

BROWN-SUGAR SHORTCAKES

Makes 8 to 10 shortcakes

Forget fancy gènoise or sponge cake; in the South, a shortcake is really just a sweet biscuit. Granted, this recipe is a step above, flavored with orange zest and sprinkled with raw sugar that sparkles like amber on the golden tops. At Martha Stewart Living Television, we served miniature versions of these buttery brown sugar shortcakes filled with peaches, strawberries, and blueberries at a luncheon attended by President Clinton.

SHORTCAKES

3 1/2 cups all-purpose flour, plus more for dusting

1/3 cup granulated sugar

4 teaspoons baking powder

1 teaspoon fine sea salt

3/4 cup (1 1/2 sticks) unsalted butter, chilled and cut into small pieces

Grated zest of 1 orange, or 2 tablespoons Grand Marnier

1 cup heavy cream, plus more for brushing

1/2 cup whole milk

Turbinado, Demerara, or raw brown sugar, for sprinkling

BERRIES AND GARNISH

2 pints strawberries, hulled and quartered lengthwise

Juice of 1 orange

1 tablespoon granulated sugar

Whipped cream, for accompaniment

Preheat the oven to 400°F. Line a baking sheet with a silicone baking sheet or parchment paper.

To prepare the shortcakes, in the bowl of a heavy-duty mixer fitted with the paddle, combine the flour, granulated sugar, baking powder, and salt on low speed. Add the butter and zest, and mix on low until the mixture resembles coarse meal, about 2 minutes. Add the cream and milk and increase the speed to medium; mix until the dough comes together. Remove the dough to a lightly floured surface, lightly knead a few times, and shape into a rectangle about 3/4 inch thick.

Cut out dough circles using a 3-inch round cutter. Place the circles on the prepared baking sheet. Brush the tops lightly with cream and sprinkle with the turbinado sugar. Bake until the shortcakes are golden brown, about 20 minutes. Transfer to a rack to cool.

Meanwhile, to prepare the berries, place the strawberries in a bowl. Add the orange juice and granulated sugar. Set aside.

To serve, halve the shortcakes horizontally with a serrated knife. Place the bottom halves on individual serving plates, top each with a dollop of whipped cream, then some berries, and another dollop of whipped cream. Cover with the tops of the shortcakes and serve.

The shortcakes can be stored in an airtight container for up to 2 days.

Brown Sugar

In the past, brown sugar was semirefined white sugar with some of the molasses left in. Now it is white sugar to which molasses has been added. The color, light or dark, depends on the amount of molasses added. Dark brown is slightly stronger in flavor than light brown, but otherwise interchangeable. When brown sugar comes into contact with air, the moisture evaporates and causes the sugar to lump together and become hard. Prevent this by storing brown sugar in a sealable plastic bag or in an airtight container. Also, storing brown sugar in the refrigerator will help keep it fresh and soft.

Mama's Angel Food Cake with Bourbon Crème Anglaise

Makes one
10-inch cake

It is necessary to sift the flour *before* measuring it for this cake. This is an anomaly; if flour is sifted at all these days (not that common anymore), most baking recipes call for sifting after it is measured. Here, the flour is sifted once before measuring, then an additional *four* times with the sugar to prepare this batter. It may seem like overkill, but it is completely necessary to achieve the traditional light-as-air texture of angel food cake.

There is an unusual implement for cutting these delicate cakes found in many silver chests throughout the South. These old-fashioned rakelike cutters typically have a long, slightly offset handle with 3- to 4-inch-long tines that actually split, rather than cut, the cake. They can still be found online and in gourmet catalogs.

1¼ cups sifted cake flour (not self-rising)

1½ cups sugar

12 large egg whites, at room temperature

¼ teaspoon fine sea salt

1½ teaspoons cream of tartar

½ vanilla bean, split and scraped, or 1½ teaspoons pure vanilla extract

¼ teaspoon almond extract

Bourbon Crème Anglaise (recipe follows)

Position an oven rack in the lower part of the oven. Preheat the oven to 375°F. Sift the flour with ¾ cup of the sugar. Re-sift three times. Set aside.

To prepare the batter, in the bowl of a heavy-duty mixer fitted with the whisk, place the egg whites, salt, and cream of tartar. Whisk on medium speed until foamy. Add the vanilla-bean seeds and almond extract. With the mixer on medium speed, add the remaining ¾ cup of sugar, a little at a time, until the whites are glossy and hold stiff peaks when the whisk is lifted. Sift enough of the flour mixture in to dust the top of the foam. Using a spatula, fold in gently. Continue until all of the flour mixture is incorporated.

Gently spoon the batter into an ungreased 10-inch tube pan. With a spatula or a knife, using a circular motion, cut through the batter twice to eliminate any large pockets of air. Smooth the top to remove any large peaks.

Bake until golden brown and a cake tester inserted into the center comes out clean, 35 to 40 minutes. Invert the pan over a bottle (such as a 2-liter soda bottle or wine bottle) and let rest until completely cooled, about 2 hours.

To serve, set upright, and using a butter knife or long spatula, loosen the cake from the sides of the pan. Invert onto a serving plate. Slice with a serrated knife or angel food cake cutter. Serve drizzled with crème anglaise.

The cake will keep in an airtight container for up to 2 days.

BOURBON CRÈME ANGLAISE

Makes 3 cups

2 cups whole milk

6 large egg yolks

1/4 cup sugar

Pinch of fine sea salt

1 tablespoon bourbon

Make an ice bath by filling a large bowl halfway with ice cubes and water.

In a saucepan, bring the milk almost to a boil over medium heat. In a second saucepan, blend together the egg yolks, sugar, and salt with a wooden spoon until thick and light (be careful not to make the mixture foamy). Mix in half the hot milk, then transfer the mixture to the other saucepan with the remaining milk and blend. Add the bourbon.

Decrease the heat to low and simmer gently, stirring constantly with a wooden spoon. Continue stirring the custard until thick enough to coat the back of the spoon and the mixture reaches 180°F on an instant-read thermometer. Remove from the heat.

Set a sieve over a large, clean bowl and pass the custard through the sieve.

Place the bowl in the ice bath, and stir the custard until it has completely cooled. Lay a piece of plastic wrap directly on the surface of the custard to prevent a skin from forming. Store the custard in the refrigerator for up to 24 hours.

MEME'S BLACKBERRY COBBLER

Serves 6 to 8

Wild blackberries grow prolifically throughout the South. No matter how hot the sun, when picking the musky, sweet-sour fruit it's always a good idea to wear long sleeves and gloves. Huge brambles with thick canes like barbed wire protect the berries. In the fall, we'd put on our armor, grab a few buckets, and walk toward the pond, where the blackberries grew. My sister and I ate at least one berry for every berry that went into the bucket. We'd return an hour or so later with smiles and blackened teeth and sit in the kitchen as Meme made this homey dessert. Farm-raised blackberries are much larger than wild ones, and may be used instead if you are not able to find yourself a briar patch. Other fruit may be substituted, including sliced peaches, raspberries, blueberries, plums, cherries, and apricots.

To cobble means to hastily throw together. Cobblers come in a variety of styles: biscuit, pastry, crumb, and batter. This cobbler is a batter cobbler, which is an absolute snap to assemble. And, since it's the one I grew up on, I consider it the best! The batter is poured into a hot cast-iron skillet and immediately crisps and swells.

1/2 cup (1 stick) unsalted butter

4 cups fresh blackberries

1 cup sugar, plus more for sprinkling, if needed

1 cup all-purpose flour

2 teaspoons baking powder

Pinch of fine sea salt

1 cup whole milk

1 teaspoon pure vanilla extract

Whipped cream, crème fraîche, or ice cream, for accompaniment

Preheat the oven to 350°F. Melt the butter in a large cast-iron skillet or ovenproof baking dish in the oven, 5 to 7 minutes.

Place the blackberries in a large bowl. Using a potato masher, mash them to release some of the juices. If the berries are tart, sprinkle over some of the sugar.

To make the batter, in another bowl, whisk together the flour, baking powder, and salt. Add the 1 cup sugar, milk, and vanilla extract, and stir until evenly blended. Remove the skillet from the oven and add the melted butter to the batter; stir to combine. Pour the batter all at once into the skillet, then add the blackberries and juices to the center of the batter.

Bake until the top is golden brown and a cake tester inserted into the batter comes out clean, about 1 hour. Serve, hot, warm, or at room temperature with whipped cream, crème fraîche, or ice cream.

Butter

Butter is simply over-whipped cream. In cream, the fat floats around in a water suspension. When the cream is whipped, the fat coagulates and the remaining liquid is buttermilk (see page 57). Whereas cream is an oil-in-water emulsion, after churning, the butter is a water-in-oil emulsion. This emulsion, butter, is a complex combination of milk fat, milk solids, and water. American butter contains at least 80 percent milk fat; some European or European-style butters contain between 82 and 88 percent milk fat. For simplicity and consistency of product, I use Land o' Lakes unsalted butter in my recipes, preferring unsalted to salted, because you can always add salt, but you cannot take it out.

HOMEMADE CHOCOLATE PUDDING

Serves 4 to 6

What other dessert brings out the kid in us more than chocolate pudding? If you want a pudding that is slightly more grown-up, substitute bittersweet chocolate for the semisweet.

The taste of the chocolate is heightened with the addition of vanilla extract. Use only pure vanilla extract, not imitation. To make your own vanilla extract, halve six vanilla beans lengthwise to reveal their seeds. Steep the beans in four cups of best-quality vodka in a dark place at room temperature for one month. After steeping, you'll have a flavorful extract.

6 tablespoons sugar

3 tablespoons cornstarch

1 1/2 tablespoons cocoa powder, plus more for dusting

1 teaspoon instant espresso powder (optional)

Pinch of fine sea salt

1 1/4 cups heavy cream

1 1/4 cups milk

1 teaspoon pure vanilla extract

6 ounces semisweet chocolate, finely chopped

1 tablespoon unsalted butter, cut into small pieces

Whipped cream, for accompaniment

In a saucepan, whisk together the sugar, cornstarch, cocoa, espresso powder, and salt. Combine the heavy cream with milk and vanilla extract in a large measuring cup. Whisk the liquid mixture into the dry ingredients in the saucepan until smooth.

Place the saucepan over medium heat. Cook, whisking constantly, until the mixture comes to a boil and thickens, about 5 minutes. Add the chocolate and cook, whisking constantly, until the chocolate is melted, 1 to 2 minutes.

Remove the saucepan from the heat. Whisk in the butter until melted. Divide the mixture equally among 4 to 6 serving dishes such as dessert coupes or ramekins. To prevent a skin from forming, place plastic wrap directly on the surface of each pudding. Chill in the refrigerator until set, about 1 hour.

When chilled completely, serve topped with a spoonful of whipped cream and dust with cocoa powder. Serve immediately.

Chocolate

Chocolate comes from the tropical cacao tree, *Theobroma cacao*, cultivated around the equator in the Caribbean, Africa, and Asia, and in the South Pacific islands of Samoa and New Guinea. To make chocolate, cacao beans are fermented, dried, and then cleaned. Next, processors roast and shell the cocoa beans, leaving only the centers, called nibs. These nibs are then pulverized or ground into a smooth liquid called chocolate liquor. Most fine chocolates, such as Valrhona, Callebaut, and Michel Cluizel are labeled with a percentage, which refers to the amount of chocolate liquor in the chocolate itself. The higher this number, the more intense the chocolate taste. Unsweetened or bitter chocolate contains nearly 100 percent chocolate liquor. Semisweet and bittersweet chocolates have added sugar, so their cocoa percentages are a little lower.

CHOCOLATE POTS DE CRÈME

Serves 6

Undeniably creamy and indulgent, these are the French version of pudding cups. Pots de crème are traditionally baked and served in individual ceramic pots with lids, how they got their name.

Much to my consternation, Mama buys Cool Whip instead of using freshly whipped cream. She recycles the tubs for food storage and other uses. I think a pet hamster was once gently laid to rest in a Cool Whip coffin. Whipping real cream is easy, and my mother's opinion aside, it really does taste better. The key is that everything must be well chilled: the heavy cream in the refrigerator, and the mixer beaters and bowl in the freezer until cold to the touch. I prefer not to add sugar or vanilla to the cream, as I think the dessert is quite often sweet enough and sweetened whipped cream is overpowering.

1 cup heavy cream

1 cup whole milk

5 ounces best-quality semisweet chocolate, finely chopped

5 large egg yolks

1/3 cup sugar

1 teaspoon pure vanilla extract

Pinch of fine sea salt

Whipped cream, for garnish

Position an oven rack in the lower third of the oven. Preheat the oven to 325°F. Place six 6-ounce ramekins in a roasting pan.

In a saucepan, combine the cream, milk, and chocolate over medium heat. Bring almost to a simmer; remove from the heat. Set aside, stirring occasionally, until the chocolate is completely melted.

In a large measuring cup, whisk together the egg yolks and the sugar. While whisking, add a little of the hot milk mixture to the egg mixture to combine. (This technique is called tempering; it makes the temperatures of two mixtures—one containing raw egg—more similar, so the egg won't curdle in the presence of heat.) Add the remaining milk mixture, and whisk to combine. Whisk in the vanilla and salt.

Pour approximately 1/2 cup of the egg mixture into each ramekin. Cover each ramekin tightly with aluminum foil to prevent a skin from forming. Fill the roasting pan with enough boiling water to come halfway up the sides of the ramekins. Bake until the custards are just set in the center, 35 to 40 minutes.

Remove the pots from the water, and place on a wire rack to cool, about 30 minutes. (I usually remove the pots with tongs and leave the roasting pan of water in the oven. Turn the oven off and let the water cool until it is safe to remove the pan.)

When the pots de crème have cooled completely, refrigerate to chill thoroughly, preferably overnight. Just before serving, top with a dollop of whipped cream.

AUNT JULIA'S CHOCOLATE PIE

(Makes one 9-inch pie)

Meme's sister, who died long before I was born, was named Julia. She also liked to cook. Meme used to tease me that I was a lot like Julia in that we both would dirty every pot in the kitchen when we cooked.

This is hands-down my favorite dessert. Mama makes it almost every time I come home to visit. When I was in culinary school, I took a look at the recipe and was certain with my newly learned techniques I could improve the consistency of the pudding. Wrong. It was a disaster, and the pudding mixture never congealed—which brings to mind the expression, "If it's not broke, don't fix it."

All-American Pie Crust (page 258), fully baked

1 cup granulated sugar

2 cups whole milk

3½ tablespoons all-purpose flour

¼ cup cocoa powder

3 large eggs, separated

½ teaspoon pure vanilla extract

Pinch of fine sea salt

1 teaspoon cream of tartar

2 tablespoons confectioners' sugar

Preheat the oven to 500°F.

To prepare the pie filling, in a saucepan, combine the 1 cup of granulated sugar and 1 cup of the milk. Set aside.

In a bowl, combine the remaining 1 cup of milk, the flour, and cocoa powder in a bowl and whisk thoroughly to combine. (Mama uses a shaker and shakes the mixture until it is well combined and frothy.) Set aside.

Heat the saucepan with the milk-sugar mixture over medium-high heat until simmering. Slowly add the milk-flour mixture and stir to combine. Bring to a boil. Add the egg yolks, whisking constantly, until it returns to a boil. Once the mixture comes to a boil, immediately add the vanilla and remove it from the heat.

Pour the mixture into the baked pie crust. Set aside.

To make the meringue topping, place the egg whites in a non-reactive bowl with a pinch of salt. Add the cream of tartar and, using a hand-held mixer, whisk on high speed until foamy. Sift over the confectioners' sugar a little at a time and whisk until the whites are glossy and hold stiff peaks when the whisk is lifted.

To finish the pie, spoon the meringue over the pie, making sure it touches the edges of the pie crust. Bake until golden brown, 3 to 5 minutes. Move to a rack to cool completely and set, then serve.

256 | Bon Appétit, Y'all

MAMA'S PECAN PIE

Makes two
9-inch pies

Too many pecan pies are mostly goo without enough pecans, making them far too sweet. The secret to the success of this pie is that its pecan-to-goo ratio is just right. As a child, I helped Mama make this pie. It was my job to help her coarsely grind the nuts. She still uses a hand-held grinder; it has a crank that forces the nuts through two opposing fork-like blades and a glass jar to catch the nut pieces. The metal top that screws into the glass jar is bent and dinged, but the tool still coarsely cuts the nuts just right.

Double recipe All-American Pie Crust (page 258)

3 large eggs, slightly beaten

1 cup sugar

1 cup light corn syrup

2 tablespoons unsalted butter, melted

1 teaspoon pure vanilla extract

1/4 teaspoon fine sea salt

3 cups coarsely chopped pecans

Preheat the oven to 350°F. Prepare 2 unbaked 9-inch pie shells.

To make the filling, combine the eggs, sugar, corn syrup, butter, vanilla, and salt in a bowl; stir until blended. Add the pecans and stir to combine. Pour into the chilled pie shells.

Bake the pies, rotating once, until a knife inserted into the center comes out clean, about 55 minutes. Remove the pies to a wire rack to cool. The pies can be stored wrapped tight in aluminum foil or in a pie safe (at room temperature) for up to 1 week.

FRENCH COCONUT PIE

Makes one
9-inch pie

Cousin Michele makes this pie for her family each and every holiday. She learned it from Aunt Dolores and has taught her daughter, Nina, and son, Walker, to make it, too. The passing of recipes from one generation to the next is a thread of continuity, of family roots and place. Sweet memories in every bite, it's a small but amazing bit of history.

Let me just say I have never had "French" coconut pie in France. This pie is more along the lines of winning a blue ribbon at a country fair, not Le Cordon Bleu.

All-American Pie Crust (page 258)

1 cup sugar

2 tablespoons all-purpose flour

Pinch of fine sea salt

1/2 cup (1 stick) unsalted butter, melted

1/2 cup buttermilk

3 large eggs, lightly beaten

1 teaspoon pure vanilla extract

1 cup flaked fresh coconut (see page 32)

Prepare an unbaked 9-inch pie shell. Preheat the oven to 325°F. To prepare the filling, in a bowl, whisk together the sugar, flour, and salt. Add the butter, buttermilk, eggs, vanilla extract, and coconut. Stir to combine. Pour into the pie shell. Bake until set and pale golden brown, about 1 hour. Remove to a rack to cool. Let cool completely before slicing and serving.

Store in an airtight container for up to 2 days. (Don't worry, it won't last!)

ALL-AMERICAN PIE CRUST

Makes one
9-inch pie crust

When I was her apprentice, Nathalie Dupree spent hours on my baking and pastry education, patiently showing me again and again how to create perfect pie crusts, homemade breads, puff pastry, and rolls, until I had the techniques down cold. She crafted this recipe for beginners: it's an easy crust for novices because it's made in the food processor and because of the combination of butter and shortening. Shortening does not melt as readily as butter does and makes for a more forgiving dough. As Nathalie knew, a beginner's first taste of sweet success in the pastry kitchen can be inspirational.

For a double-crust pie, simply double the amounts and divide the dough before rolling out.

1¼ cups all-purpose flour, plus more for rolling

½ teaspoon fine sea salt

¼ cup solid vegetable shortening, preferably Crisco, chilled and cut into pieces

4 tablespoons (½ stick) unsalted butter, chilled and cut into pieces

3 to 8 tablespoons ice water

In the work bowl of a food processor fitted with the metal blade, combine the flour and salt, then add the vegetable shortening and butter. Process until the mixture resembles coarse meal, 8 to 10 seconds.

With the processor on pulse, add enough of the ice water, 1 tablespoon at a time, until the dough holds together without being sticky or crumbly. Shape the dough into a disk and wrap in plastic wrap. Chill until firm and the moisture has distributed evenly, about 30 minutes.

Flour a clean work surface and a rolling pin. (If making a double-crust pie or 2 pie shells, work with one disk at a time, keeping the second disk chilled.) Place a dough disk in the center of the floured surface. Starting in the center of the dough, roll to, but not over, the upper edge of the dough. Return to the center, and roll down to, but not over, the lower edge. Lift the dough, give it a quarter turn, and lay it on the work surface. Continue rolling, repeating the quarter turns, until you have a disk about $1/8$ inch thick.

Ease the pastry into a 9-inch pie plate. Trim 1 inch larger than the diameter of the pie plate; fold the overhanging pastry under itself along the rim of the plate. For a simple decorative edge, press the tines of a fork around the folded pastry. To make a fluted edge, using both your finger and thumb, pinch and crimp the folded dough. Chill until firm, about 30 minutes.

To blind bake, see directions on page 64.

CRÈME BRULÉE AU VANILLE FOR MEME

Serves 6

When my grandmother became ill with cancer, I thought my heart would break. I never knew anything could hurt so badly—the pain actually seemed to make it impossible to breathe. I was living in New York, working in Connecticut, and would fly home to see her as often as possible, at least every other weekend. When I was home I would make her this soft, rich custard that she loved.

The cause of death on Meme's death certificate is actually starvation, not cancer. The cancer prevented her from swallowing, and the only solution was to feed her through a tube, something no one wanted, or needed, to face. It was a cruel irony for a woman who made so many meals with so much joy and love.

1/2 cup firmly packed light brown sugar

2 cups heavy cream

3/4 cup granulated sugar

Pinch of fine sea salt

1 vanilla bean, split and scraped, or 1 tablespoon pure vanilla extract

5 large egg yolks

For the topping, spread the sugar on a large plate or baking sheet and let dry on the counter, uncovered, for at least 3 hours or overnight. When it is properly dried, it will feel dry and sandy. If it's hard and clumped together, sift it through a mesh sieve. Set aside. (You can use an equal amount of white granulated sugar.)

Preheat the oven to 325°F. Line a baking dish with a paper towel or tea towel and set six 4-ounce ramekins in the dish.

To prepare the custard, in a heavy-bottomed saucepan, add the cream, 1/2 cup of the granulated sugar, and the scraped vanilla-bean seeds and stir over medium heat until blended, the sugar dissolves, and the mixture comes to a simmer. Cover the pan, decrease the heat to very low, and simmer gently for 10 minutes to infuse the cream with vanilla flavor. Strain into a large measuring cup, rinsing and saving the bean for another use.

Meanwhile, whisk the yolks with the salt and remaining 1/4 cup sugar in a bowl until well blended. Gradually whisk in some of the hot cream mixture just to blend, then whisk the egg mixture into the remaining cream mixture in the measuring cup. Divide the custard equally among the ramekins. Pour enough hot water into the baking dish to come halfway up the sides of the ramekins. Carefully transfer the baking dish to the oven.

Bake the custards until almost set in the center when the ramekins are gently shaken, about 35 minutes. Using a metal spatula or tongs, transfer the ramekins to a rack to cool to room temperature. (Let the water bath cool completely before removing it from the oven.) Once the custards are at room temperature, chill them in the refrigerator for at least 3 hours and up to 2 days.

To finish, evenly sprinkle about 2 teaspoons of the prepared brown sugar over each custard. Working with 1 ramekin at a time, hold a kitchen torch so that the flame is about 2 inches above the sugared surface of the custard. Direct the flame so that the sugar melts and browns. Serve immediately.

Mama's French Butter Cookies

Makes 48

When Mama makes this, it's all she can do to get it to the baking sheet. While it's refrigerated, my sister and I sneak nibbles of the sweet, raw dough. One summer years ago, my cousin ate so much of the dough that he got a stomachache. Even now, every time Mama makes these cookies, we laugh about him groaning. Shortly thereafter, she started successfully doubling the recipe to take our nibbling into account.

These cookies are somewhat similar to sablés, the real French butter cookie. The vegetable shortening also makes them softer than true French sablés, which are larger in size and have a fine, crumbly texture that resembles sand (their name means sand in French).

2 cups all-purpose flour

1/4 teaspoon fine sea salt

1 teaspoon baking soda

1 teaspoon cream of tartar

1/2 cup (1 stick) unsalted butter, at room temperature

1/2 cup solid vegetable shortening, preferably Crisco, at room temperature

1 1/2 cups confectioners' sugar, sifted

1 large egg, at room temperature

1 teaspoon pure vanilla extract

In a bowl, sift together the flour, salt, baking soda, and cream of tartar. Set aside.

In the bowl of a heavy-duty mixer fitted with the paddle, cream the butter and shortening on medium speed until light and fluffy. Add the confectioners' sugar and beat on low speed until smooth. Add the egg and vanilla extract and continue beating on low until well combined.

On low speed, slowly add the reserved dry ingredients. Beat until well combined. Cover with plastic wrap. Transfer to the refrigerator and chill until very firm, at least 2 hours.

Preheat the oven to 350°F. Using an ice cream scoop or a melon baller, take some of the dough and shape it into small 1-inch balls. (Keep the remaining dough in the refrigerator, as it must be kept chilled.) Place the dough balls on an ungreased baking sheet and press with the tines of a fork to flatten. Bake until pale golden, but not brown, 10 to 12 minutes. Cool slightly on the baking sheet on a rack. Then, using a spatula, transfer the cookies to a rack to cool completely.

Mama's Apple Pie

Even though peaches are considered the quintessential Southern fruit, the phrase "as American as apple pie" applies to the South, too. Apples grow in the cooler mountainous regions from Georgia to Virginia. There is no longer an issue with refrigeration, but apples were an important fruit for people in the country who lived off the land. When held in a cool cellar, apples lasted for months, providing much needed vitamins and nutrition in the winter.

Many factors affect an apple's juiciness: the age of the apple, the weather and climate where it was grown, and how it has been stored. In a pie, there's sometimes a fine line between juicy and sopping wet. Flour is one ingredient that will help absorb some of the cooking juices.

This is my sister's favorite dessert and she always requests it on special occasions.

Double recipe All-American Pie Crust, in 2 disks (page 258)

7 Granny Smith apples, peeled, cored, and thinly sliced

3/4 cup to 1 cup sugar, plus more for topping the pie

2 tablespoons all-purpose flour

1/2 teaspoon ground cinnamon

Pinch of freshly grated nutmeg

Pinch of fine sea salt

2 tablespoons unsalted butter, cut into bits

1 tablespoon water

Prepare the pie pastry. To shape the crust, on a lightly floured work surface, roll out one disk of the dough into a 13-inch round about 1/8 inch thick. Transfer the dough round to a 9-inch pie plate. With a sharp paring knife, trim the dough flush with the rim of the plate. Freeze until firm, at least 30 minutes.

To make the filling, place the apples in a bowl; sprinkle over the sugar, flour, cinnamon, nutmeg, and salt. Stir to combine and coat. Place the apple mixture in the unbaked pie shell. Dot with butter bits.

Roll out the remaining half of the pie crust on a lightly floured surface. Cover the filled pie crust with the round of dough, and trim so that 1 inch overhangs the pie plate. Fold the dough under, and crimp the edges by pressing with a fork or your fingers. Chill in the refrigerator until the crust is firm, about 15 minutes.

Meanwhile, to bake the pie, preheat the oven to 400°F. Brush the top of the pie with the water. Sprinkle over a teaspoon or so of sugar. Bake until golden brown, about 50 minutes.

Transfer to a rack to cool slightly before slicing and serving.

Keeping the Oven Clean

Apple pie and cheesy gratins sometimes have a tendency to bubble and dribble, resulting in a burnt, smelly mess on the bottom of the oven. Or, if you place a baking sheet underneath, you still have to clean the baking sheet. To avoid both messes, place a silicone-lined baking sheet under the baking dish. If the juices spill, they are very easy to clean off with warm soapy water.

Aunt Louise's Red Velvet Cake

Makes one
9-inch cake

Red velvet cake has inspired as many theories about its provenance as there are recipes in a Junior League cookbook. The question cannot be definitively answered. We do at least know why the cake is red: most red velvet cakes use acidic ingredients—buttermilk and vinegar—and cocoa, which contains a reddish pigment called anthocyanin. The acidic buttermilk reacts with the cocoa and actually makes this red pigment appear even redder. Somewhere along the line, someone decided the cake needed a little more rouge and added red food coloring. Some chefs try to gussy it up using beet juice or deconstruct it into something it's not.

My friend Angie Mosier, who is an incredible baker in her own right, once very aptly described red velvet cake as "the Dolly Parton of cakes—she's a little bit tacky, but you love her."

2 1/2 cups all-purpose flour

2 teaspoons cocoa powder

1 teaspoon baking soda

1 teaspoon fine sea salt

1 cup buttermilk

1 teaspoon pure vanilla extract

1 teaspoon distilled white vinegar

2 cups vegetable oil

1 1/2 cups sugar

2 large eggs

1 (1-ounce) bottle red food coloring

CREAM CHEESE FROSTING

8 ounces cream cheese, at room temperature

1/4 cup (1/2 stick) unsalted butter, at room temperature

1 (16-ounce) box confectioners' sugar

1 teaspoon pure vanilla extract

2 to 3 teaspoons whole milk, as needed

1 cup chopped pecans, for garnish

Preheat the oven to 350°F. Butter and flour three 9-inch round cake pans and line the bottoms with waxed or parchment paper. Butter and flour the paper. In a bowl, sift together the flour, cocoa, baking soda, and salt. Set aside. In a measuring cup, combine the buttermilk, vanilla extract, and vinegar. Set aside.

To prepare the batter, in the bowl of a heavy-duty mixer fitted with the paddle, combine the oil and the sugar on medium speed. Add the eggs, one at a time, and mix well after each addition. With the mixer on low speed, add the food coloring. Add the flour mixture alternating with the buttermilk mixture, beginning and ending with flour, scraping down the sides of the bowl as needed. Mix until just combined.

To bake the layers, divide the batter among the prepared pans. Bake until firm and a toothpick inserted into the cakes comes out clean, 25 to 30 minutes. Let the cakes cool in the pans on a rack for 5 minutes. Invert the cakes onto the rack to cool completely.

Meanwhile, to prepare the frosting, in the bowl of a heavy-duty mixer fitted with the paddle, cream the cream cheese and butter on medium speed until smooth. Sift over the confectioners' sugar. Beat until light and fluffy. Beat in the vanilla. If too stiff, add the milk, 1 teaspoon at a time, to achieve the correct consistency.

To assemble, place one layer on a cardboard cake round. Spread with frosting. Repeat with the remaining 2 layers, placing the final layer bottom-side up. Finish with the remaining frosting. Sprinkle over the pecans. Serve the cake immediately, or store it in an airtight container in the refrigerator for up to 5 days.

Lemon Squares

When I was older, Meme and Dede would travel to Florida in the winter and stay near a citrus farm. They would return with bulging sacks of oranges, lemons, and grapefruit. I know Dede enjoyed the trip, but I sometimes wondered about Meme. She must have been in her eighties when she derisively commented, "There's nothing but old people in Florida."

Citrus fruit has a strong presence in Southern cooking. Lemons and other citrus from Florida and the Caribbean were used in Southern cooking as early as the Colonial period. A recipe for lemon pudding appeared in Mary Randolph's 1824 cookbook, *The Virginia Housewife*, the first regional cookbook published in America. Lemon meringue pie holds a special place in people's memories, as do lemon curd and lemon squares like these. Store these bars tightly wrapped in the refrigerator for up to 3 days.

1½ cups (3 sticks) unsalted butter, at room temperature

3⅔ cups all-purpose flour

¾ cup confectioners' sugar, plus more for dusting

¼ teaspoon fine sea salt

3 cups granulated sugar

7 large eggs

Grated zest and juice of 5 lemons (about 1 cup juice)

Take a few bits of the butter and, using your hands, grease an 18 x 13-inch (half-sheet size) rimmed baking sheet.

To make the crust, in the work bowl of a food processor fitted with the metal blade, combine 3 cups of the flour, the ¾ cup of confectioners' sugar, and half of the salt; pulse until well combined. Add the remaining butter and pulse until the mixture starts to pull away from the sides of the bowl. Transfer to the prepared baking sheet and, using your fingers, press into the pan. To ensure that the dough is a smooth, uniform layer, cover with a sheet of plastic wrap, then, using the back of a spoon, spread the dough evenly in the pan. Chill in the refrigerator until firm, about 30 minutes.

Preheat the oven to 350°F. Bake the chilled dough until golden brown, rotating once, about 30 minutes; remove to a rack and leave the oven on.

Meanwhile, to make the filling, in the work bowl of the food processor (no need to worry about residual dough), combine the remaining ⅔ cup of flour, the granulated sugar, the remaining pinch of salt, eggs, grated lemon zest, and lemon juice.

To assemble, pour the filling on top of the still-warm crust. Bake until set and just beginning to color, 30 to 35 minutes. Transfer to a rack to cool completely, about 2 hours. Sift over additional confectioners' sugar. Slice into squares and serve.

CHESS PIE

Makes one
9-inch pie

Buttermilk, eggs, and sugar are the main ingredients of a chess pie. The mixture is thickened with a little flour or cornmeal, and often flavored with vanilla or lemon. The origin of the name is hazy. One theory holds that it is a variation on cheese pie, an English dessert made of lemon curd. I tend to accept this version. Meme made an old-fashioned white cake layered with lemon curd that she called "cheese cake," even though it contained no cheese (the recipe is on page 268). The verbal association between curd and cheese seems logical and in time, cheese simply became chess.

Another theory is that, before refrigeration, wooden cupboards called pie safes or pie chests were obligatory in Southern kitchens. Since the pie will hold up at room temperature, it may have been called chest pie, which became chess pie. Finally, imagine a waitress in a "meat and three" diner, her hair piled up high on her head, as her customer asks, "What kind of pie you got today?" She looks up from wiping the table and says, "It's ches (just) pie."

4 large eggs, at room temperature

1 1/2 cups sugar

1 tablespoon white or yellow cornmeal

1 tablespoon all-purpose flour

1/4 teaspoon fine sea salt

1/2 cup melted butter, cooled to room temperature

1/2 cup buttermilk, at room temperature

Grated zest of 1 lemon

Juice of 1/2 lemon

1 teaspoon pure vanilla extract

All-American Pie Crust (page 258), blind baked and still warm (see page 64)

Preheat the oven to 350°F. In a bowl, whisk the eggs until smooth. Add the sugar, cornmeal, flour, and salt. Whisk well to combine. Add the butter, buttermilk, lemon zest, lemon juice, and vanilla extract. Whisk well to combine. Pour into the warm pie shell.

Bake until golden brown and a knife inserted into the center comes out clean, 35 to 40 minutes. (The pie may puff and crackle during baking, which is fine. It will settle as it cools.) Remove to a rack to cool completely before slicing and serving.

MEME'S POUND CAKE

This cake has been a constant in my life and it has been my birthday cake many times. Our family holidays would not be complete without it. The best part is the crispy, dark-brown sugary edges. Much to my mother's consternation, more than once, little pesky elves raided the opaque Tupperware cake container and nibbled away those tasty bits.

1 cup (2 sticks) unsalted butter, at room temperature, plus more for the pan

3 cups White Lily or other Southern all-purpose flour

1/2 teaspoon baking powder

1/2 teaspoon fine sea salt

1 cup whole milk, at room temperature

5 large eggs, at room temperature

1 vanilla bean, split and scraped, or 1 tablespoon pure vanilla extract

1/2 cup solid vegetable shortening, preferably Crisco, at room temperature

3 cups sugar

Preheat the oven to 300°F. Generously grease a 16-cup (measure to the rim) bundt pan with butter. In a bowl, sift together the flour, baking powder, and salt. Set aside. In a large liquid measuring cup, combine the milk, eggs, and the scraped vanilla seeds. Set aside.

In the bowl of a heavy-duty mixer fitted with the paddle, cream together the 1 cup of butter, vegetable shortening, and sugar on medium speed until light and fluffy. Add the flour and milk mixtures to the butter mixture in 3 batches, alternating between dry and liquid, occasionally scraping down the sides of the mixing bowl, beginning and ending with the flour mixture. Fill the prepared pan with batter (it should be no more than two-thirds full).

Bake for 15 minutes. Increase the oven temperature to 325°F and bake an additional 45 minutes, or until the cake is golden brown and pulls away from the sides of the pan. Remove to a rack to cool for 10 minutes. Invert the cake onto the rack to cool completely.

This cake will stay moist in an airtight container for up to 1 week.

MEME'S LEMON CAKE

Makes one
8-inch cake

Meme called this "lemon cheese cake," which is somewhat confusing since people more often use that name for a New York–style cheesecake. This is one of the recipes that "got away." Meme often recorded a recipe on a card or on the previously mentioned interior of her cabinets. Trouble is, she only wrote down the ingredients and rarely included instructions. She used to actually cover her version of the cake in lemon curd. Normally, lemon curd is soft and not firm enough to frost a cake. I have tried to make the curd with her ingredients list every way but Sunday with no success. I'm afraid now I will never know. Instead, I fill between the layers with curd and flavor the frosting with it as well.

The cake itself is an excellent rich, moist, cake that would also be delicious with chocolate frosting or served with strawberries and cream.

CAKE

2 cups (4 sticks) unsalted butter, plus more for the pans

3 cups cake flour (not self-rising), plus more for the pans

2 teaspoons baking powder

2 cups sugar

1 vanilla bean, split and scraped, or 1 tablespoon pure vanilla extract

1 cup whole milk

8 large egg whites

Pinch of fine sea salt

LEMON CURD

8 large egg yolks

1 cup sugar

Grated zest and juice of 4 lemons

Pinch of fine sea salt

1 cup (2 sticks) unsalted butter, chilled and cut into bits

FROSTING

8 ounces cream cheese, at room temperature

3/4 cup (1 1/2 sticks) unsalted butter, at room temperature

2 cups confectioners' sugar, sifted

1/2 cup Lemon Curd (see above)

Preheat the oven to 350°F. Butter and flour two 8 x 3-inch cake pans. In a bowl, sift together the flour and baking powder. Set aside.

To make the cake, in the bowl of a heavy-duty mixer fitted with the paddle, cream the 2 cups of butter, sugar, and scraped vanilla-bean seeds on medium speed until light and fluffy, about 3 minutes. With the mixer on low speed, add the flour mixture, alternating with the milk, beginning and ending with flour, scraping the sides of the bowl as needed. Transfer the batter to a large bowl.

Switch to the whisk attachment of the mixer and use a clean bowl. Whisk the egg whites with a pinch of salt on low speed until foamy. Increase the speed to high and beat until stiff peaks form, 3 to 5 minutes. By hand, whisk one-third of the beaten whites into the batter to lighten the mixture. Using a large rubber spatula, fold the remaining whites into the lightened batter. Divide the batter between the prepared pans.

Bake until golden brown and a toothpick inserted into the cakes comes out clean, 40 to 45 minutes. Remove to a rack to cool for 5 minutes. Invert the cakes onto the wire rack to cool completely.

Meanwhile, for the lemon curd, prepare an ice-water bath by filling a large bowl with ice and water.

To prepare the lemon curd, in a stainless steel bowl placed over a saucepan of simmering water, whisk together the egg yolks, sugar, lemon juice, and salt until blended. Cook, stirring constantly (to prevent the eggs from curdling), until the mixture is very thick and reaches 170°F on an instant-read thermometer, about 10 minutes. Remove from the heat and immediately pour through a fine mesh strainer into a bowl to filter out any lumps or cooked egg. Whisk in the butter, one piece at a time, whisking until each piece of butter has melted before adding the next. Add the lemon zest and stir to combine. Place the bowl in the ice-water bath (or in the refrigerator), stirring occasionally, to cool.

To make the frosting, switch back to the paddle attachment of the mixer and use a clean bowl. Cream the cream cheese and butter on medium speed until smooth. Sift over the confectioners' sugar. Beat until light and fluffy. Add the $1/2$ cup of chilled lemon curd and beat on medium speed until combined. Set aside.

To assemble the cake, once the layers have cooled completely, halve each with a serrated knife to create 4 layers. Place one sliced layer on a cardboard cake round. Spread with about $1/2$ cup of lemon curd. Repeat with the remaining cake layers, spreading $1/2$ cup of lemon curd between each layer. Place the final cake layer bottom-side up. Using an offset spatula, cover the top and sides with frosting.

GEORGIA PECAN BROWNIES

For the most part, Mama has always made everything from scratch. Homemade cakes, cookies, and pies were the norm, but she would open one box when she made brownies. My father worked for a company that made, among myriad other things, brownie mix. I remember opening the Christmas gifts from corporate friends that contained a potpourri of company products, including the familiar red box—the brownie mix. Perhaps one of the reasons I am so fond of these brownies is that they represent my first solo forays into baking. Other than turning on the oven, I was allowed to prepare the brownies all by myself.

1 cup (2 sticks) unsalted butter, plus more for the dish

2 cups sugar

1½ cups all-purpose flour

1¼ cups cocoa powder

1½ teaspoons baking powder

1 teaspoon fine sea salt

4 large eggs, at room temperature

1 tablespoon vanilla extract

12 ounces best-quality semisweet chocolate, finely chopped

1 cup chopped pecans

Preheat the oven to 350°F. Brush a 9 x 13-inch baking dish or pan with butter.

In a saucepan, melt the 1 cup of butter over medium heat; add the sugar and stir to dissolve. Keep warm.

In a bowl, whisk together the flour, cocoa, baking powder, and salt. Add the butter mixture and stir to combine. Add the eggs, vanilla extract, chocolate, and nuts. Stir until the chocolate is fully melted and the ingredients are combined (the batter should be very thick). Alternatively, you can mix the batter in a heavy-duty mixer. Spoon the batter into the prepared pan. Smooth the top with an offset spatula.

Bake until set, 25 to 35 minutes. Remove to a rack to cool. Cut into pieces and serve. Store in an airtight container for up to 3 days.

GEORGIA PECAN-CHOCOLATE CHIP COOKIES

Makes about 30

The key to this great cookie is the mix of chocolates—semisweet, milk, and creamy white—and just enough batter to hold together the good stuff. After the boxed brownies, making chocolate chip cookies was the next step in my young baking career. I was able to make the cookies without (much of) Mama's supervision. The recipe was from my very first cookbook, *Betty Crocker's Cookbook for Boys and Girls*, given to me on my eighth birthday.

I top each of these cookies with a flawless pecan half, which makes them picture perfect. My pecans of choice are a variety called Elliot, which are petite, yet plump and rich with natural oils. For years, I've ordered them from Pearson Farms in Fort Valley, Georgia, for myself, and also have sent them as Christmas gifts to very special people all over the world.

2 cups all-purpose flour

1/2 teaspoon baking soda

1 cup (2 sticks) unsalted butter, at room temperature

3/4 cup firmly packed dark brown sugar

1/4 cup granulated sugar

1/2 teaspoon fine sea salt

1 teaspoon pure vanilla extract

1 large egg, at room temperature

8 ounces best-quality semisweet chocolate, coarsely chopped

6 ounces best-quality white chocolate, coarsely chopped

4 ounces best-quality milk chocolate, coarsely chopped

2 cups chopped pecans

30 perfect pecan halves, for decoration

Preheat the oven to 375°F. Line a baking sheet with a silicone baking sheet or parchment paper. In a bowl, whisk together the flour and baking soda. Set aside.

In the bowl of a heavy-duty mixer fitted with the paddle, combine the butter, brown sugar, and granulated sugar and cream on medium speed until light and fluffy. Add the salt, vanilla extract, and egg and stir to combine.

Add the flour mixture to the butter mixture and mix on low speed until just combined. Add the semisweet, white, and milk chocolates and chopped pecans.

Make balls of dough using a 1-ounce ice cream scoop or with your hands shape the dough into balls about the size of a gumball; place 6 dough balls on the prepared baking sheet, about 3 inches apart. Using the palm of your hand, flatten each cookie slightly. Press a pecan half into the center of each.

Bake until the cookies are just brown around the edges, 13 to 14 minutes. Using an offset spatula, transfer the cookies to a rack to cool. Repeat with the remaining cookie dough and pecan halves.

Store the cookies in an airtight container for up to 1 week. (Don't worry, they won't last that long!)

Freezing Cookies

For quick-frozen cookie dough: scoop out or roll individual balls of cookie dough and place them on a rimmed baking sheet lined with a silicone baking sheet, parchment paper, or waxed paper. Place the baking sheet in the freezer until the dough balls are completely frozen, 1 to 2 hours. Once they are frozen solid, transfer them to a freezable airtight container or bag for storage. There is no need to thaw them before baking—just increase the baking time by a minute or two.

SABAYON WITH SEASONAL BERRIES

Sabayon is the French name for zabaglione, a light foamy Italian dessert. It is served warm in glasses or coupes or spooned over a dessert, fruit, or pastry as a topping. Traditionally, it is made with Marsala or port, but it may be prepared using other wines and liqueurs. Use the freshest berries in season. Try all the same berry, or mix them up for a colorful treat.

2 pints fresh ripe strawberries, washed, hulled, and quartered, and/or blueberries or blackberries

6 tablespoons sugar

Juice of ½ lemon

Pinch of fine sea salt

6 egg yolks

1 cup sweet Marsala or port

Place the berries in a bowl. Add 1 tablespoon of the sugar, the lemon juice, and salt. Stir to combine. Set aside.

In a large, stainless steel bowl, whisk to blend the egg yolks, the Marsala, and the remaining 5 tablespoons of sugar. Rest the bowl over a saucepan of barely simmering water to create a double boiler (a standard double boiler is too small). Using a whisk or a handheld mixer (trust me, you'll prefer the latter, if you have one), whisk constantly until it has the consistency of lightly whipped cream and is thick, foamy, and tripled in volume, about 5 minutes. Remove from the heat.

Divide the berries among serving bowls or glasses and top with a spoonful of sabayon. Serve immediately.

HOT VANILLA SOUFFLÉS WITH VANILLA ICE CREAM

Serves 4 to 6

This soufflé uses the pastry-cream method as the base. Pastry cream (*crème pâtissière*) is a very stable custard thickened with flour or cornstarch, and it provides an excellent foundation for dessert soufflés. Vanilla is the bean of a variety of tropical orchid. Use the whole pod if possible to allow the tiny seeds to flavor and speckle the dish. As a substitution, use 1 tablespoon of pure vanilla extract.

3 tablespoons unsalted butter, at room temperature, for the ramekins

1/2 cup sugar, plus more for the ramekins

1 1/3 cups whole milk

1 vanilla bean, split and scraped, or 1 tablespoon pure vanilla extract

4 large eggs, separated

2 tablespoons all-purpose flour

2 tablespoons cornstarch

Fine sea salt

Vanilla ice cream, for accompaniment

Confectioners' sugar, for sprinkling

Preheat the oven to 400°F. Generously butter four 8-ounce or six 5-ounce soufflé ramekins. Put a couple of tablespoons of the sugar inside one ramekin and toss to coat, then tip the excess sugar into the next, and repeat until all the ramekins are sugar-coated. Place the ramekins on a rimmed baking sheet.

In a large saucepan, add the milk and the vanilla bean and heat just to a boil over medium-high heat. Turn off the heat, cover, and set aside to let the vanilla bean infuse for 10 minutes. Remove the vanilla bean and rinse and reserve for another use.

To make the pastry cream, in a bowl, whisk 1/4 cup of the sugar with the egg yolks until thick and light, about 1 minute. Whisk in the flour, cornstarch, and a pinch of salt. Add a little of the warm infused milk and whisk to combine. Add the remaining milk. Return the egg mixture to the saucepan and bring to a boil over medium-high heat. Decrease the heat to medium and cook, stirring constantly, until thickened, 45 to 60 seconds; it will be lumpy. Remove it from the heat and whisk until smooth. Set aside.

To beat the egg whites, in the bowl of a heavy-duty mixer fitted with the whisk, whip the egg whites with a pinch of salt on medium speed until foamy. Increase the speed to high and beat until the whites begin to form soft peaks. Slowly add the remaining 1/4 cup of sugar, beating until the whites are glossy and hold stiff peaks, 1 to 2 minutes.

Add about a quarter of the beaten egg whites to the pastry cream mixture and stir until well mixed. Pour this mixture over the remaining whites and fold them together as lightly as possible.

To assemble the soufflés, spoon the mixture into the prepared soufflé ramekins (the mixture should come up to the top). Smooth the tops with a metal spatula. Run your thumb around the inside of the rim of each dish, making a shallow channel around the edge of the batter. (This will help the soufflés rise up straight and tall.) Set the filled soufflé ramekins on the rimmed baking sheet.

Bake the soufflés until risen and just set, 12 to 15 minutes. Remove from the oven. With two forks, pull open the center of each soufflé. Place a scoop of vanilla ice cream in the opening. Sprinkle with confectioners' sugar and serve immediately.

GEORGIA PEACH SOUFFLÉS

Each summer, any peaches that were not eaten, jellied, or canned were frozen. We would peel and slice the peaches and pack them into sealable plastic freezer bags. Most often, they later appeared as a topping for Meme's Pound Cake (page 266). For a child, peach season was purgatory—it was so very hot—but I am sure Meme is smiling in heaven with satisfaction when she sees me practicing now what she taught me then.

This soufflé uses the meringue method to rise, and the flavor is delicate and light. Frozen peaches may be used when peaches are not in season; simply defrost them before using.

3 tablespoons unsalted butter, at room temperature, for the ramekins

2 to 3 peaches, peeled and sliced (about 2 cups)

Juice of 1 lemon

1 teaspoon pure vanilla extract

7 large egg whites, at room temperature

1/4 teaspoon fine sea salt

3/4 cup granulated sugar

Confectioners' sugar, for sprinkling

Preheat the oven to 400°F. Generously butter six 8-ounce ramekins. Set aside on a rimmed baking sheet.

In the work bowl of a food processor fitted with the metal blade, pulse the peaches until coarsely chopped. (The pieces should be no larger than 1/4 inch.) Remove 3/4 cup of the chopped peaches and place 2 tablespoons of them in each of the prepared ramekins. Set aside.

Add the lemon juice, vanilla extract, and a pinch of salt to the remaining chopped peaches in the bowl of the food processor. Process until very smooth and pureed. Transfer 1 cup of the peach puree to a bowl, discarding any remainder or reserve for another use, such as an ice cream topping or base for a smoothie. Set aside.

In the bowl of a heavy-duty mixer fitted with the whisk, beat the egg whites with a pinch of the salt on medium speed until foamy. Add about 1 tablespoon of the granulated sugar and beat on high speed until the whites hold soft peaks, 1 to 2 minutes. Slowly add the remaining granulated sugar and beat on high speed until the whites are glossy and hold stiff peaks when the whisk is lifted.

Add about a quarter of the beaten egg whites to the peach puree mixture and stir until well mixed. Pour this mixture over the remaining whites and fold them together as lightly as possible.

Spoon the mixture into the prepared soufflé ramekins (the mixture should come up to the top of each). Smooth the top with a metal spatula. Run your thumb around the inside rim of each dish, making a shallow channel around the edge of the batter. (This will help the soufflés rise up straight and tall.) Set the filled soufflé ramekins on the rimmed baking sheet.

Bake until puffed, golden, and gently set in the center, 8 to 10 minutes. Remove from the oven, sprinkle with confectioners' sugar, and serve immediately.

CHAPTER 12

SAUCES, CONDIMENTS, JAMS, JELLIES, AND PRESERVES

I GREW UP IN Macon County, Georgia. The next county over is Peach County, which is well known for its peach crops in the summer (and pecan harvests in the fall). Each summer Meme, Aunt Louise, or Aunt Lee would visit and the women of my family would make jelly. But first you had to pick the peaches.

You have never been hot until you have been picking peaches in the middle of a South Georgia summer. Rumor has it that hell is cooler. The air is stifling. Gnats and mosquitoes buzz and swarm. Peach fuzz covers your arms and wrists. The combination of sweat, bug spray, and itchy peach fuzz is a recipe for guaranteed misery. But the end result is that each amber spoonful of peach jelly is more precious than gold.

Somehow, picking cherries atop a tall ladder in the 300-year-old *potager* at Château du Feÿ in Burgundy was not nearly as bad. When I first arrived to study in France, Anne Willan, founder and director of École de Cuisine La Varenne, automatically (and incorrectly) assumed I could make jelly since I was from the South. I explained that I would try my best, but had never made any preserves on my own. Spending the afternoon picking the cherries was fun, but I approached my first batch of preserves as a bomb squad rookie would approach a suspicious package on the subway.

I was fearful because I only knew Meme's way. She and Dede would make gallons of preserves at a time in all-day marathons. Cooks who have never made preserves inevitably think they are going to kill someone with an exploding canner or poison them with improperly preserved food laced with botulism. Or they have images of twinkly-eyed grandmothers like my own rising at daybreak with the roosters, their spacious farm kitchens filled with bushels of vegetables. It's downright daunting. There is a grain of truth in these images, but honestly, anyone who can boil water can make jam.

Canning interrupts the natural decaying process by heating the food in a container. The heat destroys potentially dangerous microorganisms, including molds, yeasts, enzymes, and bacteria.

All foods are either high acid or low acid. High-acid foods includes all fruits and soft spreads such as jams and jellies, pickles, and tomatoes or foods that have had lemon juice, citric acid, or vinegar added to them. The water-bath canner method of processing is sufficient for high-acid foods. Foods in this category have a pH of 4.6 or lower. Low-acid foods include meats, poultry, and seafood as well as vegetables such as okra, carrots, beets, and green beans. It is necessary to process these foods at 240°F in a pressure canner. (This, frankly, is what seems like the scary stuff.) The difference is that around 212°F, which is the boiling point of water, molds, yeasts, and some bacteria are destroyed in high-acid food. However, in low-acid food the temperature necessary to destroy bacterial spores is 240°F—much higher than the temperature of boiling water. A steam-pressure canner is necessary to achieve that temperature. All of the recipes in this chapter are for high-acid preserves and use the Boiling-Water Canning method (see page 279).

If you are interested in making other kinds of preserves, more detailed information is available in these easy-to-follow resources: *USDA Complete Guide to Home Canning*, *So Easy to Preserve* (University of Georgia Cooperative Extension Service), and the *Ball Blue Book of Preserving*.

Meme put up every last bit of the harvest that wasn't eaten, but small-batch preserving is manageable with a minimum of time and effort. Buy the produce in season at your local farmer's market and make just a few pints or quarts at a time. The Refrigerator Technique (see page 279) relies on short-term storage in the refrigerator or freezer to impede mold and bacterial growth. Many of the jam, jelly, and preserve recipes in this chapter may be adapted to this technique. Small batches are easily stored in the refrigerator or freezer. Canning jars and lids can be purchased at most grocery or hardware stores. An afternoon or a weekend project becomes a wonderfully satisfying gift for your friends and family. And you won't believe how good it makes you feel when you serve your homemade preserves to guests.

BOILING-WATER CANNING

Except for a ladle, home canning kits include everything you'll need: the *Ball Blue Book of Preserving*, jars with two-piece lids, stovetop water-bath canner with cover, rack, canning funnel, plastic spatula, lid wand for removing the lids, and rubber-tipped tongs to safely lower and remove the jars from the hot water.

Sterilize the jars and lids before filling: place the jars in the rack in the canner and fill the pot with enough water to cover. Bring the water to a boil over high heat, decrease to low, and simmer for 10 minutes. Leave them in the hot water until the preserves are ready for processing. Place the lids and rings in a small saucepan and add water to cover. Bring the water to a gentle simmer over medium high heat, about 180°F. Simmer to sterilize for 10 minutes. (To help prevent seal failure, do not boil the lids and rings. Also, though used jars may be reused, it is necessary to use new rings and lids each and every time.)

Place a wire rack on a rimmed baking sheet. When you are ready to fill the jars, remove them from the hot water and place upside down to drain on the prepared rack. Remove the lids from the water and dry with a clean towel. For each jar, insert the canning funnel, then carefully ladle in the preserves, leaving $1/4$ to $1/2$ inch of headroom (the empty space between the preserves and the jar's rim), depending on the recipe. Remove the funnel and wipe the rim clean. Set the flat part of the lid on the rim of the jar and tightly screw on the ring.

Once filled and sealed, use tongs to place the jars in the rack in the stovetop water-bath canner; add enough water so the jars are covered by at least 1 inch of water. Bring the water to a boil over high heat, then process, covered, for the time specified by the recipe. Start timing *only after the water is boiling*. After the processing period is complete, turn off the heat and remove the lid. Using the jar lifter, remove the jars from the water and place them on a towel to cool. Allow the jars to cool overnight before checking for the concave seal. When the jars seal properly, they are vacuum-sealed and the lid will be slightly concave.

REFRIGERATOR TECHNIQUE

The refrigerator technique relies on the acidity of the brine and refrigeration to prevent vegetable spoilage. To prepare fresh vegetables—including cucumbers, blanched green beans, onions, beets, cauliflower, green tomatoes, and bell peppers—are combined with a mixture of vinegar, herbs, and spices, then packaged and refrigerated. No boiling-water bath or steam kettle is needed. However, the level of acidity in a pickled product, even refrigerator pickles, is critical, not only for developing texture and taste, but also for ensuring that the vegetables are safe to eat. For that reason, if you feel the vegetables are too acidic, do not decrease the amount of vinegar, but counteract with additional sugar. Choose produce that is firm, with no bruises or soft spots. Make sure that the vegetables are thoroughly washed and dried. Have the vegetables packed into the jars before making the brine.

The basic brining formula is: 5 cups distilled white or apple cider vinegar, 2 cups water, 1 cup sugar, and $1/2$ cup coarse salt. You can add different herbs and spices, such as sprigs of dill, dried chile peppers, mustard seed, cloves, or celery seed, to alter the flavor.

Combine the ingredients in a saucepan over medium heat. Cook, stirring occasionally, until the sugar dissolves and the mixture just begins to simmer. Pour the hot brine over the vegetables, leaving $1/4$ inch of headroom. Place the jars on a rack to cool. Secure the lids, and refrigerate for 2 to 3 weeks before opening. Once opened, the pickles will keep, refrigerated, for up to 2 months.

HERB BUTTER

Makes 1 cup

Use this flavorful compound butter, known in French cuisine as *beurre maître d'hôtel*, on toasts, to saute vegetables, to toss with pasta—the possibilities are endless. Vary the herbs as well. For example, try basil, garlic, and Parmigiano-Reggiano for an Italian flavor.

1 cup (2 sticks) unsalted butter, at room temperature

Juice of 1/2 lemon

2 to 3 tablespoons chopped fresh herbs, such as parsley, tarragon, chervil, or chives (see page 46)

1/2 teaspoon chopped fresh thyme

2 cloves garlic, very finely chopped

1 medium shallot, chopped

Coarse salt and freshly ground black pepper

In a bowl or sealable plastic bag, combine the butter, lemon juice, chopped herbs, thyme, garlic, shallot, salt, and pepper. Seal the bag and knead until well combined. Place the bag on the counter, and using the back of a knife or a bench scraper, push the mixture toward one corner. Snip off a corner of the bag and it's ready to go. Squeeze directly onto steaks, seafood, or vegetables (see below for a more classical presentation). Use immediately or transfer to a sealable freezer bag or an airtight container and refrigerate for up to 2 days or freeze for up to 1 month.

Compound Butter

Compound butters rolled into user-friendly logs not only look attractive when sliced but are also in an easy form to store in the refrigerator. To make a log, spoon dollops of flavored butter lengthwise down the center of a sheet of parchment paper. Fold the paper over the butter so it extends past it and the long edges of the paper almost line up. Hold down the paper with one hand, and with a straight edge (such as a ruler or bench scraper), gently push against the mound of butter to form it into a rough cylinder. Roll up the paper around the butter log and twist the ends in opposite directions (like the wrapping on hard candy). This will shape the butter into a neat, uniform log. Chill to firm, and slice as needed. To store, wrap tightly in plastic wrap and freeze for up to 1 month.

PECAN-BASIL PISTOU

Makes about
1 1/2 cups

Pistou is the French version of pesto. As in Italy, it's used with pasta or dolloped on soups or stews for additional flavoring. Make this sauce when herbs are plentiful, and freeze some for later. I like to freeze it in ice-cube trays; once the cubes are frozen solid, I transfer them to a sealable freezer bag or an airtight container and freeze for up to 1 month.

Pine nuts are traditional, and walnuts are a good choice for a delicious hint of bitterness. But pecans give the sauce a rich, buttery flavor. Try it also with other herbs—parsley, cilantro, or even nasturtium leaves for a little spicy kick.

4 cups firmly packed fresh basil leaves (about 3 bunches), washed and dried

4 to 6 cloves garlic, finely chopped

1/2 cup pecans, pine nuts, or walnuts

3/4 cup grated Parmigiano-Reggiano cheese (about 2 1/2 ounces)

Coarse salt and freshly ground black pepper

1/2 cup extra-virgin olive oil

In the bowl of a food processor fitted with the metal blade, place the basil, garlic, pecans, and cheese; season with salt and pepper. Blend until smooth, scraping down the sides of the bowl as necessary. With the machine running, slowly pour in the olive oil until it is thoroughly incorporated and the mixture is smooth.

Store in the refrigerator in an airtight container for up to 2 days or freeze for up to 1 month.

MAYONNAISE

Makes 1 cup

Mayonnaise is a subject of much debate in the South. I've even heard rumors about a veritable barroom-type brawl between chefs at the Southern Foodways Symposium in Oxford, Mississippi, that rose out of a discussion of Duke's versus Hellmann's. I grew up on Duke's mayonnaise and strongly believe that if it's not homemade, it's got to be Duke's!

This recipe uses raw eggs. Pregnant women, young children, the elderly, or anyone whose health or immune system is compromised should not consume raw eggs. Otherwise, for healthy adults, homemade mayonnaise is fine.

2 large egg yolks

1 teaspoon Dijon mustard

Juice of 1/2 lemon

1 cup oil (such as canola, olive, or a combination), at room temperature

Coarse salt and freshly ground black pepper

Whisk the egg yolks, mustard, and lemon juice together in a bowl until smooth and light. In a slow steady stream, whisk in the oil, a drop at a time, until the mixture starts to thicken. As it thickens, you may add the oil slightly faster. Season with salt and pepper. (Alternatively, this recipe may be prepared in a blender or the small bowl of a food processor fitted with the metal blade.) Use immediately or store in an airtight container in the refrigerator for up to 2 days.

VIDALIA HONEY MUSTARD DRESSING

Makes about
1¼ cups

The secret to a creamy, emulsified dressing or vinaigrette is mustard. You've probably noticed that when you combine oil and vinegar in a bowl they form separate layers. If you whisk the mixture it will combine only for a brief period, then separate out again. Mustard helps thicken liquid sauces by absorbing some of the liquid and allows the suspension of one liquid in another.

Try this savory-sweet combination over crisp salad greens or buttercup lettuce or as a dipping sauce for the Oven-fried Chicken Breasts with Pecan Crust (page 102). If Vidalias are unavailable, use another sweet onion, such as Walla Walla or Texas Sweet.

½ onion, preferably Vidalia, quartered

2 tablespoons apple cider vinegar

2 tablespoons honey (preferably tupelo, orange blossom, or sweet clover)

1 tablespoon Dijon mustard

½ cup canola oil

½ teaspoon sugar (optional)

Coarse salt and freshly ground black pepper

Place the onion in the bowl of a food processor fitted with the metal blade and pulse until smooth. Add the vinegar, honey, and mustard and puree until smooth. Add the oil in a slow steady stream until the mixture is thick and emulsified. Taste and adjust for seasoning with sugar, salt, and pepper. Store in an airtight container in the refrigerator for up to 3 days.

HOT PEPPER VINEGAR

Makes 4 cups

Almost every diner and "meat and three" establishment across the South has a jar of hot pepper vinegar on each and every table. A dash or so of this potent liquid on greens is a revelation. The longer the mixture sits, the more potent it becomes. It also makes a great gift. I prepare several batches with peppers from my garden and present them as hostess and Christmas gifts. Nothing says love like a little heat.

6 to 8 hot chiles (such as jalapeño, cayenne, or banana)

4 cups apple cider vinegar

Wearing rubber gloves, wash the chiles under cold running water. Using a paring knife, make 2 or 3 small slits in each. Pack the peppers tightly in one or more sterilized jars (see page 279). Heat the vinegar in a saucepan over high heat until simmering. Pour the hot vinegar over the peppers. Secure tightly with the lid, and refrigerate for 3 weeks before opening. Store in the refrigerator for up to 1 year.

Mama's Barbecue Sauce

Makes about
6 1/2 cups

There has seldom been a time in my life when a mason jar of this sauce wasn't in a corner of my mother or grandmother's refrigerator. The truth of the matter is, once you have had homemade you will go off the store-bought kind for good.

1 cup (2 sticks) unsalted butter

1 onion, preferably Vidalia, very finely chopped

2 1/2 cups ketchup

2 cups apple cider or distilled white vinegar

1/2 cup Worcestershire sauce

1/4 cup Dijon mustard

2 tablespoons firmly packed brown sugar

Juice of 2 lemons

2 tablespoons freshly ground black pepper

Coarse salt

In a saucepan, melt the butter over medium heat; add the onions and simmer until soft and melted, 5 to 7 minutes. Add the ketchup, vinegar, Worcestershire sauce, mustard, brown sugar, lemon juice, and pepper.

Bring to a boil, decrease the heat to low, and simmer until the flavors have smoothed and mellowed, at least 10 and up to 30 minutes. Taste and adjust for seasoning with salt and pepper. Store in an airtight container in the refrigerator. It will last for months.

COUNTRY RÉMOULADE

Makes about
1³/4 cups

Rémoulade is a cold French sauce made with mayonnaise, mustard, pickles, capers, and various herbs, and is very similar to American-style tartar sauce. It's important the onions and celery are very finely chopped. It's a dip, not a salad.

To cut the celery, first cut the stalk into even, manageable lengths. Then cut into very thin matchsticks, line them up like little soldiers and slice across in thin cuts to make small perfect dice.

1 cup mayonnaise (page 282)

1 tablespoon whole-grain Dijon mustard

1 tablespoon freshly squeezed lemon juice

1 stalk celery, very finely chopped

2 to 3 green onions (white and pale green parts only), finely chopped

1 tablespoon chopped fresh chives

1 clove garlic, finely chopped

1/2 teaspoon hot sauce

Coarse salt and freshly ground black pepper

In a bowl, combine the mayonnaise, mustard, lemon juice, celery, green onions, chives, garlic, and hot sauce. Season with salt and pepper. Cover and refrigerate for 1 hour to blend the flavors. Taste and adjust for seasoning with salt and pepper. Store in an airtight container in the refrigerator for up to 3 days. Serve chilled.

Jalapeño Tartar Sauce

Makes 1 1/2 cups

A little dab of this hotness on fried fish will set you up! Capsaicin, the chemical compound in chiles that makes them hot, is water repellent. Not only does water not stop the fire, but it also spreads the capsaicin around. However, it easily combines with fats. So, if you've had a little too much heat, reach for milk or yogurt instead of water, wine, or beer.

1 cup mayonnaise (page 282)

1 jalapeño chile, cored, seeded, and finely chopped

1/4 cup sweet pickle relish

3 tablespoons capers, rinsed, drained, and chopped

Grated zest and juice of 1/2 lemon

2 teaspoons freshly grated or well-drained prepared horseradish

2 teaspoons hot sauce

Coarse salt and freshly ground black pepper

In a small bowl, combine the mayonnaise, jalapeño, relish, capers, lemon zest, lemon juice, horseradish, and hot sauce. Season with salt and pepper. Cover and refrigerate for 1 hour to blend the flavors. Taste and adjust for seasoning with salt and pepper. Store in an airtight container in the refrigerator for up to 3 days. Serve chilled.

Homemade Creole Seasoning

Makes about 1 cup

Many of the store-bought Creole seasonings are mostly salt, sometimes with added chemical preservatives and anticaking agents. This simple seasoning blend is a mixture of salt, pepper, and dried herbs and spices. How's this for anticaking: shake the jar.

1/3 cup cayenne pepper

1/4 cup coarse salt

1/4 cup freshly ground white pepper

3 tablespoons dried thyme

1 tablespoon freshly ground black pepper

2 teaspoons dried sage

1 teaspoon onion powder

1 teaspoon garlic powder

Combine the cayenne, salt, white pepper, thyme, black pepper, sage, onion powder, and garlic powder in a small airtight container or mason jar. Stir to combine. Store in a cool, dry place for up to 3 months.

CREAMY BLUE CHEESE DRESSING

Makes about 1 1/4 cups

Roquefort is a blue-veined, smooth, and creamy French sheep's milk cheese with a strong smell and very pronounced flavor. It is one of the oldest known cheeses, having been produced in the south of France for almost two thousand years. Only cheeses made according to specific standards of production and matured in caves near the village of Roquefort, France, may be called Roquefort. Similar blue cheeses to try in this dressing include American Maytag Blue, a regional cheese from South Carolina known as Clemson Blue, English Stilton, and Italian Gorgonzola. Try this on green salad, with chicken wings, or with raw or blanched vegetables as a great crudité dip.

4 ounces blue cheese, coarsely crumbled

3 tablespoons buttermilk

1/2 cup mayonnaise (page 282)

2 tablespoons apple cider vinegar

1 teaspoon Dijon mustard

Coarse salt and freshly ground black pepper

In the bowl of a food processor fitted with the metal blade, combine the cheese, buttermilk, mayonnaise, vinegar, and mustard; season with salt and pepper. Process until well combined, but a little chunky. Store in an airtight container for up to 1 week.

OLD-FASHIONED BUTTERMILK RANCH DRESSING

Makes about 1 1/4 cups

I'm not fond of a garlic press—cleaning out all the holes is a chore. I prefer chopping garlic, but finely chopping or mashing large quantities to a paste (see page 72) can be tiresome. Recently I picked up my Microplane, a rasp-type grater, and grated the garlic directly over my saucepan. A couple of swipes back and forth and the garlic had disappeared into the pan below.

1/2 cup mayonnaise (page 282)

1/4 cup buttermilk

3 tablespoons sour cream

2 green onions (white and green parts), chopped

2 tablespoons chopped fresh flat-leaf parsley

2 tablespoons apple cider vinegar

2 teaspoons Dijon mustard

1 clove garlic, very finely chopped

Coarse salt and freshly ground black pepper

In a bowl, combine the mayonnaise, buttermilk, sour cream, green onions, parsley, vinegar, mustard, and garlic; season with salt and pepper. Store in an airtight container in the refrigerator for up to 8 hours. The garlic becomes very strong if made more than a day in advance.

RASPBERRY JAM

Makes about
8 cups, eight
1/2-pint jars

There's an incredible cookware store in Paris called Dehillerin. When I lived in France as a poor student, I would scrimp and save so I could buy one copper pot a year. Even though times eventually became richer, I still stick to my rule of one pot a year. One summer at La Varenne, after many marathon sessions making preserves, I decided my one purchase would be a copper confiture pot. This special French pot is designed specifically for making jams and jellies. It is large and wide at the rim, providing a large surface area, which allows a mixture to evaporate and thicken quickly during cooking.

Trouble was, I was purchasing this mammoth pot on my way home to the U.S. after many months in France; I had no room for it in my luggage. I'm not certain whether they would now consider it a possible weapon, but that summer I flew home with my shiny new confiture pot saddled snugly in my lap.

16 cups (8 pints) raspberries

7 cups sugar

Juice of 2 lemons

Pinch of fine sea salt

Place a wire rack on a rimmed baking sheet. Place several small plates in the freezer to use later to test the consistency of the jam.

In a large, heavy-bottomed saucepan, combine the raspberries, sugar, lemon juice, and salt, crushing the ingredients together. Let stand until the berries start rendering their juice, about 5 minutes. (You should have about 11 cups of crushed berries.) Meanwhile, sterilize eight $1/2$-pint canning jars and lids in boiling water, following the manufacturer's instructions (or see Boiling-Water Canning, page 279). Remove the jars from the water and place upside down to drain on the prepared rack. Remove the lids from the water and dry with a clean towel. Turn the sterilized jars right side up on the rack, using tongs or a kitchen towel to protect your hands. When they are cool enough to handle, dry them with a clean towel. Set aside.

Bring the raspberry mixture to a boil over high heat, stirring occasionally. The mixture will bubble up, rising high up the sides of the saucepan. Using a slotted spoon, skim off any light-colored foam as it collects on the edges. Cook the jam until it reaches the jelling point, 220°F on an instant-read thermometer, 30 to 45 minutes. (You can also dribble a few drops on the frozen plate; if the jelly is about to set, it will crinkle on the plate when you push it with your finger.)

While the jam is cooking, place the canning rack in the canner and fill the pot with water; bring to a boil over high heat.

Remove the jam from the heat. For each jar, insert a canning funnel and carefully ladle in the jam, allowing at least $1/4$ inch of headroom. Clean the rims of the jars with a clean, damp towel, and tightly secure the lids.

Using tongs, place the jars on the rack in the canner. The water should cover the jars by at least 1 inch. Cover the canner. Return

continued

the water to a boil and boil gently for 15 minutes. Using tongs, transfer the jars to a towel to cool. If the seal works and fits properly, the metal lid will be slightly concave within 24 hours of processing. Store the unopened jars of jam at room temperature for up to 1 year. Once the jam is opened, store in the refrigerator for up to 1 month.

VARIATION: For refrigerator or freezer jam, transfer the mixture to sterilized freezer-safe plastic containers or freezer-safe jars with lids, leaving 1 inch of headroom. Freeze for up to 1 year or refrigerate for up to 1 month.

BLUEBERRY JAM

Makes about
8 cups, eight
1/2-pint jars

Blueberries bring to mind fingers stained purple-blue, fruity pies and cobblers, and warm, fresh-from-the-oven muffins. When buying blueberries, look for plump, firm, fresh berries that are a light, powdery, blue-gray. If refrigerated, fresh blueberries will keep for up to three weeks. When blueberries are in season, freeze them in a single layer on a rimmed baking sheet. Once they are frozen solid, transfer to a freezer-safe container.

This is a basic formula for making jam. I've added a small amount of candied ginger at the end. The underlying ginger flavor is subtle, but it really complements the blueberry.

8 cups (4 pints) blueberries

4 cups sugar

Juice of 1 lemon

Pinch of fine sea salt

1 tablespoon finely chopped candied ginger

Place a wire rack on a rimmed baking sheet. Place several small plates in the freezer to use later to test the consistency of the jam.

In a large, heavy-bottomed saucepan, combine the blueberries, sugar, lemon juice, and salt. Let stand until the berries start rendering their juice, about 15 minutes.

Meanwhile, sterilize eight 1/2-pint canning jars and lids in boiling water, following the manufacturer's instructions (or see Boiling-Water Canning, page 279). Remove the jars from the water and place upside down to drain on the prepared rack. Remove the lids from the water and dry with a clean towel. Turn the sterilized jars right side up on the rack, using tongs or a kitchen towel to protect your hands. When they are cool enough to handle, dry them with a clean towel. Set aside.

Follow the procedure for Raspberry Jam (page 289), including bringing the blueberry mixture to a boil and cooking until the mixture reaches the jelling point, preparing the canner, filling the jars and boiling them gently for 5 minutes, and checking that the seals on the jars are good. When the jam reaches the jelling point (220°F), add the candied ginger and stir to combine. Store the unopened jars of jam at room temperature for up to 1 year. Once the jam is opened, store in the refrigerator for up to 1 month.

VARIATION: For refrigerator or freezer jam, transfer the mixture to sterilized freezer-safe plastic containers or freezer-safe jars with lids, leaving 1 inch of headroom. Freeze for up to 1 year or refrigerate for up to 1 month.

SCUPPERNONG JELLY

Makes 8 cups,
eight 1/2-pint jars

Muscadines are wild American grapes native to the Southeast. Scuppernongs are a variety of muscadines. Both grapes have a tough, thick skin that ranges in color from deep purple to greenish bronze. There are scuppernong and Muscadine arbors more than fifty years old at my family's home. The thick branches are gnarled and twisted, forming a large canopy instead of growing in a row like traditional grapes. Dede made muscadine wine and stored it in the basement. It was unfiltered and quite sweet. We recently found a bottle, at least twelve years old, that had aged and mellowed to a honey liqueur. The wine-making ended when Dede passed away, but Meme and Mama have always made jelly from the copious amounts of fruit. I think I was in first grade when I had my first taste of store-bought jelly. It was the ubiquitous Concord grape jelly of childhood, and I remember not liking it. I had never had jelly before that wasn't homemade. My friend's mother very likely thought I was either a complete brat or a complete hick.

As children, my sister and I would stand for hours at the arbor, using both hands and mechanically eating the fruit like locusts. We'd squeeze the fruit into our mouths and spit out the seeds and bitter skins. Once, I reached into the arbor to pick a greenish globe and just as my fingers started to close on the fruit, it moved. My scuppernong was the head of a green snake. Scared out of my wits, I ran screaming into the house. Meme's constant reminder about staying out of the bushes because of snakes had finally come true.

32 cups scuppernongs or muscadines (about 12 pounds)

6 cups sugar

Juice of 2 lemons

Pinch of fine sea salt

Wash the fruit and remove the stems. Place the fruit in a large bowl, and using your hands, a fork, or a potato masher, squeeze the grapes. Place the fruit in a large, stainless steel or enamel pot, and using your hands, mash until no large pieces of fruit remain. Add just enough water to keep the mixture from sticking (see page 295) and bring to a boil over high heat. Decrease the heat to low, and simmer until very juicy, about 20 minutes. Transfer the mixture to a jelly bag (see page 293) and allow to hang over a bowl for at least 6 hours or overnight. Measure the juice; you should have about 8 cups.

When you are ready to make the jelly, place a wire rack on a rimmed baking sheet. Place several small plates in the freezer to use later to test the consistency of the jelly.

Sterilize eight 1/2-pint canning jars and lids in boiling water, following the manufacturer's instructions (or see Boiling-Water Canning, page 279). Remove the jars from the water and place upside down to drain on the prepared rack. Remove the lids from the water and dry with a clean towel. Turn the sterilized jars right side up on the rack, using tongs or a kitchen towel to protect your hands. When they are cool enough to handle, dry them with a clean towel. Set aside.

In a large, heavy-bottomed saucepan, combine the scuppernong juice (you should have about 16 cups, or 4 quarts), sugar, lemon juice, and salt. Follow the procedure for Raspberry Jam (page 289), including bringing the scuppernong mixture to a boil and cooking until the mixture reaches the jelling point, preparing the canner, filling the jars and boiling them gently for 5 minutes, and checking that the seals on the jars are good. Store the unopened jars of jam at room temperature for up to 1 year. Once the jam is opened, store in the refrigerator for up to 1 month.

VARIATION: For refrigerator or freezer jam, transfer the mixture to sterilized freezer-safe plastic containers or freezer-safe jars with lids, leaving 1 inch of headroom. Freeze for up to 1 year or refrigerate for up to 1 month.

Jelly Bag

A jelly bag is used for straining pressed juice when making jelly. It may be made of several thicknesses of cheesecloth, or of cotton flannel or firm unbleached muslin. These are available online and in some hardware stores and gourmet shops. Meme used to use an old cotton pillowcase. When making jelly, it is important not to squeeze the fruit. Let the fruit hang in the jelly bag and slowly drip out into a bowl. Squeezing the mixture will produce cloudy juice, which makes for cloudy jelly.

PEACH JELLY

Pectin is found naturally in ripe fruits such as apples and citrus fruit. Naturally occurring pectin combined with the proper amount of an acid will set jams and jellies. It is also available commercially in powdered and liquid forms and is used to make jams and jellies. With commercial pectin, the powdered type is added with the uncooked prepared fruit. Liquid pectin is added to the fruit mixture after cooking. Both forms require one minute at a full boil to activate. Cooking fruit without added pectin can take fifteen to forty minutes to reach the jelling point, 220°F, depending on the amount of fruit, the stovetop, and the saucepan. It's clear that preserves made with added pectin that only require one minute of cooking will taste fresher and more like raw fruit than cooked fruit.

However, I still generally prefer the old-fashioned method of cooking fruit, sugar, and lemon juice to the jelling point with no added pectin. Many recipes call for equal parts fruit (or fruit juice) to sugar. These proportions will produce a very sweet jam or jelly. I prefer using 3/4 cup of sugar for each cup of fruit (or fruit juice), as it allows the natural flavor of the fruit to come through.

---

24 peaches (about 10 pounds), sliced, pits reserved

2 cups water

6 cups sugar

Juice of 1/2 lemon

Place the peaches and pits in a large, nonreactive pot, and using your hands, mash until no large pieces of fruit remain. Add enough water to keep the mixture from sticking (see page 295) and bring to a boil over high heat. Decrease the heat to low, and simmer until very juicy, about 20 minutes.

Place the fruit in a jelly bag and place over a large bowl (see page 293). Let rest until all the liquid has drained, about 6 hours or overnight.

When you are ready to make the jelly, place a wire rack on a rimmed baking sheet. Place several small plates in the freezer to use later to test the consistency of the jelly.

Sterilize four 1/2-pint canning jars and lids in boiling water, following the manufacturer's instructions (or see Boiling-Water Canning, page 279). Remove the jars from the water and place upside down to drain on the prepared rack. Remove the lids from the water and dry with a clean towel. Turn the sterilized jars right side up on the rack, using tongs or a kitchen towel to protect your hands. When they are cool enough to handle, dry them with a clean towel. Set aside.

Measure the amount of peach juice (you should have about 8 cups) and place it in a large nonreactive pot. Add 3/4 cup of sugar for each cup of peach juice, and the lemon juice.

Follow the procedure for Raspberry Jam (page 289), including bringing the peach juice mixture to a boil and cooking until the mixture reaches the jelling point, preparing the canner, filling the jars and boiling them gently for 5 minutes, and checking that the seals on the jars are good. Store the unopened jars of jelly at room temperature for up to 1 year. Once the jar is opened, store in the refrigerator for up to 1 month.

VARIATION: For refrigerator or freezer jam, transfer the mixture to sterilized freezer-safe plastic containers or freezer-safe jars with lids, leaving 1 inch of headroom. Freeze for up to 1 year or refrigerate for up to 1 month.

Fruit Juice for Jelly

When preparing juice for jelly, water is needed to extract the fruit juice. Wash hard fruits like apples, peaches, and pears. Without peeling or coring, quarter the fruit and measure the quantity. Place in a large saucepan. For every 1 quart of fruit, add about 1 cup of water, or just enough to keep the fruit from sticking. Simmer over low heat until the fruit is soft. For soft fruits such as berries, add 1/2 cup of water per 1 quart of fruit and simmer until soft. Finally, berries vary in size and juiciness, so the yield will also vary. Simply stick to the rule of 3/4 cup of sugar (or 1 cup if you want it sweeter) per cup of juice.

Jonagold Apple Butter

Makes about
5 cups, five
1/2-pint jars

When I see Jonagold apples at the market, I buy them, always thinking of my sister, Jona. My parents got a little creative with her name. It's feminine for John, my father's name. A blend between Jonathan and Golden Delicious, Jonagold apples are great for apple butter and applesauce. They have a tendency to soften in the refrigerator, so they are best used shortly after harvest.

5 pounds tart apples (such as Jonagold, Winesap, Jonathan, Empire, or Granny Smith), peeled, cored, and cut into eighths

1 cup apple juice or water

1/2 cup firmly packed dark brown sugar

1 to 1 1/2 cups granulated sugar

1/2 teaspoon ground cinnamon

1/2 teaspoon ground cloves

1/4 teaspoon ground allspice

Pinch of fine sea salt

Combine the apples and juice in a large, heavy-bottomed saucepan. Cover and bring to a boil over high heat. Decrease the heat to low and simmer, stirring occasionally, until the apples are very soft, 30 to 45 minutes. Add the brown sugar, granulated sugar, ground cinnamon, cloves, allspice, and salt. Continue to cook until the apple butter is thick enough to mound when spooned onto a plate, about 45 more minutes.

Meanwhile, place a wire rack on a rimmed baking sheet. Sterilize the 1/2-pint canning jars and lids in boiling water, following the manufacturer's instructions (or see Boiling-Water Canning, page 279). Remove the jars from the water and place upside down to drain on the prepared rack. Remove the lids from the water and dry with a clean towel. Turn the sterilized jars right side up on the rack, using tongs or a kitchen towel to protect your hands. When they are cool enough to handle, dry them with a clean towel. Set aside.

When the apple butter is cooked, fill the hot jars according to the procedure for Raspberry Jam (page 289), and process them in a boiling-water canner for 10 minutes. Store the unopened jars of apple butter at room temperature for up to 1 year. Once a jar is opened, store in the refrigerator for up to 1 month.

VARIATION: For refrigerator or freezer apple butter, transfer the mixture to clean airtight containers and refrigerate for up to 1 month. Or spoon into airtight freezer-safe containers, leaving at least 1 inch of headroom and freeze for up to 1 year.

PICKLED PEACHES

Makes about 2 quarts

Dede loved pickled peaches and all manner of preserves. Every year, there was a garden of fruits and vegetables. In the summer, my family would put up quart upon quart of green beans, peaches, and canned tomatoes, and in the fall, golden pears in syrup and muscadine preserves. He'd seal the lids tightly with his strong hands and place them in rows on shelves in the basement.

The name of this recipe reminds me of the tongue twister, "Peter Piper picked a peck of pickled peppers." Dede would often recite similar silly phrases, play word games, and come up with whimsical names for foods: "cat head" was a large biscuit. "Wasp's nest" was loaf bread. "Floppy motus" was gravy. And Jell-O was appropriately called "nervous pudding."

12 peaches (about 5 to 6 pounds)

1 lemon, halved

1 quart distilled white vinegar

4 cups sugar

4 sticks cinnamon, halved

2 tablespoons whole cloves

1 tablespoon whole allspice

2 inches fresh ginger, peeled and cut into 1/8-inch-thick slices

Score each peach at the blossom end with an X. Make an ice-water bath by filling a large bowl with ice and water.

Bring a pot of water to a boil over high heat and blanch the peaches for 30 seconds (the skin should begin to peel away at the X). Transfer immediately to the ice-water bath.

Using a paring knife, peel the skin from the peaches. Halve and pit the fruit and rub with lemon juice to prevent browning.

In a large, heavy-duty pot, combine the vinegar, sugar, cinnamon sticks, cloves, allspice, and ginger and bring to a boil over high heat. Cook, stirring occasionally, until the sugar dissolves, about 15 minutes. Place the peaches in the hot syrup and decrease the heat to low. Simmer until the peaches are tender when pierced with the point of a knife, but not too soft, about 10 minutes.

Meanwhile, place a wire rack on a rimmed baking sheet. Sterilize two 1-quart canning jars and lids in boiling water, following the manufacturer's instructions (or see Boiling-Water Canning, page 279). Remove the jars from the water and place upside down to drain on the prepared rack. Remove the lids from the water and dry with a clean towel. Turn the sterilized jars right side up on the rack, using tongs or a kitchen towel to protect your hands. When they are cool enough to handle, dry them with a clean towel. Set aside.

Fill the hot jars according to the procedure for Raspberry Jam (page 289), and process them in a boiling-water canner for 20 minutes. Store the unopened jars at room temperature for up to 1 year. Once the peaches are opened, store in the refrigerator for up to 1 month.

VARIATION: For refrigerator preserves, skip the boiling-water canner and refrigerate for up to 1 month.

PEAR PRESERVES

There's an ancient pear tree at the edge of Mama's driveway. The pears have thick green skin, are very aromatic, and have an intense pear flavor. Most certainly a now-nameless heirloom variety, they appear to be similar to an Anjou or a Bartlett. Remember the canned pears often served with cottage cheese in the school cafeteria? Those are Bartlett pears. Anjou pears are distinctive in that they remain green even when fully ripe.

Meme and Dede preserved the pears from the yard in quart containers packed in heavy syrup. Meme served them chilled for dessert and topped with grated Cheddar cheese for "salad." One of our favorite treats was the deep-fried, half-moon-shaped pies she made with pureed pears and biscuit dough.

6 cups sugar

6 cups water

12 Bartlett pears, peeled, halved, and cored

In a large, heavy-bottomed saucepan, combine the sugar and the water and bring to a boil over medium heat. Cook until the sugar is dissolved, 3 to 5 minutes. Add the pears and decrease the heat to low. Simmer until the pears are tender and transparent, an additional 20 to 25 minutes. Remove from the heat and transfer to a rack to cool. Cover and let rest overnight in a cool place, up to 24 hours.

Place a wire rack on a rimmed baking sheet. Sterilize five 1-pint canning jars and lids in boiling water, following the manufacturer's instructions (or see Boiling-Water Canning, page 279). Remove the jars from the water and place upside down to drain on the prepared rack. Remove the lids from the water and dry with a clean towel. Turn the sterilized jars right side up on the rack, using tongs or a kitchen towel to protect your hands. When they are cool enough to handle, dry them with a clean towel. Set aside.

Remove the pears from the syrup. Fill the hot jars according to the procedure for Raspberry Jam (page 289), and pour over the hot syrup, leaving $1/4$ inch of headroom. Process the jars in a boiling-water canner for 20 minutes. Store the unopened jars at room temperature for up to 1 year. Once the jars are opened, store in the refrigerator for up to 1 month.

VARIATION: For refrigerator preserves, skip the boiling-water canner and refrigerate for up to 1 month.

MEME'S PEAR CHOW-CHOW

Makes 4 quarts

A Southern tradition, chow-chow is a spicy, pickled fruit-and-vegetable relish that utilizes the produce at the end of the harvest.

The fruit and vegetables can vary from recipe to recipe, and can include green tomatoes, sweet peppers, onions, cabbage, carrots, and cucumber. Since Meme and Dede had a pear tree in their yard, they made chow-chow with pears.

When I called Aunt Louise to ask for this recipe, she started reciting, "A peck of pears, peeled, cored, and sliced." I laughed. Members of my family teasingly offer loving sentiments accompanied by the phrase, "A bushel and a peck, and a hug around the neck." But that is pretty much the extent of my definitive knowledge about a peck. However, a peck is an actual measurement: one-fourth of a bushel, which is about fifty pounds, depending on what is being measured. Bushel and peck baskets made of curved wooden slats with thin wire handles are still seen at farmer's markets and farm stands all across the South.

One peck (12$1/2$ pounds) pears, peeled, cored, and thickly sliced

2$1/2$ onions, preferably Vidalia, chopped

2 green bell peppers, cored, seeded, and coarsely chopped

1 red bell pepper, cored, seeded, and coarsely chopped

2$1/2$ cups distilled white vinegar

1 pound sugar (scant 2$1/2$ cups)

2 teaspoons pickling salt (see page 300)

2 teaspoons pickling spices

2 teaspoons ground turmeric

In the bowl of a food processor fitted with the metal blade, working in batches, combine the pears, onions, and bell peppers, and pulse until ground but still slightly chunky. Place the mixture in a large, nonreactive pot and stir to combine.

Add the vinegar, sugar, pickling salt, pickling spices, and turmeric and stir to combine. Bring to a boil over high heat. Decrease the heat to low and simmer until thick, about 30 minutes.

Meanwhile, sterilize four 1-quart canning jars and lids in boiling water, following the manufacturer's instructions (or see Boiling-Water Canning, page 279). Remove the jars from the water and place upside down to drain on the prepared rack. Remove the lids from the water and dry with a clean towel. Turn the sterilized jars right side up on the rack, using tongs or a kitchen towel to protect your hands. When they are cool enough to handle, dry them with a clean towel. Set aside.

Fill the hot jars according to the procedure for Raspberry Jam (page 289), leaving $1/4$ inch of headroom, and process them in a boiling-water canner for 10 minutes. Store the unopened jars at room temperature for up to 1 year. Once the jars are opened, store in the refrigerator for up to 1 month.

VARIATION: For refrigerator preserves, skip the boiling-water canner and refrigerate for up to 1 month.

SPICY PICKLED OKRA

Southerners are almost as fond of pickling as we are of frying. Submerging fresh produce in vinegar or a combination of sugar and vinegar meant there would be vegetables to eat in the winter months. Pickling recipes encompass not just simple cucumbers, but also more unusual ingredients, such as watermelon rind, green tomatoes, and okra. Okra responds very well to pickling; the vinegar virtually eliminates the slime factor, the main reason people don't eat okra. I like to use one of these crisp, spicy pods instead of an olive for a Southern-style martini.

2 pounds medium okra pods

4 small dried chiles

2 teaspoons yellow mustard seed

1 teaspoon whole black peppercorns

8 cloves garlic, peeled

4 cups distilled white vinegar

2 cups water

2 tablespoons pickling salt (see sidebar)

Wash the okra and trim the stems to $1/2$ inch. Place 1 chile, $1/2$ teaspoon mustard seed, $1/4$ teaspoon peppercorns, and 2 cloves of garlic in the bottom of each of 4 sterilized pint-sized canning jars (see page 279). Divide the okra evenly among the jars, placing the pods vertically, alternating stems up and down.

In a medium saucepan over medium heat, bring the vinegar, water, and salt to a boil. Carefully pour the boiling mixture over the okra in the jars, leaving $1/4$ inch of headroom between the top of the liquid and the lid. Seal the lids.

Process the jars in a boiling-water canner for 15 minutes (see page 279). Store the unopened jars at room temperature for up to 1 year. Once the jars are opened, store in the refrigerator for up to 1 month.

VARIATION: For refrigerator pickles, skip the boiling-water canner and refrigerate for up to 1 month.

Pickling Salt

Pickling salt is fine-grained, highly pure, and free of additives, including iodine and anticaking agents that cause the pickles to turn dark and the pickling liquid to turn cloudy. Although sea salt does not contain additives, it does contain various minerals and elements that can cloud the mixture. Also, flaked salts vary in density and are not recommended for pickling. Pickling salt is labeled as such, and it's available in many grocery stores and online.

300 | Bon Appétit, Y'all

SOURCES

BACON
Nueske's Hillcrest Farm
Tel. 800-392-2266
www.nueskes.com

CHEESE
Sweet Grass Dairy
Tel. 229-227-0752
www.sweetgrassdairy.com

CRAWFISH
Tel. 866-LA-CFOOD
www.livecrawfish.com

FLOUR
White Lily Flour
Tel. 800-264-5459
www.whitelily.com

CORNMEAL, GRITS,
AND RICE
Anson Mills
Tel. 803-467-4122
www.ansonmills.com

HEIRLOOM PORK AND
GRASS-FED BEEF
Riverview Farms
Tel. 706-334-2926
www.grassfedcow.com

White Oak Pastures
Tel. 229-641-2081
www.whiteoakpastures.com

PECANS AND GEORGIA
PEACHES
Pearson Farm
Tel. 888-423-7374
www.pearsonfarm.com

PROSCUITTO AND
COUNTRY HAM
**Benton's Smoky Mountain
Country Hams**
Tel. 423-442-5003
www.bentonshams.com

HONEY
Savannah Bee Company
Tel. 912-234-0688
www.savannahbee.com

SPICES
Vanns Spices
Tel. 800-583-1693
www.vannsspices.com

Zatarain's
www.zatarains.com

VIDALIA ONIONS
Bland Farms
Tel. 912-654-1426
www.blandfarms.com

ACKNOWLEDGMENTS

I WOULDN'T BE THE woman, person, or chef I am today without the love and support of my Mama. Like it or not, you can't help growing up to be like your parents. If I grow to be as half as generous as my mother, I will have achieved far more than I ever thought I would.

Becky makes me smile, keeps me grounded, and is my one true love. I look forward making biscuits for her *as long as old men sit and talk about the weather, as long as old women sit and talk about old men. . . . Forever and ever, amen.*

My sister Jona, who has all the common sense, also has unconditional love, support, and belief in me—as I do in her. Thank you for still being here.

The first years of my life were spent in a home next door to my grandparents, Meme and Dede, who instilled in me a love of food and family—and taught me how to clean a deer.

I thank Sara Minchew for taking me in to Sara's "home for the homeless," loving me as a daughter, and helping make my dream a reality with her endless understanding.

Lisa Ekus is a phenomenal woman whom I am incredibly happy to have in my life as a friend and guide. My love, respect, and admiration for her and her work are beyond words.

Without the guidance of my mentor, Nathalie Dupree, I would not have found my way *to* this complicated path, much less *on* it. She has had a hand in so much of what I have been able to accomplish in my career.

Anne Willan taught me how to write a recipe. My first drafts to her were returned soaking in red ink corrections, but I finally learned the La Varenne Way.

Martha Stewart allowed me the opportunity to learn something new every day and exposed me to the infinite possibilities of a career in food.

Heartfelt gratitude and deep appreciation go to the following:

Gena Berry, for her precious friendship and unending energy, and for being my indefatigable cheerleader.

Mary Moore of The Cook's Warehouse, who helped me get my career off the ground in Atlanta—and became one of my dearest friends.

Angie Mosier for her astonishing work and her clear vision of what Southern food can and should be.

Jeannette Dickey, my Atlanta editor, who helped me corral both my proposal and my manuscript and helped me stay true to my voice.

The members of the Atlanta chapter of Les Dames d'Escoffier, Georgia Organics, and Southern Foodways Alliance—because it's all about teamwork.

Cheryl Galway of Whole Foods Market for her generous support, for helping local make a difference, and for her community involvement.

Francois Dionot, founder and chef of L'Academie de Cuisine set me off on the right track with a sound knowledge of classic technique.

The recipe testers and photo shoot assistants: Wendy Allen, Alison Berry, Sue Clontz, Adeline Craig, Cecelia Jenks, Caroline Joe, Shirley Lawrence, Marta Luce, Elise Luce, Megan McCarthy, Rachael Milder, Michelle Moore, Steve Moorman, Wayne Naihe, Michele Phillips, Calvin Rouse, Paula Skinner, Gloria Smiley, Alison Stockum, Donna Taylor, Nancy Waldeck, and Linda Wilson.

To the incredible culinary professionals who agreed to put their name on this book, answered questions along the way, or have just been helping me spread the love: Alton Brown, Tamie Cook, Shirley Corriher, Nathalie Dupree, John T. Edge, Damon Fowler, Scott Peacock, Susan Puckett, Anne Willan, and Marvin Woods.

To the Serenbe community, inn, and organic farm, for allowing us to share the beauty of rural Georgia in these pages.

Thank you to a host of very special friends and loved ones who are always there: Lisa and Terry Allen, Leslie Allen and Got-Any-Leftovers-Lloyd Prince, Lee Babbitt, Evan Bernstein and Rich Wilner, Melita Easters, Michele Minchew, Claire Perez, Lindy Shallcross, Mike Thomas, and Louise Waites.

Finally, thanks to Clancy Drake, Ellen Silverman, and the talented folks at Ten Speed Press for making such a beautiful book.

Bon appétit, y'all!

INDEX

1¼ C (cake flour)
½ C sugar) sift together

3 C flour
3 tsp BP
1 " salt.

1½ C (12) egg Whites beat
with ¼ tsp salt + 1½ cream of T
1 tsp Vin 1½ C sugar B. 350 30 mi

350°

SHORTCUT PAN ROLLS
Makes 3 dozen rolls

1 cup Quaker Instant Grits
¼ cup sugar
1 tablespoon salt
3 cups hot water

⅓ cup vegetable oil
6 to 6½ cups sifted all purpose flour
2 pkg. dry yeast

Combine instant grits, sugar and salt in large bowl of mixer.
Add water, oil and 2 cups of the flour. Beat 2 minutes on low
speed. Add 1 cup additional flour and yeast. Beat 1 minute
on low speed. Stir in enough additional flour to make soft
dough.
Turn out on well floured board or canvas, knead until smooth
and elastic, about 10 minutes.
Divide dough in half. Shape each half into 18 balls; place in
greased 8-inch round cake pans. Cover; let rise about 1
hour until nearly double in size. In preheated 350°
F. 30 to 35 minutes or until brown.
pans, brush with butter.

2 lb - 1 pt
325°

LEMON CAKE
(Makes 12)

1 package Duncan Hines Lemon
Supreme Deluxe Cake Mix
1 package lemon instant
pudding mix (4 serving size)
1/2 cup Crisco Oil*

1 cup water
4 eggs

325° 1 hr

Blend all ingredients in a large bowl, then beat at
medium speed for 2 minutes. Bake in a greased and
floured 10-inch tube pan at 350° for about 45-55
minutes, until center springs back when touched
lightly. Cool right side up for about 25 minutes,
then remove from pan.
Glaze: Blend 1 cup confectioners sugar with either
2 tablespoons milk or 2 tablespoons lemon juice.
Drizzle over cake.

BUTTERMILK BISCUITS

3 tablespoons SACO Buttermilk Powder
2 teaspoons baking powder
1/2 teaspoon soda
2 cups all-purpose flour
1 tablespoon salt
2 teaspoons sugar
1/3 cup shortening
2/3 cup water

Preheat oven to 450°F. Sift dry ingredients together
into a mixing bowl. Cut in shortening thoroughly until
mixture resembles corn meal. Add water and mix until
dough is pliable. Do not overbeat.

Turn dough on lightly floured surface and knead
lightly, for about 30 seconds (20 to 25 times). Roll or
pat ½-inch thick, no less. Cut with floured biscuit
cutter. Place close together on ungreased baking
sheet. Bake 10 to 12 minutes or until golden brown.

ONE DOZEN 2½-inch biscuits